Congress, the Bureaucracy, and Public Policy

Congress, the Bureaucracy, and Public Policy

Fourth Edition

Randall B. Ripley
Professor and Chairperson
Department of Political Science

Grace A. Franklin
Research Associate
Mershon Center

both of
The Ohio State University

The Dorsey Press
Chicago, Illinois 60604

ISBN 0-256-05592-0

Library of Congress Catalog Card No. 86–71438

Printed in the United States of America

1 2 3 4 5 6 7 8 9 0 K 4 3 2 1 0 9 8 7

Preface

We expect a student who reads this book to come away with an understanding of the critical nature of the relationship between Congress and the federal bureaucracy. The examples we have used should give the student a feel for part of the substantive business of the United States government and should also give the student a better sense of how and where to seek additional examples of that business. We also think the student who uses this book will be able to use simple English to explain to herself or himself and to others a number of patterns in American policy making.

Public policy making at the national level in the United States is both important and complicated. It is important because it affects the daily lives of all residents of the United States and sometimes affects the lives of people in other nations. It is complicated because of the vast number of items on the agenda of the national government and because of the large number of individuals and institutions that get involved in decisions about public policy.

Central to the complex and important business of public policy making is the interaction between Congress and the federal bureaucracy. Existing books about public policy usually either ignore this relationship or merely allude to it, implying that it is too mysterious to be comprehended. In fact, it is comprehensible and—happy thought!—there are patterns in the relationship that help reduce the confusion surrounding national policy making. We have sought to portray those patterns in clear terms. And, above all, we have sought to give concrete, interesting, and timely examples of the relationships that illustrate the patterns.

A further word is necessary about our choice of examples. Because of the necessities of the publishing process, we could have no examples later than the end of 1985. We have sought to sprinkle our examples over the last few decades rather than concentrate them all in the last few years or only in the Reagan years. We feel no necessity in bringing every example up to the minute. We seek to describe and explain patterns of behavior. To be sure, every short period of time—whether measured by president, by Congress (two years), or annually—will have its own variations. But the patterns we observe transcend all of these artificially created time periods. Reagan brought different values and styles to the presidency. But so did every other president. And the president, as an institutional figure, only has so much weight and then vanishes from a future scene. The continuities in the patterns we discuss are more important than variations introduced by any given policy actor or any given dominant ideology in the United States government. Where Reagan (or any other president or policy actor) seems to have made an important difference in terms of introducing change, we say so. But the popular, journalistic proclivity to proclaim "new eras" that are assumed to wipe away basic institutional relationships is alien to this volume. In fact, we think such proclamations are almost always false and misleading, especially to any serious student of American politics.

We do not intend to describe all that either Congress or the bureaucracy does with regard to public policy. Our focus is on those areas and activities in which constant interaction occurs between them and has at least the potential for major substantive results. Our attention, therefore, is primarily directed to *policy formulation and legitimation*. The *implementation* of policy by bureaucracy is a vast and important topic by itself. We do not address implementation in the present volume because the patterns are substantially different in terms of actors (although not in terms of what is at stake). We systematically analyze implementation in a companion volume to this one, *Policy Implementation and Bureaucracy* (Dorsey Press, 1986).

We are grateful to the Mershon Center at Ohio State University for providing a good location in which to write and think and interact with other people interested in public policy. This book stems both from a number of projects on policy making sponsored in part by Mershon, in which we have been involved since 1970, and from our teaching—both formal and informal and to a number of audiences—about public policy.

In preparing this fourth edition we had the benefit of thoughtful reviews of the third edition by Roger H. Davidson and Glenn R. Parker.

Randall B. Ripley
Grace A. Franklin

Contents

List of Figures

List of Tables

1

The Nature of Policy and Policy Making in the United States

Policy is a common word, one that you encounter frequently—you hear it on the radio and TV, you use it in conversation, you read it in the press—but it is a difficult concept to define, despite its familiarity. Political scientists have filled many pages defining and arguing about the meaning of policy and its relatives—policy making and policy process. That policy is complex, both conceptually and substantively, is undeniable. Nor should the importance of government policies be underestimated; one reason the media report so frequently about policy is that the policies of government are pervasive in their direct and indirect impact on you and all citizens.

To help sort out the complexities, we offer the following very simple statements:

Policy is what the government says and does about perceived problems.

Policy making is how the government decides what will be done about perceived problems.

Policy making is a process of interaction among governmental and nongovernmental actors; policy is the outcome of that interaction.

Figure 1–1 presents a highly simplified overview of the chain of activities in the making and implementing of policy.

In the first stage of the policy process—*agenda setting*—a problem exists in society, and through various means it comes to the attention of government actors, who perceive it to be an issue that should be addressed by government. Some parts of the government recognize that an issue or problem should receive attention. The agenda of the government can be thought of as the sum of all the issues and problems that the government is addressing at any given time. In the 1970s, for example, some of the issues on the government agenda included environmental preservation, energy

1

FIGURE 1-1
An Overview of the Policy Process

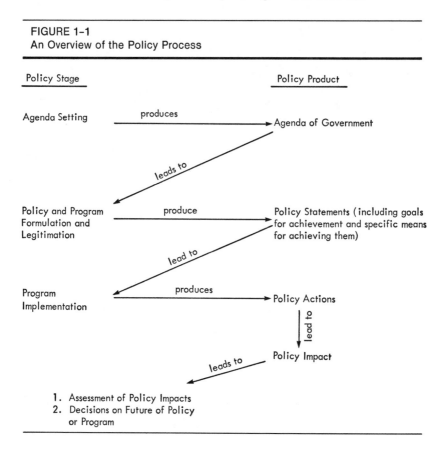

Policy Stage   Policy Product

Agenda Setting   produces
                                              Agenda of Government

                      leads to

Policy and Program   produce   Policy Statements (including goals
Formulation and   for achievement and specific means
Legitimation   for achieving them)

                      lead to

Program   produces
Implementation   Policy Actions
                                                    │ lead to
                                                    ▼
                                              Policy Impact
                      leads to

1. Assessment of Policy Impacts
2. Decisions on Future of Policy
   or Program

resources, unemployment, and inflation. In the 1980s the most visible issues changed. Emphasis was given to defense spending, tax policy, and the extent of deregulation and assignment of federal responsibilities to the states or the private sector.

Having acknowledged that a problem deserves governmental attention, government must say what it is going to do and specify how it plans to accomplish its goals. In the stage of *formulation and legitimation*, government and nongovernment actors propose alternative methods of problem solution, and they choose a plan of action. The presence of often vehemently different points of view necessitates negotiation and compromise if a decision is to be reached. The typical product of this stage is a congressional statute creating a new program or amending an existing one.

Once a plan of action has been selected, the decisions must be *implemented* by responsible individuals and agencies. The agencies must acquire resources, interpret the legislation, write regulations, train staff, and deliver services in order to put flesh on the bones of the statute.

The actual operation of a program designed to address a problem will have some *impact* on society. It may or may not achieve its intended purposes (assuming those were clear), and it may also have unintended consequences, both beneficial and detrimental. Several kinds of assessment of impact are always undertaken. Political considerations dominate these assessments, and the assessments are usually informal. Sometimes more formal analyses may be undertaken. The results of such formal analysis may become incorporated into the adversarial process. Often the governmental users are primarily looking for support for positions they already hold rather than considering more-or-less objective analyses on their own terms. The results of assessment, regardless of type or number, can lead to changes in the operation of the program or to additional formulation and legitimation as revised programs are debated. They can occasionally, but very rarely, lead to temination of existing programs. However, the result most often is no change, or only minor change, in the existing policies.

A full treatment of the entire policy process is beyond the scope of this book (see Jones, 1984, for an excellent introduction to it). We are going to focus on one part of the policy process—the formulation and legitimation of public policies and programs. At the heart of the policy-making process lies the relationship between Congress and the bureaucracy, a relationship that is not usually given sustained attention in the literature on American government and policy making. In order to set the relationship in perspective, we will first describe policy making in American national government in terms of major actors, relationships, and characteristics.

The model portrayed in Figure 1–1, the definitions of policy phenomena, and the brief description of the policy process above vastly oversimplify the rich variety of the real policy world. Our generalizations impose order on a very complex world whose activities and interactions are messy, not neat. On the other hand, we find distinct patterns are present when policy formulation and legitimation in the United States are analyzed. We present those patterns in the firm belief that a grasp of patterns is far better than a store of unconnected observations or anecdotes. Throughout the book, however, we illustrate our patterns with policy examples from the last several decades in order to avoid analyzing a fascinating process only in the language of abstraction.

AN OVERVIEW OF THE GOVERNMENT POLICY PROCESS

Actors and Relationships

The core of the American national governmental policy process is located in Congress and in the executive branch. These public institutional entities and actors are often supplemented by nongovernmental institutions and actors. Especially important among the latter are the great variety of interest groups active in American politics and policy making. They are important and influential in many cases, but it is essential to note that their importance is not all-encompassing. One of the principal contributions of the present volume, in fact, is to specify when, where, and how interest groups are important in shaping policy. There is an interactive relationship between interest groups and official institutions and actors. The importance of each varies systematically in ways that will occupy us in detail throughout this book. It is also worth noting that the relationship between interest groups and policies can flow in both directions. Interest groups can sometimes help shape policy, and, equally important, the creation of policies often involves the identification and specification of interests that help generate groups to perpetuate and "refine" those policies.

Both Congress and the executive branch can be understood in terms of key component parts. Congress has party leaders, committee and subcommittee leaders (typically, committee and subcommittee chairpersons and ranking members), and rank-and-file members of the House and Senate. The executive branch consists of the president personally, the presidency collectively in the form of the Executive Office of the president and the presidential appointees, and the civil servants throughout all of the agencies.[1] Each of these six component parts of the central Washington policy-making institutions interacts with every other part, but all of the relationships are not equally important. Figure 1-2 indicates the interactions most important to national government policy making.

Within the executive branch two relationships are critical—that of the president with Executive Office personnel and presidential appointees throughout the government (the institutional presidency in a broad sense), and that of Executive Office personnel and presidential appointees with civil servants throughout the government. The bureaucracy is so vast that the president cannot hope to have direct relationships with civil servants (except for a few career civil servants in the Executive Office and a few career ambassadors in the foreign service). Thus, the Executive Office personnel and presidential appointees scattered throughout the various departments and agencies take on special importance in serving as links between the president and his programmatic ideas and the development of and implementation of those ideas in the bureaucracy.

Three relationships are critical within Congress. Committee and subcommittee leaders play an intermediary role between party leaders and rank-and-file members, but party leaders also need and maintain direct ties to the rank and file. This relationship is relatively easy to achieve in

---

[1]That part of the federal bureaucracy in which we are most interested comprises those career officials—both civilian and some military equivalents—who are high enough in grade or rank to be considered as involved in national policy making. Typically, this would mean individuals who are supergrades (GS 16, 17, or 18) or equivalents in other career services, including the military.

FIGURE 1-2
Critical Relationships for Policy Making in the National Government

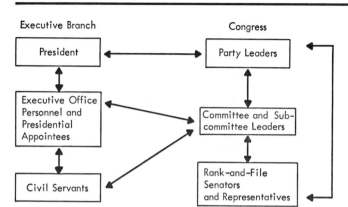

physical terms, given the limited size of the House and Senate. The committee and especially subcommittee leaders are typically the most important individuals in deciding what emerges from Congress in substantive terms. The party leaders make the strategic and tactical decisions about how best to get the work of committees and subcommittees approved by the full House and Senate. The rank and file are approached by committee and subcommittee leaders and party leaders in their respective spheres of expertise.

There are also three critical relationships between the executive branch and Congress: those between the president and the party leaders (largely on strategic and tactical matters), between the Executive Office personnel and presidential appointees and committee and subcommittee leaders (on substantive matters), and between policy-level actors in the civil and military service and committee and subcommittee leaders in Congress (on substantive matters).

In order for substantial and relatively rapid policy movement to occur, the eight relationships portrayed in Figure 1-2 must all be marked by a high degree of mutual confidence and trust, and there must also be a high degree of agreement on the nature of the problems facing society and the proper solutions to those problems. These conditions are absent more than they are present, which helps explain the normal posture of the government as moving very slowly on only a few problems at a time. Rapid movement on major issues occurs, but when it does, it is unusual enough to warrant special notice.

More often, minor changes are misleadingly touted as major ones. Policy makers often give in to the temptation to overstate incremental legislative compromises, attributing to them panacean qualities, in order to create a favorable public image. This kind of hyperbole was much in evidence throughout 1985 as Congress and the president labored to bring the federal budget deficit under control. A variety of formulas were billed as responsible solutions by various parties to the debate. Some seemed to believe the final compromise really offered a solution to the problem; others denounced the "solution" as a public relations sham.

This book focuses primarily on the relationship between civil servants (and equivalent military officers) and committee and subcommittee leaders as portrayed in Figure 1–2. The other relationships included in the figure will be discussed as necessary to set the context for the central relationship to be examined.

In some policy areas the other actors and relationships will appear more frequently because they are very important. In addition, some of the unportrayed relationships that occur more rarely (for example, a relationship between the institutional presidency and committees or bureaucracies and rank-and-file members or bureaucracies and party leaders) will also appear in some of the empirical material in subsequent chapters.

In general, the role of the president personally will receive attention only when it becomes critical. Given the vast workload of the federal government and the limits on any one individual, the president personally becomes involved only rarely. The institutional presidency has more routine contact with Congress, and so parts of the institutional presidency—especially the White House office and the Office of Management and Budget—will receive more frequent attention.

Principal Characteristics

Policy making in the U.S. government is an extremely complex phenomenon. This complexity results from a variety of factors—the sheer size of the government, the number of participants (both governmental and nongovernmental) that can become involved in policy making, the proliferation of specialization within agencies and committees and subcommittees, the involvement of various levels of government, the separation of institutions that share powers as outlined by the Constitution, and the vast range of substantive issues to which government addresses itself and the complexity of most of those issues. Four of the most important characteristics, each of which contributes to complexity, are described in the following paragraphs. These characteristics also interact with each other to multiply the complexity.

The first characteristic is the widespread occurrence of *subgovernments* in important positions in various issue areas. Subgovernments are small groups of political actors, both governmental and nongovernmental, that specialize in specific issue areas. Subgovernments in part are created by the complexity of the national policy agenda, and they help sustain that complexity. They are also most prevalent and influential in the least visible policy areas. Subgovernments do *not* dominate *all* policy making, but the gradations in their importance require serious attention.

A second major characteristic of policy making is the great variety of governmental institutions—federal, state, and local—that share the responsibility for developing and implementing a number of policies and programs and also have some programs exclusively their own. Thus, a national program is very likely to involve actions not only in Washington but also throughout a number of states and cities in both federal field offices and offices of state and local governments. The pattern of which level of government is responsible for what varies over time. For example, states became considerably more important during the Reagan years (see Beam, 1984; Peterson, 1984; Chubb, 1985).

A third important characteristic of federal policy making is the existence of separated institutions (the legislative, executive, and judicial branches) that share powers. The separation of institutions stems from a decision by the founders not to place all powers of government under a single body or person—hence, the basic governmental functions were subdivided and delegated to three distinct branches. However, in order to limit the autonomy of each branch, checks and balances were written into the Constitution that force the institutions to share their powers to some extent. The separation makes some jealousies and conflicts over turf inevitable. The sharing necessitates cooperation among the branches to prevent the governing apparatus from ceasing to function with any effectiveness. In addition to the separation and sharing of powers prescribed in the Constitution, a commingling of legislative, executive, and judicial powers has evolved as the branches have interacted. Congressional delegation of authority to the executive branch is a particularly notable example of this sharing.

A final dominant characteristic of national policy making is the tremendous variety and volume of issues facing government. The substantive spectrum of government policy ranges from acreage allotments for cotton, wheat, and corn growers to child care and legal assistance for poor people to military and economic aid for developing nations. The relative specificity of governmental policy also varies greatly—a law may spell out in infinite detail every guideline, or it may be highly general. Naturally, different types of policy have different rewards and penalties for various groups, and the anticipated outcome of a proposed policy can affect the process by which the policy is made.

The remainder of this chapter will explore the above four characteristics in more detail.

THE SUBGOVERNMENT PHENOMENON

Subgovernments are important throughout a broad range of American public policy. They afford an important channel by which nongovernmental actors help determine policy and program content. They are not equally dominant in all policy fields, and their level of influence changes from time to time within a single field. Later in this chapter we suggest that the level of subgovernment dominance varies in a predictable way depending on which of several broad policy types is involved.

Note that we have made two important statements about subgovernments. First, they *are* widely present and important. But they are *not* dominant in all policy making.

Subgovernments are clusters of individuals that effectively make most of the routine decisions in a given substantive area of policy. The existence of subgovernments has been noted and documented in a number of studies of American government (see, for example, Cater, 1964; Davidson, 1977; and Freeman, 1965). A typical subgovernment is composed of members of the House and/or Senate, members of congressional staffs, bureaucrats, and representatives of private groups and organizations interested in the policy area. Usually the members of Congress and staff members are from the committees or subcommittees that have principal or perhaps exclusive jurisdiction over the policy area dominated by the subgovernment. The congressional members of the subgovernment are also usually the most senior members of a relevant subcommittee. The bureaucrats in a subgovernment are likely to be the chief of a bureau with jurisdiction paralleling that of the congressional subcommittee and a few of his or her top assistants. The nongovernmental members of a subgovernment are most likely to be a few lobbyists for interest groups with the heaviest stakes in the nature of governmental policy in the area.

Most of the policy making in which subgovernments engage consists of routine matters. "Routine" policy is simply policy that is not embroiled in a high degree of controversy. The substance of routine policy changes slowly over time, and the participants most interested in it are also thoroughly familiar with it and quietly efficient in both its implementation and minor alterations in its legislative base.

Because most policy making is routine, subgovernments can often function for long periods without much interference or control from individuals or institutions outside the subgovernment. If the members of a subgovernment can reach compromises on any disagreements about policy, they can reduce the chances of calling a broader audience together that might become involved in their activities and output. When more participants enter, the chances of basic policy realignments increase because there are a greater number of interests to satisfy, and such realignments might not be perceived to be in the best interests of the members of the subgovernment. Thus, there is strong incentive for them to reach compromises and avoid broadening the number of participants.

In general, there are three ways that the normally closed, low-profile operations of a subgovernment can be opened to "outsiders." First, as just indicated, if the subgovernment participants themselves disagree on some point fundamentally, this disagreement may become publicized and stimulate attention and intrusion from nonmembers of the subgovernment.

Second, the president, other high administration officials, and members of Congress can draw on a variety of formal and informal resources if they choose to be aggressive in inquiring into the functioning of a subgovernment. Formal resources include budget limitations, staff size limitations, vigorous legislative oversight of program activity, and restraints on agency communications (Freeman, 1965: 62). Informal resources consist mainly of using personal influence on an individual-to-individual basis. This is especially true for the president, who can exert influence on persons he has appointed. Whether the president, administration officials, and congressional members will be aggressive with respect to subgovernments depends on the extent to which they perceive interests important to them to be threatened by the subgovernment's behavior. For example, the president or a department secretary may be stirred to an aggressive stance if the bureau chief member of a subgovernment strays too far too often from officially announced administration policy.

Third, a new issue that attracts the attention of outsiders can be introduced into the subgovernment's jurisdiction. The new issue can upset normal decision making if it is more important than or different in character from the issues the subgovernment is used to dealing with, especially if the issue involves regulation of private activities or redistribution of wealth to one group at the expense of another. In recent years, for example, both the increased concern for the environment and the energy crisis have intruded into the world of the various subgovernments dealing with oil, coal, and natural gas. Now these subgovernments must handle major regulatory issues as well as the familiar issues of subsidy.

The "rules of the game" of American politics—as practiced, regardless of what the law or popular myth may say—minimize the distinction between governmental and nongovernmental institutions and actors. In practice, the supposed line between the two realms is easily crossed, and this practice is widely thought to be proper by those both inside and outside the government. This results in a general belief on the part of those involved that individuals and groups most affected by governmental actions should have almost continual access to governmental officials during the policy-making process (Lowi, 1979).

Not only are the lines between governmental and nongovernmental institutions blurred by the norm of open, continual access during policy making, but there is also a constant flow of personnel between governmental and nongovernmental institutions that further blurs the distinctions. People from Congress (both the members and staff) and the executive branch agencies move into jobs in the private sector to work in the same substantive policy areas they worked in during their government tenure. This flow of personnel enhances the importance and stability of subgovernments, and the magnitude of this type of personnel interchange is so large that subgovernments have also been called "incest groups" (Lewis, 1977).

It is worth emphasizing that participation in subgovernments offers the most pervasive and effective channel for interest-group impact on policy and program decisions. But the impact of interest groups will not be uniformly important—rather, they will have a great deal of importance in some areas and minimal importance in other areas (Hayes, 1981). In part their impact varies with the policy area and in part it varies with the groups' resources.

When all organized interest groups are considered together, a strong "business or upper-class bias" becomes evident (Schattschneider, 1960). The more well-off members of society, especially the private business sector, are particularly strongly represented. This helps explain why much substantive policy that emerges is favorable to these interests.

FEDERALISM IN POLICY MAKING

Geographic Dispersion of the National Government

Washington, D.C., is synonymous with the national government, and it is true that much of the decision-making apparatus of the government is concentrated there. But the Washington area contains only a small proportion of all federal employees. Of all federal civilian employees (more than 2.7 million persons in the mid-1980s), about one in eight was stationed in the metropolitan Washington area. The rest worked elsewhere in the United States, with the exception of a few who were stationed outside the United States, either in U.S. territories or in foreign countries. It is the regional and local outposts of the federal government where the primary federal responsibility for delivery of benefits and services resides.

Nearly every federal agency has some regional and local field offices. There is no standard summary of agency field offices, and the patterns among agencies vary—some have a profusion of installations in every state, while others have very few. Even at the regional level, there is considerable variation among agencies, despite the Standard Federal Regional Boundary System established in 1969 that prescribes ten standard regions to which agencies should conform. A glance at any local telephone book of reasonable size under the heading "U.S. Government" will reveal how extensively the federal government is represented on the local and regional level.

Federal, State, and Local Government Interaction

In addition to being complicated by the dispersion of purely national institutions and employees, policy making and implementation in the United States are also complicated because numerous state and local governments are also important in implementing national programs. Numerous ties bind federal, state, and local governmental units and employees together: federal money, limited exchanges of personnel, and daily interaction on programs.

State and local government employment is much larger than federal government employment. In 1983, 82 percent of the more than sixteen million civilian government employees were state and local. The federal share of total civilian governmental employment has been shrinking steadily since World War II. (In 1950, for example, it was 33 percent compared with 18 percent in 1983.)

The financial impact of the federal government on state and local governments grew dramatically during the 1950s, 1960s, and 1970s. Table 1–1 summarizes the growth of federal grants-in-aid from 1950 through an estimate for 1990. The amount of aid in this form has risen enormously. Until

TABLE 1–1
The Growth of Federal Grants-in-Aid to State and Local Governments, 1950–1990

| | | Federal Grants as a Percent of | |
| | | --- | --- |
Fiscal Year	Amount (Millions)	Total Federal Outlays	State-Local Expenditures
1950	$ 2,253	5.3	10.4
1960	7,019	7.6	14.7
1965	10,910	9.2	15.3
1970	24,065	12.3	19.2
1975	49,791	15.0	23.0
1980	91,451	15.5	26.3
1985 (Estimate)	107,016	11.2	NA*
1990 (Estimate)	105,442	8.9	NA*

*NA = not available.
Source: *Special Analyses, Budget of the United States Government, Fiscal Year 1986,* (Washington, D.C.: U.S. Government Printing Office 1985), H-19.

TABLE 1–2
Percentage Distribution of Federal Grants to States and Localities by Function, 1960–1990

	1960	1970	1980	1990 (est.)
Energy	*	*	1	*
Natural resources and environment	2	2	6	3
Agriculture	3	4	1	*
Transportation	43	19	14	16
Community and regional development	2	5	7	4
Education, training, employment, and social services	7	27	24	18
Health	3	16	17	29
Income security	38	24	20	28
General-purpose fiscal assistance	2	2	9	2
Other	*	1	1	*
Total	100	100	100	100

*0.5% or less.
Source: *Special Analyses, Budget of the United States Government, Fiscal Year 1986,* (Washington, D.C.: U.S. Government Printing Office 1985), H–17.

the 1980s this amount also represented a continuously increasing percentage of all federal outlays. And, during the same period, it also represented a continuously increasing percentage of all state and local spending.

The purposes for which these federal grants-in-aid to states and localities are spent have changed considerably. Table 1–2 summarizes the distribution of grant spending by function from 1960 through an estimate for 1990. When examining the table, note that health has been the consistent large gainer in terms of purposes served and that transportation has become relatively less important. Education, training, employment, and social services peaked in the 1960s and 1970s and went into decline during the Reagan era. Income security remained very important throughout the period, although it fluctuated. General-purpose fiscal assistance (general revenue sharing for the most part) was used largely for education by state governments and for public safety and transportation (mass transit) by local governments.

The grant system was altered in the early 1970s by the development of several major "special revenue sharing" efforts, particularly in the community-development and employment and training areas. The system was altered again in the Reagan era by the collapsing of some specific categorical grants into block grants. These alterations did not change the percentage distribution of dollars by function, but they did change some of the patterns of control and some of the necessary interrelationships between federal, state, and local governments.

But regardless of how much flexibility and influence is granted to state and local governments in any particular version of federalism that happens to be in vogue at the moment, two central facts remain that are pertinent to the analysis in this book. First, Congress and the federal bureaucracy still are at the heart of the interactions that lead to the statutes prescribing the nature of the relationship between the territorial levels of government and the scope and objects of the fiscal aid. Second, no version of the federalistic relationship is likely to be permanent. Congress and the bureaucracy will both continue to review what happens during the implementation of various grants, regardless of form. They may diminish their own role, but they rarely eliminate it; and they certainly retain the option—with appropriate presidential initiative and support necessary in some cases—to change the basic relationships. The long-term "natural" pressures are for members of Congress and the bureaucracy to keep states and localities dependent on them in many ways so they can continuously claim credit for programs and spending for their individual constituencies.

SEPARATE INSTITUTIONS, SHARED POWERS

Cooperation and Conflict

The Constitution created three branches of government that have distinct identities in terms of their powers and their mode of holding office. Yet it also distributed powers in such a way that interaction and some cooperation is necessary if anything is to be accomplished. Institutional jealousies about preserving powers and competition to serve different constituencies mean that the three branches will inevitably have some conflicts. But an overriding desire to achieve some policy goals also means that most participants in all three branches understand and operate on the values of cooperation and compromise. The existence of subgovernments serves to reinforce the values of cooperation and compromise for the participants (Morrow, 1969: 156–158). Institutional jealousies and competition among constituencies remain within the subgovernmental system, but their effects are muted in its day-to-day operations. The premium is placed on the production of policy that is usually an extension of the status quo or some incremental variant of it. More policy production also creates more bureaucracy, which in the course of implementing programs creates more occasions for members of Congress to serve their constituents in dealings with the bureaucracy. Such service generates benefits to the members at election time (Fiorina, 1977).

Most of the literature dealing with Congress and the bureaucracy usually focuses on the conflictual aspects of the relationship because conflict is a more exciting topic than cooperation. But the bulk of policy making is based on cooperation. One of the tasks of this volume will be to develop suggestions in the literature (Bernstein, 1958; Bibby, 1966; Fiorina, 1977; Morrow, 1969; Scher, 1963; Sharkansky, 1965a, 1965b) about the conditions that promote cooperation or conflict. The following brief survey indicates some of the conditions to be addressed:

First, personal compatibility between key congressional (usually subcommittee) personnel and key agency personnel is important. A high degree of compatibility will promote cooperation, and lesser amounts of compatibility (or greater amounts of hostility) will promote conflict.

Second, the degree of ideological and programmatic agreement between key individuals in Congress (usually on the relevant subcommittee) and in the agency is important. A high degree of agreement will promote cooperation; a low degree of agreement will promote conflict. Similarly, a high degree of unity *between* different individual members of Congress thought by bureaucrats to be important is likely to make the bureaucrats less inclined to pursue their own interests that may conflict with united congressional opinion. Disunity among members of Congress may tempt bureaucrats to form alliances with those agreeing with them, thus provoking conflict with the other congressional faction.

Third, the amount of genuine participation by Congress (generally, members of a subcommittee) in the development of programs is important. If executive branch officials simply present Congress with finished products—either in the form of proposed legislation or in the form of major administrative decisions—conflict may result. If the executive officials adopt a habit of consulting as they undertake either legislative or administrative courses of action they enhance the chances of cooperation.

Fourth, if an issue is of relatively low salience to constituents and/or interest groups, then the chances of congresssional-bureaucratic cooperation are enhanced. However, if constituents and/or interest groups are heavily involved, the potential for conflict increases.

Fifth, agencies that are highly aggressive in seeking to expand their authority and their funding run a greater risk of conflict with Congress (committees and subcommittees) than agencies that are less aggressive.

Sixth, if the presidency and Congress are controlled by the same political party, the chances for cooperation are enhanced. If different parties control the two branches, the chances for conflict increase.

Delegation of Authority

Delegation of authority occurs when Congress writes general statutes that leave varying degrees of room for the executive branch (primarily career bureaucrats) to specify some of the detailed content of the legislation when it is put into practice. There is nothing nefarious or unusual about this practice. Some degree of delegation is necessary in most cases because of the overall volume of legislation and because of the complicated nature of any large topic addressed. Congress, in theory, sets clear standards and guidelines in the legislation for the bureaucracy to follow in administering a program. In practice, the clarity and specificity of those standards and guidelines vary a great deal. For example, Congress may direct the National Labor Relations Board (NLRB) to ascertain that "fair standards" in labor negotiations are adhered to and leave the determination of what constitutes fair standards up to the agency. The interpretation of "maximum feasible participation" of the poor in the Economic Opportunity Act of 1964 was similarly left up to the Office of Economic Opportunity (OEO). On the other hand, Congress may specify extremely precise standards that eliminate agencies' discretionary power, as it did in the Securities Act of 1933. The existence and size of the *Federal Register* testify to the amount of freedom agencies have in making formal, published interpretations of congressional intents. Agencies are required to put the regulations they use in administering their programs in the *Register.* The amount of informal, unrecorded administrative rule making that occurs is no doubt equally voluminous.

Delegation of authority to the executive branch allows Congress to keep its workload manageable. Government has assumed increasing responsibility in an ever-expanding number of issue areas in the twentieth century, and Congress, of necessity, has delegated a great deal of authority vested in it by the Constitution to various parts of the executive branch. The sheer volume and technical complexity of the work are more than Congress, with its limited membership and staffing, can manage alone.

Congress sometimes intentionally uses delegation to delay making a final decision. A clear-cut policy decision may result in penalizing or angering some groups, which can manifest their unhappiness by withdrawing their support from members of Congress. If the members perceive that they would lose a great deal of support, they may choose not to state a clear policy and leave the policy outcome ambiguous by delegating decision making to parts of the bureaucracy, or to regulatory commissions, or to the courts, with only vague congressional guidance. Thus the winners and losers affected by the policy are less clearly defined, and the responsibility for decision making is deflected from Congress to other agencies.

The propriety of congressional delegation of authority was challenged during the New Deal, and the Supreme Court ruled on a few occasions that certain delegations were unconstitutional because of vagueness. But that check has not been exercised since then. In effect, Congress can follow whatever course it wishes with respect to delegation—its form will change only when Congress decides to rewrite the legislation containing the delegation. In summarizing this fact and the continuing trend toward very broad delegations, Woll (1977: 170) says "It is possible to conclude that there are no constitutional or legal restrictions that have impeded in any substantial way the trend toward greater delegation. This situation has not, of course, resulted from administration usurpation, but from congressional desire." Delegation, in sum, is a result of necessity, but it is also a matter of will, not coercion.

While the principle of delegation of authority is well established, the question of what form delegation ought to take is not so well settled. Some scholars, like Harris (1964), argue explicitly that Congress should be only minimally involved in administration and by implication that its delegations of authority should be broad and vague to allow bureaucrats to make interpretations best suited to meeting problems faced in program administration. Others, like Lowi (1979), argue that delegation of authority without accompanying clear guidelines limits congressional policy impact to relatively marginal details and is, in effect, an abdication of responsibility by Congress. By implication, Congress should publish clear expectations and guidelines along with its delegations.

It is clear from examining legislation that the forms of delegation vary. The reasons for relatively clear guidelines in statutory language in some cases and very broad and vague language in other cases are numerous and vary from case to case. One important consideration may be the mood of Congress at any given time with reference to the agency to which the delegation is being made. Or, more precisely, the most important consideration may be the attitude of the responsible congressional subcommittees toward the relevant agencies.

An example of how patterns of delegation are affected by changing congressional attitudes is evident in the degree of discretionary power allocated to the Federal Trade Commission (FTC) in the Securities Act of 1933 and to the Securities and Exchange Commission (SEC) in the Securities and Exchange Act of 1934 (Landis, 1938: 52–55). The FTC's discretionary power was severely limited in part because of congressional lack of confidence in the agency's membership. Its duties were defined so precisely that administration was almost a matter of mechanical routine. In contrast, attitudes toward the FTC had changed by 1934, and the new confidence was reflected in the broader administrative authority granted to the new SEC.

The type of issue involved also affects the nature of congressional delegation. In highly complex issues, particularly those in the jurisdictions of the regulatory agencies, Congress is often unable or unwilling to make specific judgments. The result is the unusually large size of both the area of discretion and the accompanying set of political pressures in the regulatory commissions, such as the Federal Trade Commission, Securities and Exchange Commission, Federal Communications Commission, and Federal Power Commission.

A desire to shift responsibility for decision making may also be a factor in congressional delegations of authority to the bureaucracy. Unpopular decisions can be laid at the bureaucracy's door, rather than that of Congress. Landis (1938: 55–60) makes the point that, to the extent that Congress avoids making clear pronouncements of policy in its statutes, the conflict over which policy will be enforced is shifted from Congress to the administrative agencies involved. This congressional stance seems particularly prevalent in the area of regulation of business.

The implication of congressional delegation of authority is that a good deal of public policy gets made by the bureaucracy without any explicit attention from Congress. Congressional access to the routine matters of public policy is in practice, although not in theory, limited. Even in initiating new formal statutes, the bureaucracy is important and sometimes dominant (Woll, 1977: 170–200).

Legislative Oversight

Congressional delegation of authority does not necessarily mean congressional abdication, however. Congress still has access to administrative policy making through a variety of activities that are collectively known as legislative oversight. In effect, legislative oversight could be construed as a counterbalance to congressional grants of policy-making authority to the bureaucracy. On the one hand, Congress gives away parts of its own powers to the executive branch. But, on the other hand, it reserves the right to monitor the way the executive branch is exercising that authority. We use *oversight* as a neutral term, avoiding any implication that it is good or bad. We certainly do assert that oversight in general is necessary in a representative government, but we do not want to prejudge any given exercise of it as either proper or improper.

Legislative oversight is not just a single activity that occurs on a regular basis. Oversight, broadly conceived, consists of all of Congress's involvement in the affairs of the bureaucracy (Keefe and Ogul, 1985: chapter 12; Ogul, 1973). The oversight activities of Congress fall into five categories: concern with the substance of policy, concern with agency personnel, concern with agency structure, concern with agency decision-making processes, and concern with agency budgets. A brief survey of the techniques of oversight follows, and the topic will also receive further treatment in Chapters 3 and 8.

Congressional concern with the substance of policy is manifested at any of the three stages: passage of legislation, implementation of legislation, and societal impact of legislation. The content of legislation at the time of its passage identifies congressional intents as modified during the legislative process. The legislation may allow the bureaucracy considerable discretion in interpreting and applying the law. To monitor administrative interpretation, Congress can hold regular hearings (for both authorization and appropriations) and focus on aspects of this issue; it can hold special investigations; or it can exercise a variety of informal contacts (phone calls and visits with bureaucrats, lobbyists, and affected constituents, for example). If Congress determines that it has overdelegated or underdelegated, it can rewrite a statute to include additional and clearer guidelines. To monitor the impact of legislation on society, Congress can require program evaluations, which may be done by Congress, by an outside body (for example, the General Accounting Office), or by the agency itself. The findings will suggest how legislation, or administrative patterns, could be altered to improve the fit between intended and actual impact.

The personnel who develop and apply government programs are just as important to policy impact as the content of legislation. Congress is involved with a variety of agency personnel matters—size of total staff or certain staff components, confirmation of top administrators (civil service, foreign service, and military officers) appointed by the president, compensation for federal employees, and the conduct of personnel (political activity, loyalty, and conflict of interest).

Congress is also involved in agency structure and organization in a fundamental life-and-death sense in that it is responsible for creating new agencies or for granting the president reorganization powers, usually with provision for possible congressional disapproval. Congress also controls the lifeblood of all agencies—their budget—and can kill an agency by refusing to fund it. This happened, for example, when Congress eliminated the Area Redevelopment Administration in 1963. In addition, Congress becomes involved in the details of agency organization when the president submits executive reorganization plans for congressional approval. A congressional veto can stop the reorganization. Congressional action killed President Kennedy's proposed department of urban affairs in 1962.

Congress inserts itself into the decision-making processes of agencies in at least two ways—by requiring reports and other data to be submitted by the agency, and by the use of the legislative veto, which requires the executive branch to submit its proposals either to the whole Congress or to a particular committee for approval.[2] Both of these techniques allow Congress to maintain at least the form of reviewing bureaucratic activities in a regularized fashion, especially in legislative areas involving substantial delegation of authority.

[2]In theory, the Supreme Court declared the legislative veto unconstitutional in 1983. In practice, the legislative veto's importance has not been diminished by that ruling. Chapter 3 discusses the present situation in more detail.

Congressional oversight occurs at all stages of agency budgets—authorizations, appropriations, and expenditures. Authorizations establish the legitimacy of a program and set a ceiling on appropriations for subsequent years; authorizations must be passed before a program can receive appropriations. The authorization process for a new or existing program consists of hearings before the relevant legislative committee in the House and Senate, at which the past and expected program performances are reviewed. The frequency of authorization hearings varies from yearly to longer periods, depending on the program. The appropriations hearings are an annual event for most agencies, and they occur before the relevant subcommittee of the House and Senate appropriations committees, where, among other things, the performance of the agency's program is reviewed. Unfortunately it has been difficult for Congress to coordinate the program reviews that occur in the separate authorization and appropriations hearings, and the quality of the oversight, if not its quantity, has been criticized for focusing too much on detail and too little on program effectiveness and impact. Congress is also concerned with expenditures made by an agency after the appropriations process. This concern manifests itself during the appropriations hearings ("How did you spend the $10,000 for chicken wire at the ASCS field office in Ogden?") and also in special audits and investigations by the General Accounting Office (GAO) commissioned by Congress. Congress has removed considerable federal funding from the appropriations process, thus further dispersing responsibility for fiscal oversight among a greater number of committees.

TYPES OF POLICY

The national government has assumed responsibility for a mushrooming variety and volume of issues over the years. Trying to discuss and analyze governmental policy without a classifying scheme can be confusing and misleading, and many scholars have proposed different schemes to ease the task of analysis. Policies have been categorized in many ways: by the subject matter (education, agriculture, environment); by the relative size of the budgets of different policies (presidential requests, congressional appropriations, agency expenditures); by the beneficiary or target group affected (students, farmers, consumers); by the impact on society or some other outcome measure; or by the process through which the policy is made.

The key to any useful typology is to identify shared characteristics of different types. We have developed a sevenfold classification scheme for governmental policy based on our reading of the policy literature (particularly Lowi, 1964; also Froman, 1968; Hayes, 1981; Huntington, 1961; Lowi, 1967, 1972; Salisbury, 1968). In our scheme there are four types of domestic policy: (1) distributive, (2) competitive regulatory, (3) protective regulatory, and (4) redistributive. We identify three types of foreign and defense policy: (1) structural, (2) strategic, and (3) crisis.

We intend to account for the vast majority of policies considered by the federal government, especially in the framing of legislation. A few policies do not easily fit into the scheme. But these are policies that occur only rarely, even if some of them get lots of popular journalistic coverage for a while because they are politically "hot." The so-called social issues in the late 1970s and 1980s fit this characterization. A few—school busing is a clear example—also fit well into the basic scheme (in this case, busing for racial equality in public schools is an instance of redistributive policy). Others—abortion and school prayer are two examples—may well be hybrids or idiosyncratic cases that do not fit very well into the scheme. There are certainly elements of class conflict over values in both issues, but the fit with class issues based on economics (what we call redistributive issues) is not perfect. However, policy formulation and legitimation processes and actors rarely deal with such issues. Even in the presumed peak of concern over school prayer and abortion, Congress rarely had to decide about a legislative stance on them. We could proliferate the categories to account for these rare occurrences, but we think the values of keeping the scheme with relatively few categories far outweigh the possible defect of omitting a few idiosyncratic or hybrid cases that somehow look "different."

The basic notion behind our scheme is that each type of policy generates and is therefore surrounded by its own distinctive set of political relationships. These relationships in turn help to determine substantive, concrete outcomes when policy decisions emerge. Table 1–3 summarizes the characteristics of the political relationships surrounding policy making for each type of policy. The main features of the political relationships that we are concerned with in Table 1–3 are the identity of the primary actors, the basic nature of the interaction among those actors, the stability of their interaction, the visibility of the policy decisions to individuals not immediately involved or concerned, and the relative influence of different individual actors.

We have excluded competitive regulatory policy from Table 1–3 because it is a type of policy that is rarely formulated and legitimated. Competitive regulatory policy is primarily implemented on the basis of relatively few statutes. Responsibility for competitive regulatory policy is almost totally delegated to bureaucratic agencies, regulatory commissions, or courts for implementation. It focuses on decisions about individual cases, and the actors involved are limited to relevant bureaucratic, judicial, or quasi-judicial agencies, the individuals or corporate units competing for benefits being awarded, and occasional members of Congress who have a specific interest in the outcome. We have included a brief discussion of competitive regulatory policy below to contrast it with the other types of policy, but because this book focuses on formulation and legitimation, we have not included competitive regulatory policy in the analysis in the remainder of this book.

Domestic Policy

Distributive Policy. Distributive policies and programs are aimed at promoting private activities that are said to be desirable to society as a whole and, at least in theory, would not or could not be undertaken without government support. Such policies and programs provide subsidies for those private activities and thus convey tangible governmental benefits to the individuals, groups, and corporations subsidized. (A subsidy is a payment of some kind designed to induce desired behavior.) Many governmental policies turn out to be subsidies, even if they do not seem to be subsidies at first glance. Decisions about subsidies are typically made with only short-run consequences considered. The decisions are not considered in light of each other; they are disaggregated. Thus there appear to be only winners and no losers.

The cast of characters (usually individuals or groups that comprise a subgovernment) involved in distributive decisions in a particular field (such as agricultural price supports, water resources, or subsidies for health research) is fairly stable over time, and their interactions are marked by low visibility and a high degree of cooperation and mutually rewarding logrolling. The congressional subcommittee generally makes the final decisions after receiving input from the other actors. The recipients of distributive subsidies are not aware of each other, and there is no sense of competing for limited resources—anyone can be a potential recipient, and resources are treated as unlimited. Distributive decisions embody the federal pork barrel in its fullest sense.

Typically, many people, groups, and corporate units are granted bites of the federal pie. Distributive decisions, both within a field and between different substantive fields, are made individually, without consideration for their interrelation or overall impact—they are decentralized and uncoordinated. Chapter 4 will discuss the nature of the congressional-bureaucratic relationships when distributive policies are being made.

Examples of distributive policies include direct cash payments for purchase of agricultural commodities; grants for scientific research in universities and private laboratories; grants to localities for airport construction, hospital construction, sewage facilities, and mass transit facilities; promoting home ownership through tax provisions allowing deductions for interest on home mortgages and local property taxes; and issuing low-cost permits for grazing on public lands.

TABLE 1-3
Political Relationships in Policy Formulation and Legitimation

Policy Type	Primary Actors	Relationship among Actors	Stability of Relationship	Visibility of Decision
Distributive	Congressional subcommittees and committees; executive bureaus; small interest groups	Logrolling (everyone gains)	Stable	Low
Protective regulatory	Congressional subcommittees and committees; full House and Senate; executive agencies; trade associations	Bargaining; compromise	Unstable	Moderate
Redistributive	President and his appointees; committees and/ or Congress; largest interest groups (peak associations); "liberals, conservatives"	Ideological and class conflict	Stable	High
Structural	Congressional subcommittees and committees; executive bureaus; small interest groups	Logrolling (everyone gains)	Stable	Low
Strategic	Executive agencies; president	Bargaining; compromise	Unstable	Low until publicized; then low to high
Crisis	President and advisers	Cooperation	Unstable	Low until publicized; then generally high

TABLE 1–3 (*concluded*)

President, Presidency, and Centralized Bureaucracy	Bureaus	Influence of Congress as a Whole	Congressional Subcommittees	Private Sector
Low	High	Low (supports subcommittees)	High	High (subsidized groups)
Moderately high	Moderate	Moderately high	Moderate	Moderately high (regulated interests)
High	Moderately low	High	Moderately low	High ("peak associations" representing clusters of interest groups)
Low	High	Low (supports subcommittees)	High	High (subsidized groups and corporations)
High	Low	High (often responsive to executive)	Low	Moderate (interest groups, corporations)
High	Low	Low	Low	Low

Competitive Regulatory Policy.   Competitive regulatory policies and programs are aimed at limiting the provision of specific goods and services to only one or a few designated deliverers, who are chosen from a larger number of competing potential deliverers. Some decisions allocate scarce resources that simply cannot be divided, such as television channels or radio frequencies. Some decisions maintain limited rather than unlimited competition in the provision of goods and services by allowing only certain potential deliverers to provide them and excluding other potential deliverers. Some decisions are aimed at regulating the quality of services delivered through choosing the deliverer periodically and imposing standards of performance. If those standards are not met, a new deliverer can be chosen. This type of policy is a hybrid, which subsidizes the winning competitors and also tries to regulate some aspects of service delivery in the public interest. Examples of competitive regulatory policies include the granting and reviewing of licenses to operate television and radio stations; authorizing specific airlines to operate specified routes; and authorizing certain trucking companies to haul specified commodities over designated routes.

Decisions on basic overall policy in this area are rare. Most decisions are delegated to bureaus, regulatory commissions, and courts. The influence of the competitors is high, and over time most of them can be expected to get some benefits. Thus, at the general level the policy resembles one of subsidy, especially for the largest competitors that can enter many competitions. For example, before airline deregulation, a major airline would not win every route for which it competed before the Civil Aeronautics Board. But it would win enough routes over time to enhance its profitability. Congressional influence on individual decisions is sometimes present, usually in the form of intervention from specific senators and representatives on concrete, individual decisions affecting constituents. But because of the lack of much policy formulation and legitimation at a level and volume comparable to the other policy types we consider, we have omitted competitive regulatory policy from the remainder of the book. It also needs to be noted that the importance of positive policy formulation in this area has been diminished in recent years by the spread of deregulation to most modes of transportation and some aspects of communication.

Protective Regulatory Policy.   Protective regulatory policies and programs are designed to protect the public by setting the conditions under which various private activities can be undertaken. Conditions that are thought to be harmful (air pollution, false advertising) are prohibited; conditions that are thought to be helpful (the publication of interest rates on loans) are required.

Protective regulatory policies are not as disaggregatable as distributive decisions because they establish a general rule of law and require that a certain segment of the population conforms to the law. The actors (coalitions of members of the full House and Senate, executive agencies, and representatives of trade associations) involved in protective regulatory decisions are much less stable than in the distributive arena, partially because of constantly shifting substantive issues. The ultimate decisions get made on the floor of the House and Senate. Chapter 5 examines the congressional-bureaucratic relationship in shaping protective regulatory policy.

Examples of federal protective regulatory policies include the requirement that banks, stores, and other grantors of credit disclose true interest rates; prohibitions of unfair business practices, unfair labor practices, and business combinations that lessen competition; limits on the conditions under which strip mining can be undertaken and requirements for the postmining restoration of land; the prohibition of harmful food additives; and high taxation to reduce the consumption of sometimes scarce commodities such as gasoline.

Redistributive Policy. Redistributive policies and programs are intended to manipulate the allocation of wealth, property, rights, or some other value among social classes or racial groups in society. The redistributive feature enters because a number of actors perceive there are "winners" and "losers" and that policies transfer some value to one group *at the expense of* another group. Thus, the more well-off sometimes perceive themselves to be losers in relation to a program that seeks to confer some benefits on the less well-off. Whites sometimes perceive themselves to be losers in relation to a policy or a program that confers special benefits on minority groups.

Redistribution runs in several directions. Some programs redistribute items of value from the less well-off to the more well-off or from minorities to whites, but usually such programs are not perceived as redistributive. They do not generate the hot political controversy that is associated with redistributive attempts in the other direction. Thus, the policies of redistribution almost always involve situations in which the intended beneficiaries are the relatively disadvantaged in society.

Because redistributive policy involves a conscious attempt to manipulate the allocation of wealth, property, rights, or some other value among broad classes or groups in society, the actors perceive that there will be distinct winners and losers. The stakes are thought to be high, and this fact means the policy-making process will be marked by high degrees of visibility and conflict. The coalitions that form over any redistributive issue may change in composition depending on the issue (integrated schools, open housing, welfare programs), but they can generally be identified as a proponent ("liberal") group and an opponent ("conservative") group. Their debate on the issue is cast in ideological terms. Whether redistributive policy will emerge from the coalitions' conflicting viewpoints depends on the presence of strong presidential leadership and the willingness of participants to retreat from ideological stances and adopt compromises. The principal political consideration among the participants during the process is who gets what at the expense of whom. Chapter 6 focuses on the congressional-bureaucratic relationship when redistributive issues are at stake.

Examples of redistributive policy include setting progressive personal income tax rates so more affluent people pay a higher percentage of their incomes in taxes than do less affluent people; requiring housing, public accommodations and facilities, and public education be available to all, without racial discrimination; requiring affirmative action in hiring by federal contractors to increase the employment of women and minorities; and providing employment and training programs, food stamps, or special legal services for the disadvantaged.

Foreign and Defense Policy

Policy typologies in nondomestic issue areas are less clear-cut than in domestic areas. Lowi (1967: 324–25) suggests that there are three distinctive patterns of politics in foreign policy. The first is crisis foreign policy. In this situation the perception of a threat to national security cuts across normal channels of decisions, and an elite of formal officeholders within the executive branch makes the decisions with a minimum of conflict. In the absence of a crisis, there is time for "normal" patterns and concerns to emerge. Institutions become involved, and interactions occur over a number of questions. Foreign policy then is basically either distributive or regulatory with much the same sets of characteristics as domestic distributive or regulatory policy types.

In the area of defense policy, which has both domestic and foreign-policy aspects, Huntington (1961) has identified two types—strategic and structural defense policy. Strategic defense policy is oriented toward foreign policy and international politics, and it involves the units and use of military force, their strength, and their deployment. Structural defense policy focuses on domestic politics and involves decisions about the procurement, allocation, and organization of personnel, money, and material that constitute the military forces. Structural decisions are made primarily within the context of strategic decisions and are made to implement those decisions.

We have drawn on both Lowi and Huntington in developing our ideas about the three categories of foreign and defense policy: structural, strategic, and crisis. All three types will be examined in more detail in Chapter 7.

Structural Policy.   Structural policies and programs aim primarily at procuring, deploying, and organizing military personnel and materiel, presumably within the confines and guidelines of previously determined strategic decisions. Because the federal government has no competitors in providing defense, the element of total subsidy for the enterprise is a given. But the details of that subsidy can vary greatly.

Structural policies are closely related to distributive policies. The process is characterized by the presence of subgovernments, by decentralized decision making, by nonconflictual relationships among the actors, and by decisions that treat internal resources as unlimited and separable. Policy decisions emerge from the formal legislative process (bill introduction, committee hearings, passage by the House and Senate). Although Congress is generally responding to executive requests rather than initiating policy in this area, it nonetheless has final decision power.

Examples of structural policies include specific defense procurement decisions for individual weapons systems; the placement, expansion, contraction, and closing of military bases and other facilities in the United States; the retention, expansion, or contraction of reserve military forces; and the creation and retention of programs that send surplus farm commodities overseas.

Strategic Policy.   Strategic policies and programs are designed to assert and implement the basic military and foreign-policy stance of the United States toward other nations. Policy planning and proposals resulting from that planning stem primarily from executive branch activities. A number of executive branch agencies compete, bargain, and sometimes engage in conflict during policy development. Decisions are made by these agencies, with the final approval of the president. Public debate and congressional involvement usually occur after the formal decisions are announced. Congress may get involved in several ways—committees or individuals may lobby executive agencies for decisions. Congress may respond to an executive request for legislation to implement a decision already made, or Congress may protect and alter an action already completed. Congress does not make strategic decisions by itself. Thus, although the influence of Congress as a whole can be high, that potential influence is often used to respond supportively to executive branch initiatives.

Examples of strategic policies include decisions about the basic mix of military forces (for example, the ratio of ground-based missiles to submarine-based missiles to manned bombers); foreign trade (tariffs and quotas for specific goods and nations); sales of U.S. arms to foreign nations; foreign aid; immigration; and the level and location of U.S. troops overseas (both in general and in relation to specific trouble spots).

Crisis Policy.   Crisis policies are responses to immediate problems that are perceived to be serious, that have burst on the policy makers with little or no warning, and that demand immediate action. The occurrence of crisis situations is unpredictable and tied to external (nondomestic) events. The principal actors are elite executive branch officeholders who work cooperatively together with a minimum of publicized conflict. Visibility of the decision-making process is also low, except to the extent that press releases and press conferences inform the public. The involvement of Congress is informal and limited and is usually made in the mode of consultation with key individuals. The full body may get involved formally, usually after the crisis, to make the action legitimate or to forbid similar exercises of executive power in the future.

Examples of crisis policies include decisions about the U.S. response to the Japanese attack on Pearl Harbor in 1941; the impending French collapse in Indochina in 1954; the Soviet Union's placement of missiles in Cuba in 1962; the North Korean seizure of a U.S. Navy ship in 1968; the Cambodian seizure of a U.S. merchant ship in 1975; the Iranian seizure of U.S. hostages in late 1979; the seizure of the Mediterranean cruise ship *Achille Lauro* in 1985; and the seizure of an American commercial airplane in the Mideast in 1985.

THE REST OF THE BOOK

In the remainder of this volume we will develop the notions that have been introduced in this chapter—especially the varying nature of the involvement of subgovernments in policy making, the need for cooperation and the potential for conflict between Congress and the bureaucracy, and the presence and effect of different policy types.

Chapter 2 will discuss the actors in the congressional-bureaucratic relationship: members of the House and Senate, congressional staff, politically appointed members of executive branch agencies, and civil servants (and their military and foreign service equivalents) in policy-making positions in agencies.

Chapter 3 will focus on the occasions for interactions among the actors and will describe the resources available to Congress and the bureaucracy in those interactions.

In Chapters 4 through 7 we will use a variety of case materials to illustrate congressional-bureaucratic relations in each of the six policy areas identified above. We will focus on the subgovernment phenomenon where it is present. In the absence of a subgovernment, we will describe the broader congressional-executive interactions that do occur. A caveat might be offered at this point regarding the policy categories we use. Reality in government is never as simple or clear-cut as analysts and students might wish. The policy categories we have suggested are not mutually exclusive—some policies will display attributes of more than one category. We have selected examples that best fit each policy type, and where individual policies fall into more than one category, we have distinguished the different parts.

In Chapter 8 we will summarize our findings about congressional-bureaucratic interactions in the various policy arenas and make an overall assessment of the substantive impact of the relationship between Congress and the bureaucracy.

2

Actors in the Relationship

As Congress and the bureaucracy interact on policy matters, it is clear there are a number of actors involved and they behave differently from one another in a variety of both general and specific ways. For example, members of authorizing (legislative) committees and appropriations committees behave differently from each other. Staff members in the two houses vary in their approaches to legislation, and staff members serving a committee work differently from those assigned to individual members' offices. Presidential appointees in the White House or Office of Management and Budget (OMB) may act quite differently from presidential appointees at the cabinet and subcabinet levels. Civil servants may take very different views of the policy world depending on whether their assignment places them in a line operating position, a staff position (especially one dealing with budgetary matters), or a legislative liaison position. Their attitudes and activities may vary with their assignment to a Washington office or to a field office.

Differences in behavior not only distinguish different groups of actors but also have important implications for the nature of the relationship among the actors (the degree of cooperation or conflict) and for the policy emerging from that relationship (its substance, direction, and magnitude). In this chapter we will begin to make some observations about the nature of the relationships among and between congressional and bureaucratic actors and about the effects of those relationships on policy and policy change. The next two sections present a description and comparison of four major classes of actors—members of the House and Senate, congressional staff members, political appointees in the executive branch, and civil servants. The elements described, when taken together, present a picture of the institutional setting in which the actors work, as well as a portrait of traits that characterize them in the aggregate. The various elements described—political expertise, method of selection, loyalties, demographic factors, and so on—were selected for two principal reasons: their demonstrated importance as evidenced by their treatment in the literature and their comparability across at least several classes of actors.

These profiles of institutional setting and group characteristics of actors are presented in part to familiarize the reader with the actors by conveying basic descriptive information. They are also intended to serve as an aid for subsequent analysis of factors that explain the cooperation or conflict present in their relationships and the policy that results from those relationships. In the concluding section, we assess the impact of specific role orientations on the likelihood of conflict or cooperation and on the nature of that conflict or cooperation. Various institutional and role constraints suggest that some conflicts between individuals in different positions and roles are almost surely going to crop up because institutional loyalties sometimes push in different directions and because the scope and substance of policy interests are likely to be different.

It should be noted that some institutional changes (often called "reforms") were made in Congress in the first half of the 1970s. The following discussion takes account of those changes where they seem to have had an impact, although in many cases the impact has been somewhat minimal (Davidson and Oleszek, 1977; Dodd and Oppenheimer, 1977; Rieselbach, 1977; and Welch and Peters, 1977). In 1978 Congress passed a civil-service reform bill that, theoretically, could have had some impact on the way the bureaucracy conducts business and on the relationships between bureaucrats and other actors, especially their nominal political masters (Cooper, 1978). The Reagan administration sought to impose more ideological tests of loyalty on career bureaucrats than previous administrations. The 1978 act gave the administration more flexibility than it would have had previously in dealing with the most senior career bureaucrats (Goldenberg, 1984; Lynn, 1984; Moe, 1985).

In general, change in both congressional and bureaucratic institutions occurs slowly. New forms and behavior prescribed by statute are often absorbed into customary modes of conducting business with only minor adjustments.

THE INDIVIDUALS INVOLVED

This section presents aggregate profiles of major clusters of participants in the relationships between Congress and the bureaucracy: members of Congress, congressional staff members, political appointees in the executive branch, and civil servants.

Geographical Representation

Congress, by definition, is geographically representative. Since the reapportionment decisions of the federal courts applying to the House of Representatives in the 1960s, rural, suburban, and urban areas are all represented roughly in accord with their proportion of the total population. If there is any geographical bias in Congress it may be in the overrepresentation of smaller towns in terms of where members were born and raised. This is true of House leaders, for example (Nelson, 1975).

Many congressional staff members, particularly those on personal staffs, come from the state of their first employer. Once established, however, they may well go to work for a member from a different state. A recent study showed that close to two-thirds of personal staff members in the Senate retained a legal residence in the same state as the senator for whom they worked (Fox and Hammond, 1977).[1] Although reliable figures are scarce, it is reasonable to conclude that staff members in Congress initially come from all over the United States (with a few from foreign countries) and are probably broadly representative in geographical terms. Regardless of their own place of birth and upbringing, some personal staff members will have responsibility for tending to the welfare of the geographic constituency of the legislator for whom they work—assignment to constituency work is not limited to staff who come from the same geographic area as their employing legislator.

Regardless of place of origin, there is good evidence, based on a study of House staff in 1977 (Brady, 1981), that congressional staff members essentially become identified with the metropolitan Washington area in geographical terms. They tend to get their graduate education there, and many "new" jobs on the Hill go to individuals already in some Hill staff job. Thus, the number and volume of outsiders from Boise, Waco, or Akron shrinks.

Federal political executives—the major appointed figures in the executive branch—are also generally geographically representative of the entire population (Stanley, Mann, and Doig, 1967: 9–12, 110).[2] Compared to

---

[1]Fox and Hammond, 1977, is a major source of detailed data on congressional staff members. The samples vary in size depending on the characteristic discussed and the method of data collection; the samples range between about 160 and 480 Senate personal staff members, between about 50 and 450 House personal staff members, and about 300 committee staff members. Fox and Hammond focus on staff professionals (omitting clerical and secretarial positions). That focus is useful for our purposes because it is the staff professionals who are in a position to have some impact on the shaping of policy. Another good source on House staff members only is the summary and interpretation of 1977 data gathered by a House Commission on Administrative Review published in Brady, 1981.

[2]Stanley, Mann, and Doig, 1967, will be used frequently in the following pages. Their study is based on data on about 1,600 appointments to about 180 top federal positions from early 1933 through part of 1965. These positions include the secretaries, undersecretaries,

the general population in terms of birthplace, political appointees were underrepresentative only of the East South Central census region (Kentucky, Tennessee, Alabama, Mississippi). Compared on the basis of legal residence at the time of the appointment, only the South Atlantic census region was overrepresented (simply because Washington, D.C., is in this region). And on the basis of location of principal occupation at the time of the appointment, the distribution for political appointees again roughly mirrored that of the general population, although the Washington area overrepresentation was even more pronounced.

Federal political executives did heavily overrepresent larger cities, however, when the size of their city of principal occupation at the time of appointment was compared to the general population. Individuals from Washington (28 percent of all those appointed) and New York City (14 percent of all those appointed) dominated.

Members of the higher civil service (defined as GS 14s and above in this instance)—the policy level of the civil service—overrepresent the East and urban backgrounds when compared to the general population. The South is underrepresented. The Midwest and West are represented almost perfectly (Meier, 1979: 171). Thirty-nine percent of the higher civil servants in 1974 came from the East and 22 percent from the South. The population in general was located 28 percent in the East and 31 percent in the South. In terms of birthplace, 51 percent of the general population had an urban birthplace, but 76 percent of the higher civil service had urban birthplaces.

Education

Virtually all of the principal actors in Congress (both members and professional staff) and the actors in the policy-making positions in the executive branch have a considerable amount of formal education, and all groups are about equally well educated. Table 2-1 summarizes data on specific groups and compares them to the general population. Note that the data come from slightly different periods so they are not precisely comparable, but they sustain the point that the policy makers are very well educated. A very large proportion of these groups have education beyond the college level—either in graduate school or in law school. This held true, for example, for 60 percent of the representatives, 69 percent of the senators, 46 percent of higher civil servants defined as GS 15s and above (Stanley, Mann, and Doig, 1967: 18; data for 1963), and 63 percent

---

assistant secretaries, and general counsels of the cabinet-level departments and the three military services; the administrators and deputy administrators of a number of major independent agencies; and the members of seven regulatory commissions and boards. We shall use their terminology of "federal political officials" when presenting their results. Despite the fact that this study is two decades old nothing has replaced it.

TABLE 2-1
Formal Education of Policy Makers and the General Public

Group	Date of Data	Level of Education (Percentages)		
		Less Than College	Some College, No Degree	College Degree or More
U.S. representatives	1966	7	14	79
U.S. senators	1966	4	13	83
Congressional staff (professionals)	1972	6	5	89
Federal political executives	1961–65	2	5	93
Higher civil service (GS 14 +)	1974	1	3	96
General adult population	1974	69	18	13

Sources: For representatives and senators, Jones, 1967: 49; for congressional staff, compiled from data in Fox and Hammond, 1977: 175; for federal political executives, Stanley, Mann, and Doig, 1967: 18; for higher civil service and general adult population, Meier, 1979: 171.

of "supergrades" (GS 16, 17, and 18 and equivalents) in the civil service (Corson and Paul, 1966: 166; data for 1963). These figures have no doubt risen in the last few years for all groups. The policy makers remain much more highly educated than the general public.

Occupation

Reliable comparative figures on occupation of various policy-making groups *before* they attained their present position are hard to come by for several reasons. First, many individuals begin their careers in public service, either elected or appointed, and so their occupation is simply one of public service/politics. Second, when asked, many individuals, particularly in Congress, list several occupations. But examination of various figures leads to support for some general statements (although a table with nice percentages would be misleading).

In Congress slightly less than 45 percent of House members are lawyers and about three-fifths of senators are lawyers. About one-third of each house comes from a business background (some of them are also lawyers). Educational backgrounds are well represented too (9 percent of House members and 10 percent of Senate members in 1985–86).

Most committee staff members on the Hill come from other public-service positions (35 percent in the executive branch and 30 percent from other congressional positions, mostly positions on personal staffs). Only a few come from business (3 percent) or from the private practice of law (9 percent) (Fox and Hammond, 1977: 175).

Federal political executives between 1933 and 1965 came to their government positions predominantly from business or law backgrounds (about one-quarter from each category). Another 7 percent came from educational backgrounds (Stanley, Mann, and Doig, 1967: 34).

Analysis of a sample of higher civil servants in the late 1960s and early 1970s showed that most higher civil servants (GS 15s and above and their equivalents) began their careers in public service (40 percent); a large proportion came from business (30 percent); and a smaller but sizable proportion came from educational backgrounds (15 percent) (U.S. Civil Service Commission, 1976: 35).

What stands out in a comparative review of the backgrounds of the four groups of actors is (1) the public-service orientation of all categories of actors except federal political executives, (2) the dominance of a legal background in Congress, (3) the importance of a business background in all groups, and (4) the large representation of education (public and private schools, colleges, and universities) in all groups of actors. Thus, it is not fanciful to imagine that, in discourse among these groups, the concepts and language of the law and business are often predominant, with some familiarity with the concerns peculiar to educational institutions. It also seems likely that, because of their much weaker public-service orientation and experience, federal political executives probably find it most difficult to become accepted as fully legitimate (see Heclo, 1977).

Age

Members of Congress and others in top-level policy-making positions in the executive branch do not differ greatly in terms of average age. Only congressional staff members are somewhat younger, although not enough to put them clearly in a different "generation" (a vague notion at best). In 1985 the average age of senators and representatives together was slightly more than fifty (about fifty-four for the average senator and almost fifty for the average representative). Federal political executives averaged forty-eight years when appointed, and higher civil servants (GS 15s and above) averaged forty-eight years when appointed (Stanley, Mann, and Doig, 1967: 28). (The average age of all civil servants was forty-three in 1973.) Congressional staff members, rather than being in their late forties, tended to be just about forty in the mid-1970s (Fox and Hammond, 1977: 173). Whatever difficulties individuals on the Hill and both career and appointed bureaucrats have in communicating with each other would not seem to stem from a "generation gap."

Gender and Race

All of the groups we are discussing are dominated by white males. The Ninety-Ninth Congress (1985–86) had only two women and no blacks or Hispanics in the Senate (out of a total of 100 members), and only twenty-one women, nineteen blacks, and ten Hispanics among the 435 voting members of the House.

There are relatively few women in top congressional staff jobs at the professional level. One survey of professional staff (Fox and Hammond, 1977: 174) showed that 23 percent of Senate personal staffs, 31 percent of House personal staffs, and only 11 percent of committee staffs were women. A *Washington Post* story June 8, 1976, showed that only 6 percent of the 644 best-paying Senate staff positions were held by women. There are also relatively few blacks in these positions.

The higher civil service (GS 14s and above) is even more the preserve of white males. In 1974, 96 percent were white and 98 percent were male (Meier, 1979: 171). By 1981, despite concentrated affirmative action efforts, only 6.6 percent of the Senior Executive Service of about 7,000 of the top-level civil servants were women, and only 5.1 percent were black (Sawyer, 1982). No systematic data on sex and race are available for political appointees, but it is accurate to say that the numbers and percentages of women and minorities are very small and have shrunk in the Reagan administration compared to the Carter administration.

Previous Governmental and Political Experience

Individuals in the highest positions—senators, representatives, and federal political appointees—are highly experienced in government and political service before they reach their positions. Congressional staff members are less experienced, and high civil servants gain experience during their careers.

Members of the House and Senate are, generally, experienced public servants before they are elected to Congress. Most have held one or more elected positions at the state or local level.

Most congressional staff members, in large part because they are often younger than the other groups, have had less governmental experience before joining a personal staff, although those on committee staffs are more likely to have had such experience. Many congressional staff members have gained considerable political experience, however, usually through working in political campaigns, before joining a staff on the Hill.

Higher civil servants are not likely to have much governmental or political experience except that gathered through their careers, usually just in their own agency.

Of all federal political executives appointed between 1933 and 1965, only 15 percent had no federal service of any kind before assuming office, and more than three out of five had federal administrative experience (Stanley, Mann, and Doig, 1967: 42, 45).

Beliefs

Although there is a lot more to learn, some research has been done that characterizes both the beliefs about government and the political ideology of the groups of policy makers being considered here (Aberbach and Rockman, 1976, 1977, 1978; Fox and Hammond, 1977; Meier, 1979; Meier and Nigro, 1976; Rothman and Lichter, 1983).

Members of Congress, federal political executives, and higher civil servants all seem to believe in the legitimacy of subgovernments. They also generally believe that interest groups should have a high degree of access to both Congress and the bureaucracy (Aberbach and Rockman, 1977, 1978). No specific examination of congressional staff attitudes has been undertaken but it would be surprising if they differed on these points from their appointing members. Legislators and bureaucrats in the United States deal with each other on a regular basis, much more so, for example, than in Western European countries, and so the beliefs that they *should* deal with each other are both sustained and generated by actual practice (see Aberbach, Putnam, and Rockman, 1981, for the comparison of the U.S. experience with European experience). Some Reagan political appointees may be less disposed to believe in the desirability of subgovernments than their predecessors. But political executives are always the most likely group to register some dissent because they are often shut out of well-integrated subgovernments.

The political ideology of members of Congress can be expected to change, probably slowly, over time, depending on the outcome of elections. There is some evidence that at any given time Congress's ideology is probably not too far out of line with that held by higher-level officials in the bureaucracy (Aberbach and Rockman, 1977). The higher civil-service levels of the bureaucracy seem to hold abstract beliefs slightly more liberal than the general public but not far different from the public on specific issues (Meier, 1979: 172–73; Rothman and Lichter, 1983).

The ideology of congressional staff members, not surprisingly, mirrors rather closely the individuals in Congress for whom they work and by whom they were appointed (Fox and Hammond, 1977). The ideology of federal political executives, in theory, reflects that of the appointing president but, in practice, also comes to mirror that of the agency or department in which they work.

Thus, there is widespread agreement among different groups of actors with regard to some key beliefs about the functioning of government. And, even with regard to political ideology, there are forces that minimize differences between groups, although party affiliation may still divide Democrats from Republicans and may make relationships between a president and political executives of one party and a Congress controlled by another party somewhat difficult.

*   *   *   *   *

Table 2–2 summarizes the personal characteristics just discussed.

TABLE 2-2
Personal Characteristics of Major Congressional and Bureaucratic Policy Actors

Characteristics	Senators and Representatives	Professional Congressional Staff Members	Higher Career Civil Servants	Federal Political Executives
Geographical representativeness	Broadly representative geographically; over-representative of small towns	Broadly representative geographically	Overrepresentative of the East and urban areas	Broadly representative geographically; over-representative of large cities (especially New York and Washington)
Education	Highly educated	Highly educated	Highly educated	Highly educated
Occupation	Heavily in law and business; some educators; many professional politicians	Occupational specialty tied to job; many professional public servants; some generalists	Occupational specialty tied to job; many professional public servants; many with business background; some educators	Heavily in business and law; some educators
Age	Median: about 50 (senators slightly older)	Median: about 40	Median: late 40s	Median: late 40s
Gender and race	Mostly white males	Mostly white males	Mostly white males	Mostly white males
Previous governmental and political experience	High experience in both government and politics	Considerable Hill and political experience; limited executive branch experience	High government experience through civil service career	Moderately high experience in federal service
Beliefs	Believe in subgovernments and interest-group access; ideology shifts with election results	Believe in subgovernments and interest-group access; ideology reflects that of congressional employer	Believe in subgovernments and interest-group access; ideology reflects that of agency	Usually believe in subgovernments and interest-group access, with limits; ideology reflects that of agency and/or president

THE INSTITUTIONAL SETTING

The institutional settings in which various congressional and bureaucratic actors work help shape their behavior. The settings vary for each of the principal subgroups of actors in terms of method of selection, job tenure and orientation, principal loyalties and representativeness, degree of substantive specialization, degree of professionalism, degree of political expertise, and degree of visibility. These factors are relatively unchanging over time, regardless of the individuals holding the positions.

Method of selection means simply how actors achieve the positions they hold. The principal options are election, political appointment, or merit advancement. *Job tenure and orientation* are related to the means of selection and involve the length of service and careerist aspirations associated with different actors. *Principal loyalties* involve the actors' perceptions of the entity to which they feel they owe primary allegiance. *Representativeness* of various actors varies both according to the geographic area represented (national versus local) and the breadth of interests represented (broad-gauged interests versus narrow, special interests). Do actors tend to become experts in a few issues (specialists) or do they tend to have a general understanding of many issues (generalists)? The notion of *degree of substantive specialization* addresses these questions. An actor's identification with a profession, in addition to identification as a government employee, is the focus of the discussion of *degree of professionalism*. The *degree of political expertise* inherent in different actors' jobs involves how political those jobs are and how much political skill is necessary for holding them successfully—skill in bargaining, negotiations, and competing for limited amounts of power and resources. The final factor is the *degree of visibility* (or conversely, *anonymity*) associated with the actors—how publicly visible are different groups as they perform their daily routines?

Method of Selection

Of the four groups, only one—members of the House and Senate—is elected. This simple fact is enormously important in the kinds of considerations that are most salient to members as they deal with policy. Concern for job security nurtures a predisposition for members of Congress to provide the voters back home with sufficient tangible benefits that they will reelect the providers. Legislators usually evaluate their behavior, either consciously or unconsciously, in terms of the impact it will have on the electoral constituency and the constituency's reaction to it (Mayhew, 1974).

Once in Congress, members seek appointment to specific committees and subcommittees for a variety of reasons (Fenno, 1973). A number of members consciously seek a certain position because of the electoral advantage it can bring them. Even those who pursue memberships primarily because of their policy interests and because of their interest in increasing their influence within their chamber are mindful of opportunities a given assignment might afford them to serve their constituents. As members become more senior, they are generally less vulnerable at election time and can afford to pursue policy views that are particularly congenial to them as they work in committee and subcommittee settings.

The congressional staff is appointed by members of Congress and so reflects some of the members' concern with reelection and constituents. But, given the fact that an experienced staff member with an individual senator or representative can probably find another such job with a different member if the first employer should lose an election, the employee's personal stake is not nearly as strong as the member's stake.

Political appointments in the executive branch are made by the president. At least in theory, he is responsible for selecting the appointees, but in practice, many appointees are chosen by other high-ranking officials in the administration, either because they know and want a particular individual or because that person comes highly recommended by an important party figure—such as a major contributor of funds or an important senator or representative. Financial disclosure required by the 1978 Ethics in Government Act has made some potential political appointees reluctant to accept appointments.

Civil servants and their military and foreign-service equivalents are appointed on the basis of competitive examinations, and they advance on the basis of merit after that. In the upper levels of the civil service, political considerations are also used in filling selected top positions.

Job Tenure and Orientation

Not surprisingly, job tenure and orientation are related to the way an individual acquires office. Personnel turnover in positions dependent on electoral results is greater than in nonelective positions among civil servants. The shortest length of service occurs among political appointees in the executive branch. Median tenure in the mid-1960s was only twenty-eight months in a position and thirty-one months in an agency (Stanley, Mann, and Doig, 1967: 57; Heclo, 1977: 104). Because of their short tenure, political appointees generally have their careers in some field other than government service.

Tenure for individual legislators will always be uncertain because of the vagaries of elective office, but overall length of service in Congress has increased (not always steadily). The average number of years of service for members of both houses has dropped a bit in recent years but is still high: in the Ninety-Eighth Congress (1983–84) the average senator had served 9.6 years and the average representative was in his or her fourth two-year term. Careerist aspirations are now well entrenched among most members of Congress (Huntington, 1973; Polsby, 1968; Price, 1971; Witmer, 1964).

Although data are relatively scarce, it seems that many congressional staff members have become oriented toward a career in legislative staff work and are able to realize their ambitions, in many cases, for two reasons: First, the long service of the members (the appointing authorities) helps them stay in their positions. Second, even if their original patron is unseated, they are often sought by new members of the House and Senate and offered jobs because of the high value placed on their experience. (On the development of a congressional staff career, see Fox and Hammond, 1977: 62–65.)

Data from 1977 on tenure in current jobs in the House—both committee staff and personal staff—show that tenure in specific positions was relatively short. But this fact was offset by the additional fact, documented in the same study, that more than half the top positions on both personal and committee staffs were taken by individuals with experience on the Hill. Thus, even those who have worked in a specific top job for a short time are likely to have been a staff member in Congress for a much longer time (Brady, 1981).

The numbers of congressional staff have expanded dramatically in recent years. Between 1967 and 1983, for example, House personal staff increased by 86 percent, and Senate personal staff increased by 132 percent. Between 1965 and 1983 House committee staff increased by 245 percent, and Senate committee staff increased by 111 percent.

Careerism among bureaucrats at the policy-making levels is characterized by long service and low mobility in terms of shifting occupational specialties, shifting between agencies, and shifting between Washington and federal field installations (Corson and Paul, 1966: 22, 175, 176; Stanley, 1964: 27, 32–34, 102–3). In the early 1960s, for example, the higher civil servants had an average length of service of twenty-three years. Almost three-quarters of these individuals had served for more than twenty years. More than 86 percent of them had spent their entire careers in no more than two departments (almost 56 percent had been in only one department), and more than 68 percent had served in no more than two bureaus (more than 37 percent had been in only one bureau). Movement between Washington headquarters and field offices was very low (almost 90 percent had never left headquarters to go into the field). Figures published by the U.S. Civil Service Commission (1976) show the same lack of mobility in the 1970s.

Corson and Paul's (1966) figures on supergrade civil-service employees in 1963 show the same pattern: two-thirds had worked in no more than two bureaus and about 40 percent in only one. About half had worked in the same agency or department for their entire careers. Only 15 percent had ever worked outside the federal government once they had begun service, and more than three-fourths had held all of their federal jobs in the same occupational field.

The civil servants are the most career oriented of all the four groups and are also most likely to serve a full career wholly within a single institutional location. For example, a sample of federal civil servants interviewed in 1960 and 1961 showed that most were highly intent on staying in federal service; 88 percent of the general employees were very sure or fairly sure they wanted to stay in federal service, and only 7 percent planned to leave. Among executives in the civil service, 94 percent were very sure they wanted to stay and only 3 percent planned to leave. Even among professionals (natural scientists, social scientists, and engineers whose major loyalties might have been to their professions and not to the government organization with which they were employed), there was a high propensity to stay with federal service. Between 69 and 82 percent of these three professional groups were either sure or fairly sure they wanted to stay in federal service, and only between 10 and 18 percent planned to leave (Kilpatrick, Cummings, and Jennings, 1963: 188). Predictably, civil servants who were older and had more service were the most wedded to remaining.

Principal Loyalties and Representativeness

The principal loyalties of members of the House and Senate are generally split between loyalty to their constituencies (or, more accurately, to their perceptions of various constituencies—see Fenno, 1978) and loyalty to their congressional parties. In general, congressional life is structured so the two loyalties do not compete in head-on fashion often. When they do compete directly, a member will ordinarily stick with his perceptions of the constituency's interest.

Congressional staff members are primarily loyal to their appointing authority—that is, to the individual senator or representative responsible for having put them in their present jobs. If a staff member's "sponsor" is highly oriented toward constituency interests, the staff member is also likely to reflect that concern. If a sponsor is more oriented toward maintaining a given programmatic or ideological stance, then the staff member is more likely to take that tack too.

In theory, executive political appointees are primarily loyal to the president, the president's program, and the administration as a collectivity. In practice, political appointees are also at least partially loyal to the organization to which they are appointed. Thus, a secretary of agriculture will try to be responsible to the president who made the appointment, but if career bureaucrats within the department perceive their interests to be at odds with the president's policy initiatives, the secretary will encounter cross-pressures. Ordinarily the secretary will try to find some compromise that will avoid direct disagreement with the president, at least publicly, while still not "selling out" the department. Even in the Reagan administration, unusual for its greater-than-normal reliance on ideological criteria for making presidential appointments, some of those same ideologues turned out to defend agency budgets against severe cuts proposed by the OMB (the president's budget arm).

Civil servants are primarily loyal to the organizations in which they work and in which they are likely to make their career. They are perhaps less cross-pressured than the other major actors. Those in agencies who also belong to a nationally recognized profession (lawyers, engineers, scientists, doctors) may also feel considerable loyalty to the standards of their profession and may sometimes be cross-pressured by the perceived competing demands of profession and agency (Wilensky, 1967). The Reagan administration was also unusual in terms of the ideological demands made on top civil servants. These demands, coupled with staff reductions and reassignments, helped render many of the domestic agencies inefficient and demoralized, and less able to promote and implement programs the administration did not like.

Members of the House and Senate are concerned with representing their geographical areas—their districts or states—and are usually also concerned with representing a variety of interests they perceive to be important. While the notion of representation may be interpreted differently by senators and representatives, they are all concerned with being representative. For some, this may mean focusing mostly on tangible benefits for the district and for the most important organized groups in the district. For others, this may mean thinking about the broader needs of the district and of national interests and groups—both organized and unorganized. For most members, representation probably involves a range of activities—from seeking a new post office for some town in the district or state to worrying about the welfare of all poor people or all cotton farmers or all black people or whatever group seems to the member to be important.

Congressional staff members are also interested in representation in the same senses in which members are interested. Their interest is largely a reflection of the interests of their sponsors, although some individuals may also feel strongly about their representative capacities serving in a staff role.

Executive branch officials are also concerned with representation, but they are not concerned with a specific constituency in the same sense as individuals on Capitol Hill. The geographical ties to a local constituency of both political appointees and civil servants stationed in Washington are weaker than those of members of Congress and usually weaker than those of congressional staff members. They may retain some ties to the region in which they grew up, or, more likely, their program may have a particular regional focus (an Agriculture Department official working with cotton price supports is, of course, going to be concerned mostly with the cotton-growing regions of the South; an official in the Bureau of Reclamation is going to be concerned mainly with the arid lands of the West). But many Washington officials are involved with programs that have a national scope, and they are likely to think about the program in national terms.

But the great majority of federal bureaucrats in the United States are not located in the metropolitan Washington, D.C., area. These individuals are scattered throughout the country in a variety of federal field installations such as state, regional, and local offices. The bureaucrats who populate these field installations have regional and local geographic loyalties tied to their agencies' programs, and they undertake their work in such a way as to maximize the size of their operation in their region, state, or locality.

In addition to geographic interests, bureaucrats—both political appointees and civil servants—are also typically concerned with representing interests they perceive to be important to their programs and worthy of their attention. In general, political appointees are expected to be supportive of and sympathetic to the programmatic interests of the president and to represent these interests to Congress. They also may be concerned with representing the interests thought to be important to their political party, and thus their concern with specific representation may not be very well developed, although it seems reasonable to argue that a Republican secretary of labor, for example, will be concerned with representing managerial interests at least some of the time and that a Democratic secretary of labor will be concerned with representing organized labor's interests most of the time. To survive politically, appointees in departments and agencies are most likely to be representative of many interests involved with their agencies rather than representing only one or two interests. An appointee who advocates a single, narrow interest is apt to be a controversial figure and a political liability for the president's program and in the national electorate.

Political appointees can be representative in the critical sense of allowing competing points of view to be heard in the executive branch on controversial matters before final action is taken. Sometimes policy debates take place almost wholly within the executive branch, and the major decisions are made and the major compromises are struck before the matter becomes an important item on the congressional agenda. This was the case, for example, with the bargaining and arguments that led up to the passage of the Communications Satellite Act of 1962 and the Economic Opportunity Act of 1964 (Davidson, 1967: 390–93).

Civil servants often become very concerned with representing interests and organized groups they conceive to be important in the fields in which they are working. Sometimes this representational activity simply takes the form of advocacy by strategically placed civil servants on behalf of interests and groups. In other cases the advocacy of specific interests by a bureaucracy becomes more institutionalized. For example, some agencies use a variety of advisory committees to make and enforce decisions at the local level. These committees operate in several policy areas, including agriculture and land use (Foss, 1960; Lowi, 1973a). A potential problem with advisory committees is that they may become captives of some segment of the served clientele, and bureaucrats, in heeding their advice, are thus responding to only a narrow interest group. This was the case with federal lands grazing policy in the 1950s and 1960s. (Foss, 1960: chapter 6; Culhane, 1981).

Degree of Substantive Specialization

Members of the House and Senate are both subject-matter specialists and generalists. They are generalists because they are given the constitutional power—which they exercise with considerable, even if uneven, vigor—to oversee the entire range of federal governmental activities. They must consider and vote on everything the federal government does, at least in broad outline. Any individual is going to have a number of substantive areas in which his or her knowledge is minimal, but most senators and representatives who serve for more than a short time begin to develop familiarity with and some competence in a variety of areas.

At the same time members have also become specialists through their service on the standing committees and subcommittees of the two chambers. The committee system emerged in large part as the congressional response to a bureaucracy constantly growing in size, specialization, and expertise. Especially in the House—where in the Ninety-Eighth Congress (1983–84) the average member had assignments to only 1.7 standing committees and 3.6 subcommittees—members who serve for more than a short time become genuine experts in some piece of the policy world. In the Senate the members are spread more thinly because each senator has more assignments—an average of 2.9 standing committees and 7.5 subcommittees in 1983–84 (Ornstein and others, 1984: 111).

The congressional urge to specialize in order to compete with the bureaucrats is reinforced by the staff on the Hill. In both houses, staff members have become genuinely expert in some bounded portion of the policy universe, although staff members working in the offices of individual senators and representatives have much less time for work on substantive legislative matters than staff working for committees. Senate staff members—both those on committees and a few working in individual senators' offices—are particularly important as specialists because of the limited time and attention the typical senator can give to committee and subcommittee assignments. Senators often rely principally on a staff member to do most of the substantive work in some subcommittees to which the senator is formally assigned (Ripley, 1969a: chapter 8). Many staff members, including those on committees, are also expected to attend to political matters and to deal with constituents in a variety of ways.

In the civil service the degree of substantive specialization is very high. The main reason for the emergence of a large bureaucracy is, after all, to facilitate dealing with technical and complex topics. On the other hand, the degree of specialization among political appointees is typically very low. Commonly, political appointees in the executive branch have little experience in the subject matter with which they are expected to deal and usually do not stay in office long enough to develop much expertise through on-the-job training.

Degree of Professionalism

Professionalism is used to denote allegiance on the part of individuals to a profession other than that of government employee. For example, chemists employed by the Food and Drug Administration (FDA) may remain loyal to the norms of the chemistry profession, attend meetings of the American Chemical Society, and subscribe to a variety of professional journals. Such individuals are likely to be as concerned with national professional standards and judgments as with the narrower interests of the FDA as an agency.

Most professionalism in this sense resides in the civil service. Scattered throughout the bureaucracy are social scientists, natural scientists, engineers, dentists, physicians, and others whose professional identification is very high.

In the rest of the government—the appointed parts of the executive branch and both the elected and appointed parts of the legislative branch—the degree of professionalism is much lower. There are many lawyers, particularly in Congress, but they seem to retain little identification with abstract norms of the profession. For many, law was both a form of academic training and a natural entry into public service but not a profession actively practiced for long.

Degree of Political Expertise

By definition, senators and representatives are and must be politicians. A member needs the political skill of assessing the mood of his or her constituency. Members also are likely to develop considerable bargaining skills as they pursue their daily tasks in Congress. Staff members typically possess a number of the same kinds of political skills. Some are hired expressly for their political skills that can be used to help the member gain reelection and/or have the maximum impact on substantive policy questions.

Executive branch political appointees presumably possess considerable political skills—both in advancing the interests of the administration and the party of the president and in bargaining. Some political appointees are very adroit politically. In fact, some are so skillful that they develop their own constituency and support apart from the president, who is presumably their sponsor. A classic case is that of Jesse Jones, secretary of commerce under President Franklin Roosevelt (Fenno, 1959: 234–47). His ties with powerful business interests and his excellent relations with Congress allowed him to take policy stands contrary to those desired by Roosevelt. Yet the president tolerated Jones's behavior for more than four years because, on balance, his independent strength helped the administration more than it hurt it.

Some political appointees turn out to be quite inept politically. President Eisenhower's secretary of defense, Charles Wilson of General Motors, was usually in hot water with some congressional committee for his seemingly thoughtless remarks ("What's good for the country is good for General Motors, and vice versa.") and behavior. Reagan's first secretary of the interior, James Watt, also drew constant fire from environmental groups and congressional committees but received continued backing from the president anyway. In speaking of the cabinet specifically, Fenno (1959:207–8) concluded that, politically, a skillful secretary "maintains legislative-executive relations in an equilibrium and prevents them from deteriorating to the point where they hurt the President. What the ordinary Cabinet member supplies is a kind of *preventive assistance*. . . . The best that he can ordinarily do is to help the President in small amounts—probably disproportionate to the time he consumes doing it." The same generalization probably applies to the whole range of political appointees in the executive branch.

In theory, civil servants are supposed to be apolitical. They are barred from overt partisan activity by federal statute. The textbooks proclaim them to be "above politics" and concerned only with rational, economical, and efficient implementation of public-policy objectives determined by their political superiors.

In the United States, however, the textbook model does not apply in large part. Senior civil servants are fully political actors, and in many respects the governmental system in which they work expects that they will be if they are to be successful (Aberbach, Putnam, and Rockman, 1981; Heclo, 1977; Kaufman, 1981; and Yates, 1982).

The political stance of the bureaucracy is the result of several factors—grants of administrative discretion, congressional reliance on the bureaucracy, and competition in advancing the agencies' perceived interests. Broad administrative discretion to fill in the gaps of basic legislation does not promote "neutral" administration. Bureaucrats' decisions have political repercussions, and bureaucrats experience pressure for and against their administrative decisions. Congress relies on the bureaucracy as a primary source of policy ideas and initiatives, and policy is rarely neutral—it almost always conveys benefits to some and deprives others. Who wins and who loses is, after all, what politics is all about. The continuous maneuvering by senior agency officials to maximize the interests of their agencies and programs, especially at budget time, but also throughout daily routines, requires a high degree of political skill. Agency officials cannot afford to be neutral if their agency's interests are to be advanced.

Richard Neustadt has convincingly explained the basic reason for the political nature of our top civil servants. The governmental system puts them in direct competition with other actors and thereby breeds the necessity of developing political skills in order to gain or preserve the resources to perform programmatic tasks effectively. (Neustadt, 1973: 132):

> We maximize the insecurities of men and agencies alike. Careerists jostle in-and-outers (from the law firms, business, academic life) for the positions of effective influence; their agencies contend with the committees on the Hill, the Office of Management and Budget, other agencies for the prerequisites of institutional survival, *year by year.* Pursuit of programs authorized in law can be a constant struggle to maintain and hold support of influential clients, or the press. And seeking new authority to innovate a program can be very much like coalition warfare. Accordingly, most agencies have need for men of passion and conviction—or at least enormous powers of resistance—near the top. American officialdom may generate no more of these than other systems do, but it rewards them well: they rise toward the top.

Degree of Visibility

Visibility is, of course, relative, and it may vary from observer to observer. To even an interested part of the general public, for example, virtually all of the actors being discussed here, except some senators and representatives, are anonymous. To most journalists covering Washington, only senators and representatives and a few political appointees in the executive branch are consistently visible. A really skillful reporter will also come to know important congressional staff members and, occasionally, even a civil servant or two. Skillful lobbyists will tend to know individuals in all of the major clusters of actors. Senators and representatives and the major political appointees in the executive branch, such as the president's cabinet, are the most visible to most observers. Congressional staff members and civil servants are relatively unknown to a large number of observers.

*   *   *   *   *

Table 2–3 summarizes the discussion of the institutional work setting for the four major clusters of actors.

TYPICAL RELATIONSHIPS BETWEEN CONGRESS AND THE BUREAUCRACY: THE IMPACT OF ROLE

Thus far we have examined the work settings of the principal actors in the congressional-bureaucratic relationship and the aggregate characteristics of individuals in those positions. A third factor that can also help explain cooperation and conflict in the relationship between Congress and the bureaucracy is the actors' role.

Role is a complex concept as used in sociology and psychology, but its essential meaning is the "expected pattern of behavior associated with an actor who is in a particular relationship to a social system" (Davidson, 1969: 73). The role associated with any particular actor derives from several sources—the actor's individual characteristics and disposition, his or her institutional setting, the cumulative history of previous behavior in the position (by the actor and others), and the expectations of others about how an actor in the position should act. For purposes of this volume, we will refer to role as regularities in behavior of actors—how actors have tended to behave in the past.

Several well-established relationships between Congress and the bureaucracy that are critical to policy making occur among various subgroups of actors: between congressional committees and clusters of bureaucrats; between congressional staff and bureaucrats; between executive branch liaison personnel and Congress; and among the institutional presidency, bureaucrats, and Congress. In the following pages, general descriptions of these types of interactions are presented (1) to illustrate the role of the actors (that is, the regularities in their behavior) and (2) to illustrate the kind of accommodations the actors reach in their interactions. Specific examples of these types of interactions will be presented in Chapters 4 through 7.

Bureaucrats and the Appropriations Committees

The interaction between agency bureaucrats and appropriations committee members is of critical importance because appropriations committees allocate some (although not all) of the resources that enable bureaucrats to carry out their agency's programs. This interaction has been

TABLE 2-3
The General Institutional Setting for Congressional and Bureaucratic Policy Actors

Characteristic	Members of House and Senate	Congressional Staff Members	Executive Branch Political Appointees	Civil Servants and Equivalents
Method of selection	Election	Appointment by senators and representatives	Appointment by president	Competition and merit
Job tenure and orientation	Relatively long service; careerist orientation	Relatively long service; relatively careerist orientation	Short service; noncareer orientation	Long service; career orientation
Principal loyalties	Constituencies and congressional parties	Sponsors (appointing members)	President and agency to which appointed	Agency
Degree of concern with representation	High for geographical constituencies and special interests	Moderately high for geographical constituencies and interests	Low for geographical units; moderately low for special interests	High for special interests; moderate for geographical units among non-Washington-based civil servants; low for geographical units among Washington-based civil servants
Degree of substantive specialization	Moderately high (especially in House)	Moderately high	Low	High
Degree of professionalism	Low	Generally low	Low	High for major subgroups of employees
Degree of political expertise	High	Moderately high	Moderately high	Moderately high (for highest grades)
Degree of visibility	High	Low	Moderately high	Low

extensively and well studied (Fenno, 1966; Horn, 1970; Wildavsky, 1984; also Gist, 1978; LeLoup, 1980a). These studies support several generalizations about the nature of the interaction.

First, there is a great desire on the part of executive branch officials responsible for program operations to build up confidence over time with the members of the subcommittees that have specific jurisdiction over their appropriations. They believe that long-standing relations of good quality between themselves and the members will build a solid reputational base for them and will result in better (that is, larger) appropriations. In fact, there is solid empirical evidence that the longer individuals in an agency interact with its appropriations subcommittee, the better their agency will do in its appropriations, both in terms of the absolute size of appropriations and in terms of the percentage of its requests that are granted (Moreland, 1975).

Second, the general thrust of the behavior of agency bureaucrats is to reduce uncertainty in the treatment they receive in the appropriations process. They also seek to increase their appropriations and their share of appropriations, but they do not usually do so at the risk of alienating subcommittee members and thus jeopardizing even their existing appropriations base. Basically they seek to reduce uncertainty by being solicitous of subcommittee concerns (for example, by following mandates in subcommittee reports scrupulously even though such mandates do not have the force of law), by preparing thoroughly for formal hearings, and by maintaining continuing informal contacts so the subcommittee members always feel fully informed about agency activities.

Third, the basic attitude of most members of the House Appropriations Committee is that agency budget requests always contain some "fat" and that it is the committee's duty to trim the fat. But generally the members are also concerned with providing what they perceive to be enough money for an agency so its programs are not damaged. Once a subcommittee has made its decisions, its members will usually serve as agency defenders in the full Appropriations Committee and especially on the floor of the House.

Fourth, the basic attitude of most members of the Senate Appropriations Committee is even friendlier to the agencies. They think the House committee usually cuts dangerously deep into agency requests, and they are likely to restore a substantial portion of the cuts. They will raise some questions but are more disposed to accept bureaucrats' judgments about necessary resources. The differences in outlook of the House and Senate appropriations committees stem from the personnel shortage on the Senate committee—which inclines the members to accept the executive's vision of what is needed without timeconsuming scrutiny—and from the fact that senators can choose their subcommittee assignments on the Appropriations Committee (in the House until 1975, the chair made the assignments) (Morrow, 1969: 178). This leads senators to seek subcommittees where they can dispense "pork" to their areas, and hence they are not keen on eliminating the surplus in requests.

Some of the changes spurred by Reagan's political success and Republican control of the Senate following the elections of 1980, 1982, and 1984 have, for partisan reasons, led to less predictability in the roles of the appropriations committees in the two houses. Some movement was evident even before Reagan became president and the Senate turned Republican. Schick (1981: 41) had already made the observation that the House was becoming "more an advocate" and the Senate "more a guardian."

Fifth, neither senators nor representatives on the appropriations committees seem to have much desire to engage in broad-gauged oversight of bureaucratic activities. Their oversight activity is more likely to focus on specific items of expenditure rather than to pose broader questions about the societal impact of the agencies whose proposals are being considered. Members do seem disposed, however, to seek membership on subcommittees overseeing agency budgets that are relatively more "controllable" (the product of annual appropriations rather than other statutes).

Sixth, interest-group representatives have an impact on appropriations decisions—often through the executive branch officials (sometimes at the behest of those bureaucrats) and sometimes through Appropriations Committee members, especially in the Senate. The thrust of such intervention by lobbyists is almost always to preserve advantages with which they are already blessed either in terms of level of support for a program important to them or in terms of specific report language favorable to their interests. Horn (1970: 189–90) cites a classic case of the latter kind:

> In 1965, a nationwide automobile rental firm, faced with competition in the Midwest from a small, subsidized airline that also rented cars to its passengers at various airports, successfully secured report language directing the Civil Aeronautics Board's attention to "the practice of certain air carriers to engage in noncarrier activities. . . ." The Senate subcommittee admonished the board to "continue to supervise these activities vigorously to make sure that such non-carrier operations are not being subsidized."

Finally, in general it can be said that in the appropriations process most of the important actors desire stability above all else, despite the differences in perspective indicated by the fact that members of Congress are directly responsible to constituents and bureaucrats are not. Fenno (1966: 348) summarizes the relationship between bureaucrats and the House committee very persuasively, and his description could easily be broadened to cover the Senate committee too.

> The House Appropriations Committee–executive agency relationship is characterized on the one hand by conflict and uncertainty; it is characterized on the other by a substantial agreement on what should be done and is being done

to minimize conflict and uncertainty and, hence, to keep the relationship reasonably stable.

The sources of conflict lie in the difference between the program-oriented goals of the agencies and the combination of economy-oversight goals of the Committee. . . . The existence of conflict helps to promote uncertainty. And the sources of that uncertainty lie in the difference in the political worlds inhabited by the nonelected executive and the elected representative. . . .

Both groups, however, want to stabilize the relationship—want, that is, to keep conflict and uncertainty to a tolerable and predictable level—because it is in their interest to do so. For the agency, a stable relationship is an aid to program planning and implementation. For the Committee, a stable relationship is an aid to adaptation and survival—to its continued ability, that is, to meet House member and Committee member desires.

Early in the Reagan administration the importance of the appropriations committees in both houses was somewhat diminished because the total budget package went through a reconciliation process in both 1981 and 1982 (Schick, 1981). The central purpose of reconciliation is to aggregate decisions. The normal procedure focused on the appropriations committees and especially their subcommittees is completely disaggregated. There was a return to a more disaggregated process in 1983, 1984, and 1985. However, pressure mounted to return to a more centralized process as the federal deficit continued to balloon. By the end of 1985 a new statutory requirement for reaching a balanced budget by 1991 was in place, and some observers thought the roles and strategies of various actors in the budget process could be profoundly altered by the requirements of that statute.

Bureaucrats and the Ways and Means Committee

The House Ways and Means Committee has extensive and important jurisdiction: it contributes to congressional input into governmental tax policy, the source of revenue for all agencies; it oversees the entire social security system, including medicare; it legislates welfare policy; and it makes trade policy, including tariffs and import and export quotas.

In this relationship, executive officials work so closely with the committee that, according to one member of the committee, "They become *part* of the Committee" (Manley, 1970: 350). Executive officials are invited to participate in, not just observe, the meetings of the committee at which decisions are made on the details of legislation that will be reported to the House floor. There is also a great deal of interaction between executive officials and committee members outside formal committee hearings and meetings.

Ways and Means members participate in the details of policy making (although before 1975 only a few members dominated the detailed work of the committee; since then there has been broader participation—see Rudder, 1977). They can, collectively, hold up the endorsement of some major executive branch initiatives. The members of the committee do not, however, engage in broad-gauged oversight of the agencies and major programs within their jurisdiction. They make changes and additions in programs but without seeking or obtaining much evidence on the results of their past handiwork and the agencies' interpretations of that handiwork in the implementation process (Pincus, 1974).

The desire for stability is also a dominant motivation in the interactions between bureaucrats involved in programs within the jurisdiction of the Ways and Means Committee and the members of that committee. Major changes are typically generated from the White House (medicare, health insurance, tax reform, tax increases or decreases, new trade policy, new social security benefits). Thus the system of interactions is less stable than in appropriations, and the intervention of the White House and the president personally is more frequent.

Bureaucrats and Congressional Staff

Civil servants who are experts on complex subjects and their counterparts on congressional staffs usually work together very closely (Fox and Hammond, 1977: Chapter 7 and p. 197). In general, the congressional staff members need the information the civil servants can provide, and usually it is forthcoming. This is true even when the executive branch and Congress are controlled by different political parties. In such cases the federal political executives and the majority of various standing committees may have major policy disagreements. Nevertheless, the cooperative relationships between the committee staffs and the bureau staffs continue. For example, in the Eightieth Congress (1947–48), when the Democrats still controlled the presidency but the Republicans had won control of Congress, close staff cooperation still marked the relations between the Treasury Department and the Joint Committee on Internal Revenue Taxation even though tax bills were the subject of major public fights between the president and Congress (Kofmehl, 1977: 157). Regardless of party control, there are also instances in which the executive branch and the congressional committee are clearly in disagreement on some policy, but close technical cooperation between staff members continues unimpaired. Sometimes a staff member for an interest group will also become involved in these staff interactions and will serve to transmit the technical expertise of an executive branch formally hostile to a specific initiative to congressional staff. This happened, for example, as the first federal air pollution legislation to contain federal abatement powers (which became the Clean Air Act of 1963) was developed in late 1962 and early 1963 (Ripley, 1969b).

In the area of tax policy, a particularly close relationship between committee staff and Treasury Department staff has developed (Manley, 1970: 342–46). In this case staff members from the Ways and Means Committee, from the Joint Committee on Taxation, and from the Treasury regularly meet and discuss a range of technical details. They even form "staff subcommittees" to pursue various topics. The importance of this close relationship is summarized by John Manley (1970: 344):

> First, the meetings ensure that by the time the Treasury Department sends its tax message the Joint Committee staff is well-versed in the complexities of the proposals and is therefore equipped to explain them to the members. Second, the predictions of Committee response made by the Joint Committee staff have been relayed to the top officials of the Treasury Department and become one more element in their calculation of what they should propose to Congress. Third, having worked closely together throughout the process the two staffs are better able to draft the necessary language after the Committee makes a decision and to present the issues during the Committee's deliberations on the bill.

Relations between members of appropriations subcommittee staffs in the House and Senate and civil servant technicians are also close. Wildavsky (1984: 55–56) summarizes the nature of this relationship and the reasons for it:

> Many agencies choose to keep subcommittee staff informed months and sometimes years ahead on new developments. This expedient enables the staff to have ready explanations if and when Congressmen make inquiries. . . .
>
> Although it appears that agency personnel are more dependent on committee staff than vice versa, the relationship is by no means a one-way proposition. The staff man knows that he can do a more effective job if he has the cooperation of the budget officer. For much of the staff's work is dependent on securing information from the agency about current programs and the possible effects of various changes. The staff may be blamed for not informing Congressmen of changes in agency plans and expenditures. And when complex problems arise, the agency many actually do the work for the staff. Mutual dependence is the order of the day and both sides generally regard their contacts as prerequisites to doing their best work.

In short, technicians working for both Congress and executive branch agencies have a large stake in maintaining good relations. This means that neither side should spring policy "surprises" on the other without adequate warning and full discussion ahead of time.

Executive Branch Congressional Liaison Officials and Members of Congress

Liaison officials throughout the executive branch have a particularly big stake in promoting and maintaining good relations with Congress

(Holtzman, 1970). Their job is to sell policy positions favored by the executive branch and to promote a sense of congressional confidence in whatever part of the executive branch they are representing. There are many liaison actors in the executive branch—White House office liaison officials work directly for the president and his legislative priorities; departmental legislative liaison personnel (usually assistant secretaries) are presidential appointees and promote the president's priorities, but they are also responsive to their department's legislative priorities; liaison officials within the specific agencies and bureaus of a department are concerned primarily with their agency's priorities. All of these liaison officials try to persuade Congress to adopt or not tamper with legislation to fulfill presidential, departmental, and agency priorities. Their congressional targets include party leaders, committee and subcommittee chairpersons, individual members, and congressional staff members.

There is, of course, considerable potential for tension when liaison officials face members who have different predispositions from those of the executive branch. There is also considerable room for tension (and confusion) within the executive branch liaison operation itself. Promoting the policy priorities of the president, the departments, and the agencies in an integrated and coordinated fashion is a mammoth challenge. Although in principle the president's priorities are supposed to be supported by the rest of the executive branch, in practice departments and agencies have their own legislative priorities, and these may or may not be compatible with the president's.

There is a natural tendency for liaison personnel from individual agencies to compromise with committee members and staff members in Congress, whereas the liaison personnel working directly for the White House have a stronger tendency to resist compromise. These natural tendencies contribute to tension within the executive branch liaison operation. This tension reached its height in the Nixon administration. The president and Congress were ideologically at odds on a range of domestic issues, and the White House staff believed that the liaison officials for various agencies were too quick to abandon presidential principles. Therefore, the White House attempted unsuccessfully to centralize the entire executive branch liaison operation even more than it had been previously by making the chief liaison official in each agency and department directly responsible to the White House rather than to the agency head or department secretary.

In contrast to the centralization of President Nixon's liaison activities, the liaison efforts during the first eighteen months of the Carter administration were marked by chaos. White House liaison activities were uncoordinated and repeatedly offended key members of Congress (Bonafede, 1979; Elder, 1978; Light, 1979). The effort improved in the last few Carter years but was never particularly highly regarded on the Hill.

Carter's problems with legislative lobbying stemmed from a variety of personal, political, and institutional factors. Many of the personnel appointed to White House and department liaison jobs had limited experience with lobbying, with Congress, and with the political process in general. The nature of Congress had changed from the early 1960s— congressional reforms distributed power among more members, and members were displaying a greater sense of independence from congressional leaders and the president than they had done in the past. Part of Carter's problems were the result of his righteous, "above politics" attitude and an unwillingness to engage in political horse trading.

The Reagan congressional liaison effort was highly centralized and ran quite efficiently. The White House congressional liaison office received regular reports from the liaison offices of all of the departments and agencies. The Office of Management and Budget clearance function for keeping departmental policies in accord with the program of the president was also used by the White House liaison office to help make sure agency liaison personnel did not free-lance in support of agency objectives that did not meet with White House approval. As the Department of Labor's chief lobbyist put it, in referring to Reagan's first head of White House congressional liaison, "One of the first things Max Friedersdorf said to me is, 'There is no such thing as a departmental position. There is an administration position' " (Keller, 1981b: 2392).

The Institutional Presidency, Congress, and Bureaucrats

The institutional presidency represents, or at least purports to represent, the president in dealing with the rest of the executive branch and Congress. The heart of the institutional presidency is in the White House, whose members are all political appointees, and in the Office of Management and Budget, whose members are a mix of a few political appointees and a much larger number of career civil servants. But, despite the ratio, OMB has become an increasingly political body in recent years. Even in the area of budget projections the Congressional Budget Office is now widely regarded as both more accurate and more neutral than OMB. The latter injects a political coloration into virtually all of its activities.

The principal role orientation of officials working immediately for the president as they interact with Congress is to create and/or maintain good relations with that body, simply because any president must have good relations in order to get desired legislation through Congress. At times, however, the programmatic or ideological integrity of policy positions may be viewed as more important by the president and his White House and OMB staff than smooth relations. When this occurs, tension characterizes the relationship. The degree of tension is heightened if different political parties control the presidency and Congress, and also if both sides are strongly committed to major ideological differences. In the Nixon administration, for example, tension in the relationship between Congress and the executive branch was very great, and Congress reacted by attempting to decrease the size of staff and the salary schedules for personnel in the White House and OMB. In 1974 Congress made future directors and deputy directors of OMB subject to Senate confirmation.

In the triangular relationship among members of the presidency, the bureaucracy, and Congress, the president often confronts a preexisting, entrenched relationship between bureaus and congressional committees and subcommittees. If the president's policy preferences differ from those held by members of the entrenched relationship, and if he feels intensely enough about his preferences to want to pursue them and impose them, then it is inevitable that the White House and OMB officials, acting under his direction, are going to be viewed as disturbing influences by members of the entrenched relationship—committee and subcommittee members in Congress, their staff, and officials of the affected agency. When presidentially appointed departmental secretaries seek to control the bureaus within their departments (usually under presidential directive), they also are viewed by bureau chiefs (most of whom are civil servants) as disruptions to the normal ways of doing business with their congressional committees and subcommittees.

The Reagan administration made a particularly concerted effort to put and keep the bureaucracy under its thumb and to discourage the normal semiautonomous relations between bureaus, interest groups, and congressional subcommittees that could have resulted in policies and programs opposed by the administration. The top political echelons in the various agencies and departments were kept particularly closely wedded to the central administration's view. A number of the domestic agencies had both their budget and their work force cut. Along with the cuts in work force came massive internal reorganizations and reassignments in some agencies. These cuts, reorganizations, and reassignments were supplemented by a number of firings and transfers motivated by political and programmatic considerations. In some agencies congressional mandates from the past were ignored, at least in part. The result in most of the domestic agencies was a combination of widespread demoralization (with its concomitant inefficiency), acquiescence on the part of most employees to the new situation they faced, and dramatic resignations and protests on the part of a few employees. From their point of view, the Reagan administration and its political level of departmental and agency people were seeking to transform the bureaucracy into reliable supporters of their political and programmatic preferences. They worked to break the link between the career civil servants and congressional subcommittees and interest groups they considered hostile. The efforts met with considerable success in the short run. How permanent these changes are remains to be seen.

The longer-run view suggests that, despite political successes of the moment, there are still major forces pushing for relatively high degrees of autonomy for bureaus and relatively low degrees of central administrative leadership from a departmental secretary and staff loyal to a president. A leading student of bureaucratic behavior in the United States, Herbert Kaufman, summarizes the major forces pushing against central control and in favor of relatively high autonomy: "overextended spans of control, lack of managerial talent among cabinet officers, congressional hostility toward departmental control of bureaus, . . . pressure on the secretaries and their aides to concentrate on responsibilities other than departmental administration . . ." (Kaufman, 1981: 189–90).

Even without unusually heavy presidential involvement, the institutional presidency is not viewed sympathetically by most of the bureaucracy, especially those at the operating level. By definition the White House and OMB staff play a centralizing role in the legislative process (Neustadt, 1954, 1955); also by definition this tendency poses a threat to the stable relations and the stable policy preferences centered around agency-committee nexuses.

Bureau chiefs and agency heads complain that the centralizing forces in the executive branch don't understand the political realities that they must face on a day-to-day basis. Comments by two different civil servants in the 1960s are illustrative:

> Sticky problems arise because of the political isolation of the Bureau of the Budget.[3] The Bureau does not have good comprehension of what is in the minds of key congressional committee chairmen and members we have to deal with. They find incomprehensible the political problems we try to explain to them. They see us as being more responsive to Congress than to the President. There may be an element of truth here but they don't understand Congress (Davis and Ripley, 1967: 762–63).

*　　*　　*　　*　　*

> We have to tread a pretty thin line and we're always caught in a cross fire between the Budget Bureau and Congress. I just wish those people over there (in the Budget Bureau) had to carry those requests out—just once. They'd learn what the problems were. . . . The budget is made up over there, but we have to carry the ball. . . . They have no understanding of the climate up there, of the pressures, of the personalities (Fenno, 1966: 308).

In early 1985, the head of the Small Business Administration (a Reagan appointee) attacked the position of OMB because it favored eliminating

---

[3]The Bureau of the Budget was renamed the Office of Management and Budget in 1970.

his agency. This position was espoused by David Stockman, OMB director and another Reagan appointee. The SBA chief said Stockman was
"surrounded by fanatics [who] have no real-life experience." OMB officials, in his view, "cannot expect to understand the workings of all the federal agencies. They cannot continue to deal in micromanagement. . . .
Continuing to increase the OMB's power is sheer idiocy" (*Washington
Post*, April 28, 1985). The Small Business Administration had lots of congressional support and survived the Reagan-Stockman attempt to eliminate it.

In general, bureaucrats at the operating level see themselves as caught
between unrealistic demands and pressures from their executive branch
superiors and the pressures and demands—with which they may have
more sympathy—emanating from members of the subcommittees that are
essential to the existence and prosperity of their agencies. Agency officials
often talk about this sense of being in the middle. Three statements from
such officials serve to illustrate the general theme (Fenno, 1966: 308–9).

> Sometimes you wonder just who you are working for. I haven't been in too
> many embarrassing situations. With my relations with the Congress as they
> are, I may tell them that, frankly, I don't think I ought to tell them—that I have
> to maintain my loyalty to the department. Sometimes I go against the depart-
> ment.

*   *   *   *   *

> Sometimes I'll go over to the Committee and talk about something with
> them. The first time I went, they told me it was confidential. And I said, "When
> I came through that door, I started working for the Committee. Whatever goes
> on in here just didn't happen as far as I'm concerned when I leave here." And I
> tell them that every time. Sometimes, I'm over here and the Secretary or some-
> one will try to worm it out of me what's going on. But they know I won't tell
> them.

*   *   *   *   *

> I've gone out and tried to develop contacts with congressmen, because that's
> the way the game is played. But I don't like it. You shouldn't have to lobby for
> your program. But politics being what it is, I've done a little more of that. . . .
> Some people higher up in the department object to our having any informal
> contact with congressmen, but we'll just have to get around that, I guess.

Summary

The five general congressional-bureaucratic interactions discussed
above are important ones that occur across all substantive issue areas. Although the individual actors involved may change depending on the issue
under consideration, the general patterns of interaction do not change

much. For example, House Appropriations Committee members maintain a fairly stable outlook in dealing with agency officials, regardless of the issue or the personalities involved. The committee members have close ties with many agency representatives, and they work together cooperatively, but the committee members look at agency requests with an eye toward cutting and trimming, and this can promote conflict. The preceding sections have highlighted some of the implications that different institutional outlooks have for cooperation and conflict, and the analytical material in Chapters 4 through 7 will continue to develop this notion.

3

Congressional-Bureaucratic Interaction: Occasions and Resources

Interaction between congressional and bureaucratic actors is continuous and occurs in a variety of settings and for a variety of reasons. The most basic reason is the constitutionally based governmental feature of separate institutions sharing powers. This feature necessitates that the two branches interact in order to produce, implement, and assess governmental policy. In this chapter we discuss congressional-bureaucratic interactions during the production of policy in terms of the motivations of the actors, the resources they have to trade or withhold, the settings for their interaction, and the techniques actors may use.

Some attention has been directed by scholars to congressional-bureaucratic interaction, particularly in the form of congressional oversight of bureaucratic activities (Harris, 1964; Keefe and Ogul, 1985: chapter 12; Oleszek, 1978: chapter 9). The term *oversight* has been bandied about so much that its use may generate confusion. Oversight is used here to describe many congressional activities that are designed to keep tabs on what the bureaucracy is doing. A very specific kind of legislative oversight involves systematic review and evaluation of programs. This activity is referred to here as program oversight. As the following pages will describe, program oversight does not occur as often as other kinds of oversight activities because the rewards it offers legislators are not as enticing as the rewards for other activities.

MOTIVATIONS AND RESOURCES FOR INTERACTION

Motivations

Some interactions between bureaucrats and members of Congress are necessitated by the structure of government within which these individuals work. The constitutional allocation of responsibilities discussed in

Chapter 1 mandates a considerable amount of interaction. In addition, the history of governmental and programmatic development for almost 200 years has overlaid the rudimentary constitutional necessities with a number of interactions decreed by statutes, other written documents, and custom. This overlay in a sense summarizes the motivations of the parties to the interactions.

Both bureaucrats and members of Congress have a variety of motivations for becoming involved in specific ways in policy-related interactions between the two branches. Wilson (1980: 374) offers a suggestive threefold typology of bureaucrats' motivations. He indicates that any individual may be moved by several different considerations. But the identification of three separate career-related motivations is useful.

> To simplify, government agencies have at least three kinds of employees who can be defined in terms of their motives. The first are the *careerists:* employees who identify their careers and rewards with the agency. They do not expect to move on to other jobs outside the agency or otherwise to receive significant rewards from external constituencies. The maintenance of the agency and of their position in it is of paramount concern.
>
> The second are the *politicians:* employees who see themselves as having a future in elective or appointive office outside the agency. They hope to move on to better or more important undertakings. They may wish to run for Congress, become the vice president for public relations of a large firm, enter the cabinet or subcabinet, or join the campaign staff of a promising presidential contender. The maintenance and enhancement of their careers outside the agency is of paramount importance.
>
> The third are the *professionals:* employees who receive rewards (in status if not in money) from organized members of similar occupations elsewhere. They may hope to move on to better jobs elsewhere, but access to those jobs depends on their display of professionally approved behavior and technical competence. They may also be content to remain in the agency, but they value the continued approval of fellow professionals outside the agency, or the self-respect that comes from behaving in accordance with internalized professional norms. The maintenance of this professional esteem is of major importance to these employees.

In interacting with Congress, a careerist's paramount concern is usually for the health and welfare of his or her agency. The careerist seeks either to expand the agency's resources and influence or to maintain a low-profile status quo or to fight encroachments against the agency's resources and influence. However, "politicians" and "professionals" among the bureaucratic ranks clearly will pursue goals other than collective agency welfare unless they think agency welfare contributes heavily to the achievement of their personal goals.

Some bureaucrats willingly take positions that diminish or, in a few cases, spell the end of their agency. Thus, the last days of the Community Services Administration early in the Reagan presidency were presided over by a long-time senior career bureaucrat. It is overly simple to portray all bureaucrats as having only agency welfare at heart. Personal welfare in several senses may be even more important for some. But collective agency welfare is still a dominant motive behind much bureaucratic behavior.

Members of Congress are motivated by two general desires—to survive and/or advance politically and to pursue policy interests. Political survival and advancement are tied to constituency service and local interests, which in turn are tied to a member's reelection—survival in its most basic sense. Choice of policy interests may also be tied to political advantage: members may be most interested in policies they believe will help them win reelection or advance to other desirable posts. These two factors influence all congressional activity (Mayhew, 1974) including interactions with the bureaucracy, and they are particularly important in explaining congressional exercise of program oversight (Ogul, 1973). Because members' schedules are always full and there is insufficient time to do all the things worth doing, these twin desires help them make choices and set priorities. The utility of a particular interaction with some part of the bureaucracy may be assessed in terms of explicit calculations, such as "How will this help me with the folks back home?" or "How does this mesh with my personal policy preferences?"

Resources

Both members of Congress and bureaucrats possess a range of formal and informal resources upon which they can draw as they seek to pursue their personal, organizational, and programmatic goals. These resources can be selectively granted and withheld by actors in both branches.

From the congressional perspective, the formal powers of Congress provide a number of resources upon which individual members can draw. These formal powers include, first, the decision about the existence of agencies. Second, Congress provides the jurisdictional and programmatic scope to specific agencies and the limits on that scope both through statutory authority and through money. Third, Congress provides personnel for the executive branch in several senses—through the giving or withholding of statutory authority, personnel money, and confirmation of key appointments. Fourth, Congress influences the specific structure of both programs and agencies through positive statutory action and through action on reorganization plans submitted by the executive branch.

In addition to possessing these formal powers as resources that can be drawn on in interactions with the executive branch, members of Congress also possess more intangible resources, such as the ability to provide or withhold good information on the intentions of other individuals in a policy subsystem or area, the ability publicly to praise or criticize individual bureaucrats, and the ability to build a favorable image of the agency as a whole for a variety of other actors in higher levels of the executive branch, interest groups, and the House and Senate, as well as for potential or aspiring bureaucratic competitors.

From the bureaucratic perspective, the formal powers also provide a number of important potential resources. The bureaucracy makes a variety of specific decisions that are important to members of the House and Senate. These include formal powers over regulations determining how a program will be implemented; critical personnel decisions involving hiring, promotion, and location both geographically and hierarchically; geographic and programmatic patterns of spending; the timing of spending and other programmatic decisions; decisions about location of facilities; and disposition of individual "cases" of persons seeking a specific agency ruling.

Bureaucrats also possess informal resources. Two stand out: first, the ability of bureaucrats to enhance the personal standing and reputation of senators and representatives through a variety of forms of deference; and second, the provision of timely and accurate information about both substantive matters and the intentions of other actors in the policy subsystem.

The Tie between Motivation and Resources

Given the time pressures facing members of Congress and higher-level bureaucrats, specific individual activity is most likely to occur when both motivation for the activity and resources related to some hope of success are present concurrently. When motivation and resources do not reinforce each other, individual activity by a member or bureaucrat is much less likely. A freshman representative on the District of Columbia Committee may be highly motivated to criticize the Defense Department for allegedly sabotaging disarmament talks with the Soviet Union, but little can be accomplished; resources are absent and so activity—at least of a meaningful sort—is not likely to take place. However, if the same member becomes concerned about an alleged monopoly on parking in the District of Columbia and resulting exorbitant fees, he or she may be in a position to do something about it if the chairman of the committee can be persuaded to hold a hearing or make a few phone calls to the District of Columbia government.

Similarly, a bureau chief may devoutly wish for a large increase in the agency budget. However, if the chief cannot point to specific services to the districts of the senior members of the House Appropriations subcommittee responsible for the agency, only a modest increase in the budget will likely be requested.

Resources can also be present when motivation for action is absent. A senior member of the Senate Armed Services Committee would certainly have the resources to inquire in a serious and perhaps influential way into alleged Defense Department foot-dragging on disarmament. But if the same senator is a firm supporter of the defense establishment and simply does not trust disarmament agreements with Communist nations, then those resources will not be used. To take another example, if a bureau chief has two major programs and can point to great service to important senators and representatives from both programs, then the bureau has at least some resources to pursue substantial budgetary increases in both programs simultaneously. However, it may be that the chief believes that program A will soon get into political hot water for reasons the agency cannot control, and so increases may be pursued only in program B, which the chief believes will be the backbone of agency success for many years to come.

A nice case of the tie between resources and motivation and the organizational and programmatic consequences of that tie is provided in the policy area of soil conservation (see Morgan, 1965, for a booklength treatment of many of the matters summarized in the following two paragraphs).

From the time that soil conservation districts began to be organized in 1936, a rivalry grew up between the Soil Conservation Service, representing centralized authority over the program in Washington, and land-grant agricultural colleges and their extension services, which wished to decentralize the program and gain control of it. Some members of the House and Senate with influence in agricultural matters sided with the SCS and a centralized program. Others sided with the extension service and land-grant colleges (backed strongly by the American Farm Bureau Federation). Morgan provides an analysis of the motivations of the key members on both sides of the question (which was finally settled in favor of the SCS and centralization during the Truman administration).

Constituency interests and interest-group patterns seemed more important in shaping the alliances than party lines. For example, a key House Republican supporting the Farm Bureau–extension service position was formerly an employee of the extension service in his home state. An important House Democrat taking the same position came from a state that was a Farm Bureau stronghold. Two of the leading House supporters of the SCS position—one from each party—came from areas of the country that could be expected to benefit heavily from the small-watershed program being put together by the SCS. In addition, the Republican came from a district in which the Farmers Union (a competing group to the Farm Bureau and in conflict with it on this issue) was strong. All of these individuals were relatively senior members of the House Agriculture Committee. Other interested parties in the House were on both the Agriculture Committee and the Agriculture Subcommittee of the Appropriations Committee. Critical individuals in the Senate held parallel positions, and their positions and level of intensity also were related to factors such as the relative strength of the Farm Bureau or Farmers Union in their districts or states and the relative benefits provided their constituents by the SCS (including its proposed small-watershed program) and by the extension service.

OCCASIONS AND TECHNIQUES FOR INTERACTION

Custom and law require many occasions for interaction between Congress and the bureaucracy. These include budgeting; agency organization or reorganization; creation, amendment, or dissolution of a program or agency; personnel matters; evaluation of program performance; and location of projects. In these interactions, formal routines may be used—such as a hearing before a committee or subcommittee—and there may be formal outcomes, such as statutes, votes on reorganization plans, confirmation decisions, and committee and agency reports. Equally important, all subjects are also likely to be treated in a great number of informal interactions—phone calls, impromptu visits, lunches, cocktail parties. During these occasions, a constant two-way flow of information and views on substance, procedure, individuals, and organizations is sustained. Senior bureaucrats may spend more time interacting with Congress than with their nominal supervisors in their own executive branch agency.

No single listing of the occasions and techniques used by the participants in these interactions is likely to be complete. And, as is the case with any list, reality is not likely to be so neatly organized and categorized as the list may imply. Nevertheless it seems useful to identify and discuss the major occasions and techniques used both by individuals from the Hill and individuals in the bureaucracy because, by inventorying the segments of reality, one has a better understanding of the parts and the whole to which they contribute. Naturally, different actors may be involved in different kinds of interactions, and actors may use several techniques during a particular interaction. Their decisions about when to get involved and which techniques to use also vary, but in general each actor makes decisions he or she thinks will maximize personal, organizational, and programmatic goals. The cases presented in Chapters 4 through 7 will offer a fuller illustration of techniques and occasions for interaction.

Occasions for Interaction

Budgeting.   Budgeting is the most regularly recurring occasion for interaction between the bureaucracy and Congress. Budgeting involves the allocation of dollars among competing agencies and programs. The federal budget process is lengthy and complex and is divided into two major parts—first, the president's preparation of a budget document for the entire federal government, which essentially constitutes a request to Congress for funds to run the government; and second, the congressional budget process, which is essentially a response to the president's budget. The preparation of the president's budget involves widespread interactions internal to the various parts of the executive branch. The congressional budget process—which includes the appropriations process—is the scene of extensive interaction between parts of the bureaucracy and parts of Congress.

In 1974 Congress passed the Congressional Budget and Impoundment Control Act, a statute designed to rationalize the entire congressional budget process. Before passage of the budget reform act, congressional budget decisions were made individually, in a disaggregated, piecemeal fashion. The traditional locations for major congressional spending decisions were the appropriations committees in the two houses; the sources of major revenue decisions were the House Ways and Means Committee and the Senate Finance Committee. There was no opportunity or incentive for comprehensive or integrated assessment of the individual congressional budget decisions.

The present congressional budget process, summarized in Table 3-1, differs from the previous one by creating two new budget committees with the mandate to integrate the separate budget decisions in a single comprehensive budget resolution that specifies the total amount (a "ceiling") of congressionally authorized spending and enumerates spending priorities within the ceiling, before passage of any appropriations bills.

In mid-December 1985, Congress agreed on a bill that mandated a balanced budget by 1991. The bill put even more pressure on Congress to arrive at decisions that kept the deficit within the year-by-year bounds prescribed or risk giving the president more budget power at the expense of Congress. How the procedures would work and whether they were constitutional remained to be determined.

From the outset the budget process created in 1974 had the potential for sharpening debate over spending priorities and for decreasing the fragmentation of congressional budget decisions. In the first four years in which the process was fully operational (1976 through 1979), the new budget committees proceeded cautiously. The members of the committees were intent on surviving as committees and in establishing and preserving the new process. Thus, they did not aggressively challenge the traditional budget authorities for fear of generating a hostile coalition that would re-reform the new budget process out of existence. In shaping the first budget resolution, they sought primarily to anticipate the spending and revenue actions of the other congressional decision-making bodies, thus avoiding direct confrontations. This meant that the second budget resolution was generally a ratification of budget decisions made during the summer in compliance with the relatively generous first resolution.

TABLE 3-1
Congressional Budget Timetable

Deadline	Action to Be Completed
15th day after Congress convenes	President submits budget, along with current services estimates.*
March 15	Committees submit views and estimates to budget committees.
April 1	Congressional budget office submits report to budget committees.†
April 15	Budget committees report first concurrent resolution on the budget to their houses.
May 15	Committees report bills authorizing new budget authority.
May 15	Congress adopts first concurrent resolution on the budget.
Seventh day after Labor Day	Congress completes action on bills providing budget authority and spending authority.
September 15	Congress completes actions on second required concurrent resolution on the budget.
September 25	Congress completes action on reconciliation process implementing second concurrent resolution.
October 1	Fiscal year begins.

*Current-services estimates are estimates of the dollar levels that would be required next year to support the same level of services in each program as this year's budget. The budget act originally required submission of the current services estimates by November 10 of the previous year. Since the president was still in the midst of developing budget proposals for the next year, Congress later agreed to permit simultaneous submission of the current services and executive budgets in January.
†The budget committees and congressional budget office have found April 1 too late in the budget process to be useful; hence the congressional office submits its report(s) in February, although April 1 remains the date required by law.
Source: Allen Schick, *Congress and Money: Budgeting, Spending and Taxing,* (Washington, D.C.: The Urban Institute, 1980), 4.

The new budget process did not produce substantive policy outcomes significantly different from prereform years, but the new process provided a more informed decision-making process for congressional budgeting. The relations between individual parts of the bureaucracy and individual committees and subcommittees (particularly appropriations subcommittees) were not altered in any important way by the new congressional budget process before 1980. These interactions still determined the great proportion of the policy and budgetary outcomes affecting agencies and programs.

In short, the budget committees did not seek large-scale substantive results, and they did not achieve them. Careful analysts of the process in Congress agreed that the main achievements of these first years were procedural: the process was up and running, and it helped Congress make decisions that both balanced a wide variety of interests and did so without allowing conflict to immobilize the process and the ability to arrive at conclusions (Havemann, 1978; LeLoup, 1980b; and Schick, 1980).

In 1980, 1981, and 1982, however, Congress treated the budget process in a different way by using a "reconciliation" process that had previously been available but had lain dormant. The versions in the first two Reagan years were more comprehensive than the one in the last Carter year. This process forces the adoption of a single bottom line in which direct confrontation of priorities and interests must be resolved. Both analysts and practitioners agreed that the strain placed on the "normal" way of doing business was tolerable when major retrenchments in federal spending and programs had to be made—as the president and the majority of Congress believed in 1981 and 1982. They also agreed that the strain would eventually mean that the "normal" processes would reappear and that reconciliation could be used only in extreme cases. The political costs of the new process seem to be too heavy to be borne once the Reagan retrenchment has run its course. (See Schick, 1981; Tate, 1982, on the use and future of reconciliation.)

In 1983, 1984, and 1985 the political warfare between Reagan and Congress—especially the Democratically controlled House—intensified. Under these conditions the budget process became less important in part because the deadlines were routinely missed and much of the government began to function under continuing resolutions, much as it had in the years immediately before the 1974 reform. In 1984 deficit reduction legislation was approved before the budget resolution and became the vehicle for overall budget policy. Much the same thing happened in 1985 and, at the same time, Congress passed—with much controversy—its general procedure for bringing the annual deficit to zero by 1991.

The general lesson of the events surrounding budget processes from 1975 through 1985 is that procedures do not change politics. Political actors—presidents, members of the House and Senate, bureaucrats, interest groups—will work to protect their interests and their alliances no matter what procedures they must use. Procedures can help change the format of debate but not the underlying political realities. The quest for budget reduction, for example, was not sparked by an abstract concern for rational debate over spending and taxing priorities but by a widespread perception, especially in Congress, that a deficit seemingly out of control probably would have disastrous political consequences, especially for incumbent members of Congress.

Agency Organization and Reorganization.   Proposals to create programs and, much less frequently, to dismantle them also stimulate interaction between Congress and the bureaucracy. Such proposals may originate either in the bureaucracy or within Congress, but the decision to implement a new program eventually requires consultation with the other branch at least to secure statutory authority and funding, if not for good political relations. Statutory authorization comes after the appropriate legislative committee has held hearings on the proposal. These hearings include testimony from interested parties, including those parts of the bureaucracy that believe they may be best suited to administer the new program. The decision to terminate a program generally occurs when a program has fulfilled its purpose or has had a poor record of performance.

Congress and the bureaucracy also interact on the matter of agencies' organization and reorganization proposals. Congress does not get involved in every change that is made in a bureau's structure, but it usually does get involved in changes made at the department level (often put forth as presidential reorganization plans) or within the independent regulatory commissions, which are technically arms of Congress.

In 1978 President Carter proposed creating a separate Department of Education, which would remove a number of agencies and programs from what was then the Department of Health, Education, and Welfare. Immediately after the proposal was made, affected parties in and out of government registered objections and sought to exempt their programs from inclusion in the new department. The proposal for a separate education department died in the Ninety-Fifth Congress (1977–78), but not before the Senate Governmental Affairs Committee yielded rather quickly on exempting the head start program (a program to help prepare preschool children from disadvantaged families for entering school) from inclusion in the new department. The proposal for a separate Department of Education continued to be considered, and special exemptions and exceptions characterized the content of the final decision to create such a department in late 1979.

Program Evaluation.   The evaluation of program performance (program oversight) is an important form of interaction between the bureaucracy and Congress that occurs when congressional committees examine the performance of programs they have authorized and funded. Responsibility for program oversight is shared—the government operations committees perform special investigative inquiries, the appropriations committees are responsible for fiscal oversight, and the legislative committees are responsible for monitoring and overseeing the programs for which they authorize appropriations. Oversight activities may take several forms—special hearings to investigate a program; routine hearings, such as appropriations or authorizations; or program monitoring and analyses. Overall, Congress has not performed oversight extensively. Much of the oversight that has occurred has been in the context of appropriations, but the focus there is understandably more on narrow expenditure concerns than on substantive evaluation. Several scholars (Bibby, 1966; Davis, 1970; Huitt, 1966; Ogul, 1973; Scher, 1963) have studied oversight and the conditions that contribute to it; their findings indicate that the personal and political payoffs of oversight activities are not as rewarding to members of Congress as other kinds of behavior, and hence they are not engaged in as frequently. We will address the issue of Congress' exercise of program oversight in Chapter 8.

Personnel Matters. A variety of personnel matters also provide occasions for interaction between the two branches. The Senate must confirm a number of presidential appointments, including those of agency heads. Congress is involved in setting the pay scales for government employees, and any change in the compensation schedules will generate lobbying from bureaucrats. The total amount of money that an agency head has available to pay the salaries and expenses of employees is also determined by Congress, and it may not (deliberately or not) be enough to bring an agency up to its authorized personnel strength. Congress also gets involved in creating special positions within an agency and in limiting the total size of an agency or specific grades within it. Finally, individual members of Congress are sometimes in a position to see to it that friends and associates get particularly good jobs in the executive branch.

Other Occasions. Decisions about the location of federal projects also stimulate interaction between Congress and the bureaucracy. Because such projects usually entail employment, money, and other benefits for the area, legislators are interested in having them in their home districts. Bureaucrats are responsible for making the decisions about locations. The interaction on this subject occurs in both formal and informal settings. Occasionally, a project may have unpleasant or undesirable elements, and the interaction may occur over where to put the project. For example, basing proposals for the MX missile generated strong opposition in the western states considered as possible sites.

Congress and the bureaucracy also are brought together because of "casework," which involves a constituent's problems with an agency that the representative or senator feels obliged to help resolve. Casework occurs on an individual and piecemeal basis, usually at congressional initiative, and is usually resolved through informal means between agency and congressional staff. Typical cases involve questions of tax liability, immigration, and social security and medicare benefits.

Congressional Techniques

Personal Visits and Phone Calls. Members of Congress and staff members seek information and desired actions from bureaucrats by keeping in touch with them both in person and on the phone. This kind of personal attention is often sufficient to get the attention of a key bureaucrat, and sometimes it alone is sufficient to obtain an intended result.

The Use of Third Parties.   Members often seek to mobilize support-ers of their position to reinforce the messages they are delivering to bu-reaucrats. Thus, a member may seek, for example, to have interest-group representatives, reporters, or prestigious "clients" of a bureau approach executive branch officials with the same point of view favored by the member.

Release of Written Materials.   Individual members of the House or Senate or individual committees and subcommittees can seek to influence bureaucratic decisions by releasing materials such as committee reports, staff studies, and press releases at the most propitious times.

Hearings.   Executive branch officials are constantly appearing be-fore congressional committees and subcommittees simply as a matter of course as both new authorizations and appropriations become necessary. These hearings afford members of the House and Senate recurring oppor-tunities to elicit information about programs and to make their own views known.

An excellent example of a routine appropriations hearing being used to underscore a congressional attitude is provided by a former manpower administrator, Stanley Ruttenberg (Ruttenberg and Gutchess, 1970: 77–78). When he became manpower administrator in 1965, the Department of La-bor was pushing a reorganization of the Manpower Administration that would have given line authority to regional manpower administrators over all of the operating bureaus, including the Bureau of Employment Security and the Bureau of Apprenticeship and Training, whose directors were both opposed to the reorganization because it decreased their rela-tive autonomy. The pressure generated by the proposal's opponents, who included several key congressional figures, was strong enough to prevent its implementation. An exchange between Ruttenberg and Representative John Fogarty, then chairman of the House Appropriations subcommittee responsible for the Department of Labor's budget (among other things), during the March 1965 hearings on the department budget, shows Fogarty stating the congressional view forcefully:

Mr. Fogarty: I assume you know the feeling of this committee on the proposed re-organization? If you do not, we will spell it out for you later on. . . . I am not going to belabor the point. As far as I am concerned, my mind is made up on the question of this reorganization of your department. Mr. Goodwin (the director of the Bureau of Employment Security) has been here through several adminis-trations and four or five secretaries of labor. The secretaries of labor come and go, but Mr. Goodwin stays on. I think Mr. Murphy (the director of the Bureau of Apprenticeship and Training) will stay on regardless of who is secretary to-morrow or next year, or five years from now.

Mr. Ruttenberg: I think that is unquestionably true.

Mr. Fogarty: The Congress has always supported these two agencies and there is no doubt in my mind as to how the Congress will respond to this proposal. I thought I made it clear yesterday, but I am trying to make it clearer right now. Is that clear?

Mr. Ruttenberg: Mr. Chairman, it was quite clear to me yesterday.

In addition to routine hearings, congressional committees also hold a variety of special investigations to procure additional information. These investigations may be conducted by standing committees or subcommittees, select committees, special committees, or joint committees. At the hearings, the main congressional-bureaucratic interaction occurs in the preliminary preparation stages between congressional staff and agency members.

A good example of the kinds of impact that a congressional investigation can have even when dealing with a seemingly minor topic is provided by the activities of the Senate Small Business Committee in the early 1950s in relation to the controversy over an additive designed to prolong battery life (Lawrence, 1965). The case was a complicated one, involving conflicting philosophies over regulation of private enterprise, an aggressive marketer of the product, scientists from a range of public and private institutions, three government agencies (the Commerce Department's National Bureau of Standards, the Federal Trade Commission, and the Post Office), and the Senate Small Business Committee. Near the end of the controversy, the Eisenhower administration was trying to fire the head of the National Bureau of Standards, and this action precipitated hearings by the Small Business Committee. As the hearings began, a regulatory action initiated by the Post Office against the producer of the additive was still pending. The committee was decidedly on the side of the additive manufacturer and against government intervention. By bending to the wishes of the committee, the Post Office removed itself from the controversy. As Lawrence (1965: 70) writes: "The Post Office Department weathered the storm with little or no damage. Senator Thye (Chairman of the Small Business Committee) had said at the conclusion of his Small Business Committee's hearing on AD-X2 (the name of the additive), 'Only . . . if the Postmaster General feels the mail fraud order should not be set aside, would it be necessary to find out why the order was ever issued.' " Thus the Post Office gave in to the committee's preferences in order to avoid being investigated.

Requests for Studies by Outside Sources.   Senators and representatives have a number of sources to which they can turn for independent (or at least seemingly independent) studies of problems that can presumably be used to bolster their point of view in a policy controversy. These sources include the General Accounting Office, the Congressional Research Service of the Library of Congress, the Office of Technology Assessment, the Congressional Budget Office, the government operations committees in the House and Senate, and respected outsiders (for example, universities or independent research organizations such as the Brookings Institution).

The General Accounting Office (GAO) is an arm of Congress that in part conducts audits of the expenditure of funds. The GAO also conducts much broader studies and that activity has been growing in recent years. The reports stemming from these studies can be used by members of Congress. For example, a GAO report on the proposed Cheyenne helicopter was negative, and the House Appropriations Committee used the report to help make its case for terminating the project.

The Congressional Research Service is a nonpartisan agency but can be asked for information on programs and agencies that can then be used by proponents of specific views to buttress their case.

The Office of Technology Assessment (OTA) was created by statute in 1972 and began operations in 1974. Its primary function, in the language of the statute, is to provide "early indications of the probably beneficial and adverse impacts of the applications of technology and to develop other coordinate information which may assist the Congress." Subjects for OTA staff work are decided by requests from congressional committees or by requests from the Technology Assessment Board (six senators, six representatives, and the OTA director) or by the director after consulting with the board.

The Congressional Budget Office (CBO) was created in 1974 as part of the general congressional budget reform. The professional staff of the CBO, numbering more than 200, reports to Congress on the short-term and long-term (five-year) economic consequences of legislation that is proposed and enacted. It develops an annual report on alternative budget courses for Congress to consider, with emphasis on fiscal policy and spending priorities. The CBO also responds to requests from the fiscal committees in both houses for economic and policy studies.

The government operations committees of both houses were empowered by the Legislative Reorganization Act of 1946 to conduct investigations into the operations of government activities at all levels to determine whether programs were being administered efficiently and economically. These committees work closely with the GAO in conducting their investigations.

Statutory Changes.   Congress can by statute create or dissolve agencies and programs, alter the jurisdiction of agencies, prescribe organizational structure, and intercede in personnel matters such as limits on total number of slots available, number of slots available for specific grades, and compensation.

Major statutory activities are relatively visible. But there are also more quiet and subtle uses of statutory power by Congress to achieve desired ends. For example, Congress can maximize the responsiveness of agencies to it through several statutory devices designed to weaken the control of an agency head. The illustration involving the Manpower Administration cited earlier is an example—in that case the field structure was kept decentralized and more responsive to the decentralized structure of congressional influence rather than allowing a more centralized field structure responsible to the manpower administrator. Similarly, some agencies (usually called commissions) have been given multiple executives (called commissioners) by Congress in order to diffuse the decision-making source and make the agency more responsive to Congress. The Atomic Energy Commission and all of the independent regulatory agencies provide illustrations of this technique's use. Congress has often opted to keep the staff assigned to a secretary relatively small as a way of preventing control over individual bureaus from being centralized in the hands of the secretary (Seidman, 1980).

In a few cases Congress can specify that its members be directly involved in what might otherwise be considered strictly executive branch decision making. Two members of each house were included by statute on the negotiating teams implementing the tariff-reduction provisions of the Trade Expansion Act of 1962, for example.

Although appropriations statutes are generally thought of only for their fiscal contents, they also may have a policy impact beyond the dollars they allocate to agencies and programs. This impact occurs when the statute contains specific provisions detailing how the money in the bill is to be used or not used. As Horn (1970: 181, 183) notes, these limitations are usually negative in character ("thou shalt not . . . etc.") and are directed at administrative rather than programmatic expenditures, such as travel, subscriptions, number of personnel hired, consulting fees, and entertainment. But more substantive matters are also addressed. For example, a provision inserted in the appropriations statute for the Department of Agriculture in the mid-1950s required that cotton sold abroad be sold competitively, even though the administration thought this would have a detrimental effect on foreign policy (Kirst, 1969: 5). As another example, the Defense Appropriations Act (an annual bill) contains the provisions "That no funds herein appropriated shall be used for the payment of a price differential on contracts hereafter made for the purpose of relieving economic dislocations . . . so far as practicable, all contracts shall be awarded on a formally advertised competitive bid basis to the lowest responsible bidder" (Horn, 1970: 184). That language has "maintained the preeminence of

California in defense procurement against large-scale attempts to distribute defense contracts according to the level of unemployment in an area" (Horn, 1970: 184).

Language in Reports.   In the technical sense, only statutes have the force of law. However, Congress has also made its will felt in programmatic terms through language contained in committee reports. And the executive branch often treats this language as binding.

A good example of report language having the effect of law is provided by a 1960 reorganization of the Public Health Service (Carper, 1965). The Department of Health, Education, and Welfare decision to reorganize the Public Health Service was in direct response to language contained in the 1959 report of the Health Subcommittee of the House Appropriations Committee. And a decision not to divorce the clinical training programs of the National Institute of Mental Health from that organization was directly responsive to language contained in a Senate Appropriations Committee report in 1960.

In the late 1970s photocopying machines disappeared from post offices because of language in reports from two House subcommittees (one on the Postal Service and one involving small business), even though the machines were regarded by consumers as useful additions. The subcommittees were reacting to pressure from a trade association of office equipment stores.

All committees have the technique of report language at their disposal. The appropriations committees seem particularly active in using this technique. For example, in 1965 alone the Senate Appropriations Committee issued 150 directives and suggestions in its reports. Ninety-three of these directives dealt with programmatic matters, thirty-nine dealt with budget procedure, and eighteen dealt with management (Horn, 1970: 188). Not all bureaucrats will conform precisely to all such directives, but they will certainly weigh the costs of not conforming before they decide what to do.

Legislative Veto.   In June 1983 the United States Supreme Court ruled the legislative veto used by Congress unconstitutional. However, very little happened as a result of that ruling despite early claims that provisions in more than 200 laws had been voided and the assumption that Congress would have to find other statutory means to hold executive branch agencies responsible in detail. In fact, existing provisions have continued to be observed by the executive branch and Congress alike. Some of them have been amended to meet some of the Court's objections. Even more strikingly, in the two years immediately following the Supreme Court ruling Congress enacted fifty additional legislative veto provisions (*Washington Post*, August 6, 1985). The president's position in relation to

Congress may actually be weaker than it was before the Supreme Court decision.

The core of any legislative veto provision is a requirement that Congress (or part of it) approve or at least not disapprove an executive branch action before it can become binding, usually within thirty to ninety days. The exact form of congressional action varies. A joint resolution is a common form. It seems to conform to part of the Court's ruling.

The legislative veto, regardless of form, continues to represent a powerful weapon in the hands of Congress to help make sure that agencies do not pursue lines of decision offensive to Congress (Craig, 1983; Fisher, 1985a, 1985b).

Reporting Requirements. Congress may require that parts of the bureaucracy make certain information available to it through reporting requirements in statutes. These requirements vary considerably in their form and content. Some are highly visible because they are contained in major statutes and focus on reports from the president. For example, the Congressional Budget and Impoundment Control Act of 1974 requires that the president report annually on the amount of impounded funds and the amount of tax expenditures (the amount of revenue lost through various tax "loopholes"). The War Powers Act of 1973 requires the president to report to Congress on American troop commitments.

Other reporting requirements are directed at bureaucrats lower in the executive hierarchy and are less visible. The kind of information requested can range from details about programs to rationales about decisions. The point of the reporting requirements is the same, however: to increase the amount of information that Congress has and to increase the consultation between congressional committees and bureaucrats.

The Joint Committee on Atomic Energy (JCAE) offers a good example of how a committee can use the reporting technique to extend its influence over an agency. The JCAE exercised dominant influence over the Atomic Energy Commission during its existence, buttressing its influence with a variety of reporting procedures, legislative veto provisions, and statutory rights to virtually all information held by the agency (Green and Rosenthal, 1963).

A recent analysis of all congressional reporting requirements (Johannes, 1976) shows that since World War II the number of reports required has risen from about 300 to more than 1,000. These requirements fall into three major categories. First, various parts of the executive branch are often required to submit "policy-making" reports such as evaluations of existing programs and recommendations for action. Second, "post facto" reports are often required simply recounting actions taken. Third, "advance notification" reports must be filed for a specific period before an action is taken. This gives members of Congress or of a committee a chance to object, propose changes, or react in other ways.

In the Ninety-Second Congress (1971–72), 261 new reporting requirements were included in statutes. Of these, 50 percent were of the post facto variety, 40 percent were of the policy-making variety, and 10 percent were of the advance-notification variety. Data in the same categories since 1945 suggest that policy making reporting requirements have become an increasingly important congressional technique.

The sources of the reports and the routing of them also vary a great deal. In 1974 only 18 percent of all reports to be made (about 1,050) were to come either directly from the president or through the president. Forty-eight percent came from cabinet-level departments directly to Congress; and 16 percent came from independent agencies directly to Congress. Others came from such sources as federally chartered private corporations and a variety of boards and commissions.

In 1982 the comptroller general (head of the General Accounting Office) issued a directory of more than 900 pages called *Requirements for Recurring Reports to the Congress* that contained an inventory of such requirements as of September 30, 1981. That directory described about 2,900 recurring reporting requirements applying to all federal agencies and federally chartered corporations.

Budget Decisions.   By virtue of its powers to levy taxes and appropriate funds, Congress inevitably is the focus of attention from bureaucrats requesting and defending their agencies' budgets, and budget decisions are an important congressional technique for influencing programmatic performance in the executive branch. However, budget decisions are not centralized within Congress—many committees have the power to make these kinds of decisions.

Use of the reconciliation process, as in 1980–82, reduces the power of individual committees but does not eliminate it. The following discussion describes the "normal" process (without reconciliation being used).

By far the most visible and familiar budget deciders are the appropriations committees. A steady flow of information is traded between committee members and staff and agency personnel during the fiscal year, capped by the appearance of the agency head, and other agency representatives at the annual appropriations hearings. The committees have some latitude in setting the amount of money that goes to an agency, and they also can specify limitations on how the money is spent. Even after appropriations are made, the committees have at least potential control over the uses of the money. For example, agency reprogramming of funds (shifting money from one expenditure category to another) often must have at least informal committee approval (Fisher, 1974; Horn, 1970: 192–95).

Before the appropriations committees can appropriate funds, however, authorizing legislation for the agency or program in question must have been considered by the appropriate legislative committee and passed by both houses. Authorizing legislation gives congressional approval to an activity and generally sets a ceiling on the amount of funds that can be made available for that activity. Authorization hearings necessarily encompass more than just this budget figure, but the decision about an authorization limit is an important part of the proceedings, especially from the perspective of the administrator of the activity.

Legislative committees are also involved in budget decisions that have collectively been tagged as "backdoor spending." The central feature of the numerous techniques of backdoor spending is that a funding pattern is established for some activity by a legislative committee, and funds are available without any input from the appropriations committee and without much program oversight once the pattern is set. Once an appropriations-avoiding device is in place, it becomes part of the accepted machinery of government and is very hard for Congress to dislodge or modify.

For example, a committee may legislate monetary payments (called entitlements) to certain segments of society and require that money be made available for this purpose in a special trust fund. Social security payments to the retired and disabled are automatically financed in this manner. Sometimes payments to a group like veterans are tied to the cost of living; increases in the benefits must be met by the appropriations committees—they have no choice. A legislative committee may allow an agency to conduct its business through contract obligations, as the Corps of Engineers does. It can write contracts for services without having the money in hand to perform them—the appropriations committees must provide the money when the bills come. Yet another device allows agencies to borrow money from the Treasury to finance their activities without requiring a specific authorization. Legislative committees use all of these techniques to finance agency activities, partially because they are under pressure from the agency representatives and their clients and partially because of jurisdictional rivalries with the appropriations committees.

The budget committees offer another locus for interaction on budget decisions. As already indicated, the budget committees have not played a dramatically independent role in shaping policy or budgets, although their importance temporarily increased in 1980–82. In effect, they have tried to predict what others in the budgetary decision process would do and have for the most part adjusted their budget resolutions to those realities. However, the deliberations and resolutions of the budget committees have at least created yet another forum for considering congressional-bureaucratic budget interactions.

A final setting for budget decisions concerns the source of revenue rather than its allocation. Congress, and especially the House Ways and

Means Committee, has responsibility for legislating the government's tax code, which sets the rates of taxation on personal income, corporate income, and excise taxes, and which also specifies an incredible array of tax "breaks" for various groups. A great deal of interaction occurs between the committee staffs that prepare tax legislation and the agencies that administer it, especially Department of Treasury officials.

Good relations between members of Congress who sit on the committees that make budget decisions and bureaucrats whose agencies and programs depend on the committees' decisions are very important from the bureaucrat's point of view. The appropriations process is the most visible and regular budget-deciding forum, and members of appropriations subcommittees have particularly high standing with agency administrators, as Fenno (1966) and Wildavsky (1984) have documented so well. If a senior member of a subcommittee expresses a policy view in the course of appropriations hearings, this view is likely to be taken very seriously by the bureaucrats as they make subsequent policy decisions.

Decisions on Individual Executive Branch Officials. The Senate possesses the formal power of confirmation over some critical executive branch officials, such as departmental secretaries and assistant secretaries, the director of the Office of Management and Budget; the heads of independent agencies, such as the Federal Power Commission and the Environmental Protection Agency; and the heads of numerous departmental agencies such as the Census Bureau and the Federal Bureau of Investigation (FBI). Hearings on these nominations can be used to transmit policy preferences of members and committees of the House and the Senate in a very forceful way to the nominees. Occasionally a presidental nomination will be rejected; or defeat will look so likely that a nomination will be withdrawn. In 1981 and 1982 Jesse Helms, the Republican senator from North Carolina, and his very conservative allies in the Senate forced President Reagan to withdraw a few relatively moderate nominations for positions in the State Department and the Arms Control and Disarmament Agency. In 1985 the Senate Judiciary Committee sent a policy message to the Reagan administration about civil rights by rejecting Reagan's nomination of William Bradford Reynolds to be associate attorney general. Reynolds had been and remained assistant attorney general for civil rights and was perceived by the majority of the Judiciary Committee to be seriously deficient in his commitment to civil rights.

Even if a nomination is eventually confirmed, it may be that the fight over the nomination will persuade the president to alter the nature of subsequent nominations. For example, early in the Eisenhower administration a nominee to the National Labor Relations Board won confirmation by only three votes in the Senate. The individual in question had had a career in business management, and the Senate Democrats thought this an inappropriate background for an NLRB member. Subsequent Eisenhower nominations to the NLRB did not again draw on this source. Thus, although the Democrats lost the immediate fight, they made their larger point, and the president responded (Anderson, 1970: 373–76).

Occasionally Congress will also try to extend the confirmation power to new positions. In 1973 there was a battle between Congress and the president over the proposal to make the director and deputy director of the Office of Management and Budget subject to Senate confirmation. The president successfully vetoed one such bill because it required confirmation of the incumbents (who had been particularly obnoxious in the eyes of many congressional Democrats). A bill exempting the incumbents was signed by the president in early 1974. Similarly, but with no particular controversy, a provision of the 1968 Omnibus Crime Control and Safe Streets Act required that all future directors of the FBI be subject to Senate confirmation.

Congress can make its influence felt even if formal confirmation is not required. A good case is provided in the consumer-affairs field (Nadel, 1971: 53–55). During the Johnson administration, Betty Furness had held the post of special assistant to the president for consumer affairs and had been a visible advocate of consumer interests within the administration. Early in 1969 President Nixon announced the appointment of a part-time consultant on consumer affairs and chose the director of the Good Housekeeping Institute. Although confirmation was not required, this choice was immediately attacked by Congress on two grounds. First, the Good Housekeeping Institute itself had been severely criticized by consumer advocates in and out of Congress as a sham operation. Second, the demotion of the presidential adviser from a special assistant to a part-time consultant signaled to concerned members of Congress that the new president planned to downgrade programs on consumer protection. The outcry from Congress was so strong that the president withdrew his nomination and a few months later appointed another individual as a special assistant for consumer affairs. This person's background and credentials were considerably more legitimate in the eyes of congressional supporters of the consumer movement.

Congressional influence on appointments is felt even after an agency head has been confirmed. For example, Congress can exert pressure on an incumbent that, in effect, forces firing or resignation. This occurred in 1974 when the administrator of the Veterans Administration (VA) was so severely criticized for his handling of the organization and its programs by both veterans' groups and key House and Senate members who were handling bills affecting the VA that the administration had virtually no choice but to request his resignation.

In early 1983 the resignation of Anne Burford as administrator of the Environmental Protection Agency was forced on both her and President

Reagan by his staff in part because a number of Republican members of Congress had joined the Democrats in calling for her departure. Without such congressional pressure, the president probably would have insisted that she stay, which was her own preference.

Finally, Congress can occasionally try to create a position and name the incumbent simultaneously. In 1978, for example, when Congress was working on reauthorizing the Comprehensive Employment and Training Act, the Senate tried to create a new assistant secretary position in the Department of Labor and make sure that it would be offered to a person already in the department as a deputy undersecretary. The Senate language would have waived the normal nomination and confirmation procedures to ensure the promotion quickly without presidential involvement. This individual had worked for the Senate committee with authorizing power over the department for nine years before moving to the department. The secretary and the chairperson of the Senate committee (who was the person's former boss) made clear what they expected to do. The House rebelled against this cozy form of promotion, however, and the individual remained in his deputy undersecretary position when the assistant secretary position was not created in the statute that passed in the autumn of 1978.

Bureaucratic Techniques

The above discussion may make it appear that the bureaucracy can easily be overwhelmed by the rich variety of congressional techniques. This is not the case, however, for two basic reasons. First, the bureaucracy is so vast in terms of individual employees, organizational units, and programs that even a very aggressive set of senators, representatives, and staff members can influence only a relatively small part of the bureaucracy at any given time. Second, the bureaucracy itself also possesses techniques that allow it to influence congressional attitudes and behavior. These techniques are not as numerous as those in the hands of Congress, but they may nevertheless be very effective in achieving the ends desired by the bureaucrats.

As in the case of Congress, a number of the techniques can be used simultaneously, thus increasing their impact.

Substance of Decisions.   Bureaucrats make numerous decisions in the course of administering their programs that are important to members of Congress. This decision making constitutes the bureaucrats' most important technique in interacting with Congress. These decisions cover a range of topics and occur in a variety of settings. For example, when a new program is authorized or an old one amended, bureaucrats are required to publish proposed regulations in the *Federal Register* that detail all aspects of program operation. A draft of the regulations is circulated for public comment and changes before becoming final. Congressional views during this review and comment period are an important input to the decision making that shapes the final regulations.

Usually bureaucratic decisions don't get written and circulated as the regulations do, but they show up in the way a program is implemented. For example, a statute may contain ambiguity about eligible recipients of a social welfare program. Some members of Congress are likely to favor a broad interpretation of the eligibility requirements in order to increase the coverage of the program, while others will probably favor a more restrictive interpretation. The bureaucrats making the decision can calculate the costs and benefits of pleasing one group of legislators and perhaps offending another group.

Bureaucrats also maintain a good deal of control over the use of the monies available to them. At one extreme, they may not spend all of the money for any given object—in fact, they may be formally prohibited from doing so by presidential impoundment of funds, although such presidential action was limited by the budget act in 1974. More likely, they retain considerable latitude in terms of shifting emphases among expenditures. Again, some programmatic emphases are going to be particularly attractive to some members of the House and Senate, and different emphases will be more attractive to others.

The power that bureaucrats possess to determine where major expenditures will take place and where facilities will be located is important to members of Congress and can be used skillfully by bureaucrats to build support on a range of issues, because in addition to the broad policy concerns that most members of Congress have, they also have narrower concerns about the welfare of their own particular geographical constituencies. Thus, decisions about contracts; expansion of facilities like bases, field office, and laboratories; or the closing of such facilities are usually very salient to at least some senators and representatives.

A classic case involving closing of field offices and bureaucratic calculation designed to minimize subsequent loss of congressional support is provided by the Department of Commerce in 1948 (Arnow, 1954). Because of appropriations cuts by the House Appropriations Committee, the department had to close four of its forty-six field offices. Efficiency indicators were developed to measure the workload of each office, the cost of processing the workload, and the population of the city in which the office was located. The fourteen lowest-ranking offices were judged to be candidates for closing. The decision about which four were to be closed during the Democratic administration was made on the basis of explicitly political determinations.

In mid-1985 the new secretary of labor, William Brock (a former senator), announced he was canceling plans to close three of the ten regional offices of the Department of Labor (those in Boston, Kansas City, and Seattle). Senator Lowell Weicker, a fellow Republican, was concerned that service to his constituents in Connecticut would suffer if the Boston office were closed. Weicker also chaired the Labor, Health and Human Services, and Education Subcommittee of the Senate Appropriations Committee and thus had powerful influence over matters at the Department of Labor. Simultaneously, a Democratic member of the House Appropriations Committee from Seattle indicated he would try to mobilize that committee to block closing the three offices, including the one in his city. Secretary Brock acquiesced, observing that the three offices were "vital to too many citizens." As the *Washington Post* (June 27, 1985) observed, "Everyone on Capitol Hill knew which citizens he meant."

Bureaucrats cannot exercise the power they have over expenditures, location of facilities, or expansion or reduction of services without regard to the political repercussions such exercise of power has in Congress. It is not unusual to see representatives from districts afflicted with a proposed field-office or air-base shutdown or a decrease in rail or air or postal service work vigorously to alter the negative proposal. Successful bureaucrats learn how to balance good administrative judgment with good political judgment.

Timing of Decisions.   Not only do bureaucrats possess considerable flexibility in determining the substance of decisions, but they also possess even more flexibility in determining when those decisions are implemented. Decisions can be timed to give a helpful boost to friendly members in reelection contests. They can also be timed so as to magnify the public credit a senator or representative gets for promoting a given policy development. For instance, the Department of Labor's Employment and Training Administration (ETA) has instructed its field offices to refrain from announcing budget allocations for programs to grantees until members of Congress have had a chance to make an announcement about the federal money coming into their home state or district. This seemingly minor decision by ETA bureaucrats (a pattern followed by virtually all federal agencies) helps build the legislator's public image, and it curries congressional favor and credit for the agency.

Use of Information.   Bureaucrats possess a great deal of detailed information. Only rarely is information a neutral commodity. The release of critical information in a timely fashion by agencies is often used as a persuasive technique. For example, the Department of Commerce opposed cuts that it was ordered to make in some of its field offices even before the 1948 decisions discussed above. It released a list of the offices to be closed in an effort to get congressional support in overturning or modifying the closings. At least thirty-nine representatives and sixty-eight senators from affected districts and states could be presumed to be interested in the list. Enough money was added in the congressional appropriations bill to save eight of the thirty-nine offices slated for closing.

In general, agencies that are managed skillfully will select both the content and the timing of the release of various reports and staff studies to maximize the amount of support they generate in Congress for the ends they wish to pursue. Agencies may also be more selective in the release of information and provide it privately only to a few key senators or representatives who can make some use of it in a manner that will redound both to the credit of the member and to the advantage of the agency. Agency personnel often help congressional staff members write speeches for their principals in which information is used that puts the agency in a favorable light and also makes the member appear highly knowledgeable.

Personal Visits and Phone Calls. Top administrative officials are in constant informal contact with key members of relevant congressional committees and subcommittees. In these relationships their central job is to establish personal rapport and trust. The establishment of such a relationship does not mean that all policy and program initiatives will gain congressional approval, but the chances of favorable congressional response are enhanced.

A good example of the elaborate round of personal contacts needed to make a bureaucratic decision is provided by Ruttenberg (Ruttenberg and Gutchess, 1970: 80–81) in discussing his tenure as head of the Manpower Administration (later renamed the Employment and Training Administration). In pursuing the notion that there should be regional manpower administrators (after Representative Fogarty's death had made such a change at least possible), Ruttenberg had to establish good working relationships with the new chairman of the House Appropriations subcommittee dealing with the Department of Labor's budget, with the other members of the House Appropriations Committee, including the senior Republicans, and with the chairman and key members of the House Ways and Means Committee, which had jurisdiction over one of the programs that would come under the purview of the new regional manpower administrators.

The Use of Third Parties. Like members of Congress, executive branch officials can also use supportive third parties to intervene with members of Congress by arguing their case or reinforcing their view. These individuals can include the president or other high-ranking executive officials, newspaper reporters, interest-group representatives, and prestigious constituents who also happen to be agency clients. Like Congress, agencies can also commission studies and surveys by outsiders (presumably respected) that can be widely disseminated if their conclusions are favorable to the agency and quietly suppressed if the conclusions are not flattering or supportive.

Agency heads must be wary of tapping too often at the doors of higher-ups in the executive branch to bolster their positions before congressional committees. While important issues no doubt warrant the agency's use of heavy artillery, excessive reliance on the president or secretary has disadvantages. For one thing, as Freeman (1965: 73) noted, "Many committee members do not appreciate bureaucratic attempts to exploit the halo which sometimes attends presidential leadership, especially when the bureau spokesman infers that Congress can be pushed around by a strong President." In addition, reliance on high-ranking executive branch officials may encourage agency dependence on them and increase the difficulty of obtaining a favorable response from Congress in the absence of personal support from the president or the secretary.

Interest-group representatives are most frequently mobilized by agency bureaucrats. Horn (1970: 197–98) describes an instance in 1965 when Secretary of Defense McNamara successfully used representatives of the domestic aircraft industry to obtain approval from the Senate Appropriations Committee to allow British suppliers to bid on planned ship construction projects by the U.S. Navy:

> Most members of the Defense Subcommittee were opposed to the Pentagon position. In a short period before the markup, McNamara personally contacted almost all committee members. Representatives of the aircraft industry, coordinating their efforts with McNamara's staff, also made known their interest. Potential subcontractor suppliers of various parts were enlisted in the cause. When the showdown came in the full committee, McNamara's personal effort, combined with his skilled use of a rival segment of the private economy, paid off.

In addition to mobilizing the support of interested third parties for a specific cause, agency bureaucrats maintain a steady public relations effort to keep Congress and the public informed about the good they and their programs are doing through newsletters, press releases, and other publications. Agencies also urge their clientele to communicate satisfaction with a program to relevant members of Congress, because in the absence of such feedback Congress may assume that no one other than the agency cares about a program, and its appropriations may be cut as a result. (See Wildavsky, 1984: 65–74, for an interesting overview of agency-clientele relations.)

4

Distributive Policy

In the first three chapters we have made a number of generalizations about the relationship between Congress and the bureaucracy. We have portrayed the relationship in broad strokes in Chapter 1 by talking about its place in the general institutional framework through which national public policy gets made in the United States. In Chapter 2 we focused more concretely on the individuals involved in the relationship and on some illustrative examples of the relationship in concrete institutional settings. In Chapter 3 we discussed the resources of individuals both on Capitol Hill and in the bureaucracy and the techniques at their disposal for pursuing their various goals.

Now we want to get more specific and focus on how Congress and the bureaucracy interact as policy is made in different areas. We are going to focus particularly on the presence and importance of subgovernments within the congressional-bureaucratic relationship. We expect to observe differences in the relationship depending on which of the six policy areas—distributive, protective regulatory, redistributive, structural, strategic, and crisis—is involved. A number of questions are both substantively interesting and important to a systematic analysis of the relationship between Congress and the bureaucracy. How important is the operation of a subgovernment in the policy area? With what range of issues does it deal? Do its decisions stand as final, or are they altered before a final decision emerges from the policy process? Is the relationship between congressional and bureaucratic actors in a policy area characterized chiefly by conflict or by cooperation? If conflict occurs, how is it resolved? Do the policy positions of one branch seem to emerge dominant over the views of the other branch in the resolution of conflict? In this chapter and the ones that follow, we will present empirical material to illustrate and explore these questions in different policy areas.

We begin this analysis with some expectations about how the congressional-bureaucratic relationship will look. These expectations are summarized in Table 4-1. This table can serve as a guide to the empirical chapters. Our intent is to elaborate our expectations about the shape of the congressional-bureaucratic relationship at the beginning of each empirical chapter, discuss the examples in terms of the analytical questions, and then summarize our general observations.

THE NATURE OF DISTRIBUTIVE POLICY

The essence of distributive policy lies in its decentralized award of federal largesse to a seemingly unlimited number of recipients—individuals, groups, and corporations. The mechanics of the subsidy arrangement vary. In some issue areas there may be numerous individual laws that each specify a few beneficiaries, or there may be a general law that allows numerous similar beneficiaries to collect a subsidy. The duration of the subsidy can also vary, as can its material nature. The reward may take the form of a price-support payment; a contract for procurement, construction, or service; a tax loophole; or a special indemnity payment.

The recipients of these subsidies usually do not compete directly with each other for the subsidies, but rather they each seek a high level of support for themselves without being particularly aware of the other recipients and their subsidies. The petitioners typically seek direct access to the bureaus in the executive branch and the subcommittees in the House and Senate that are primarily responsible for setting their level of subsidy. Once the level of subsidy is set, the implementation of that subsidy is also delegated to the bureau level of the executive branch—often with close involvement of personnel from the relevant subcommittees.

The interactions of the members of the subgovernment that emerge once a subsidy pattern has been established are characterized by a low level of public visibility and by a high degree of mutually rewarding cooperation (logrolling) that facilitates both perpetuation of the subsidies within the subsystem and its continued low visibility. Cooperation and logrolling also mark the relationship between legislative members of the subgovernment and the rest of the House and Senate. Eventually most members of Congress want to set up subsidies for groups they support and need cooperation to do so.

The great proliferation of interest groups in the past few decades (Schlozman and Tierney, 1986) has been both a reflection of increased activities in the realm of subsidy and a spur to such activity. Interest groups do not organize only to spur subsidy or to perpetuate subsidy, but that is a central motivation for many groups. The subsidies are often not immediately apparent. For example, in 1978 (with revisions and extensions in 1981 and 1982) Congress created an almost invisible provision of the

TABLE 4-1
Expectations about the Congressional-Bureaucratic Relationship during Policy Formation in Different Areas

Policy Area	Importance of Subgovernment in Policy Area	Range of Issues Decided by Subgovernment	Importance of Subgovernment in Determining Final Policy Actions	Degree of Conflict or Cooperation between Congress and Bureaucracy	Mode and Normal Locus of Conflict Resolution	Substance of Conflict Resolution	Dominant Institution When Conflict Persists
Distributive	High (subgovernment is major decisional locus)	Broad	High	High degree of cooperation—both have primary interest in pleasing clients	Face-to-face negotiations: resolution within the subgovernment	Compromise between initial specific positions	Congress (typically at the subcommittee level)
Protective regulatory	Low (major new decisions are made by Congress)	Narrow	Moderately low on new decisions; moderately high in existing areas of regulation	Potentially high conflict when legislators seek exceptions to general policies	Face-to-face negotiations within the subgovernment or transfer to a higher level	Compromise between initial specific positions; nonresolution; broader compromise at a higher level	Usually Congress at the collective level
Redistributive	Very low (major decisions are made by executive branch interacting with peak associations)	Very narrow	Low	Potentially high conflict based on partisan and ideological differences; possible cooperation in redefining issue as distributive	No resolution within subgovernment; resolution is transferred to a higher level	Broader compromise at a higher level; redefinition of issues in distributive terms; nonresolution	Depends on relative partisan and ideological strength in Congress

(continued on page 92)

TABLE 4-1 (concluded)
Expectations about the Congressional-Bureaucratic Relationship during Policy Formation in Different Areas

Policy Area	Importance of Subgovernment in Policy Area	Range of Issues Decided by Subgovernment	Importance of Subgovernment in Determining Final Policy Actions	Degree of Conflict or Cooperation between Congress and Bureaucracy	Mode and Normal Locus of Conflict Resolution	Substance of Conflict Resolution	Dominant Institution When Conflict Persists
Structural	High (subgovernment is major decisional locus)	Broad	High	High degree of cooperation—both have primary interest in pleasing clients	Face-to-face negotiations; resolution within the relationship	Compromise between initial specific positions	Congress (typically at the subcommittee level)
Strategic	Low (major decisions are made in executive branch)	Narrow	Low	Some chance for conflict if Congress gets involved	Subgovernment not involved in resolution; resolution occurs at a higher level	Compromise or nonresolution	Executive branch
Crisis	Very low (major decisions are presidential)	None	Very low	Little chance for either cooperation or conflict to develop during decision making; conflict may develop after event	No subgovernment involvement; post hoc legitimation (congressional resolutions, executive orders)	Sham compromise or imposed solution	Executive branch (president)

Internal Revenue Code called the Targeted Jobs Tax Credit. Almost invisible, that is, except to enterprising fast-food lobbyists, who saw considerable federal dollars flowing to their clients for hiring the kind of youths to serve hamburgers that they hired anyway (Keller, 1981a). This is an instance in which Congress created the initial program without much pressure from lobbyists, but when renewal was at stake the lobbyists were present in force to make sure that the subsidy continued.

There is an urge throughout the entities—both public and private—responsible for designing policy to put subsidy aspects into many policy and program designs. For example, when the Postal Service and its congressional overseers and its commercial mailers began talking about a nine-digit ZIP code to replace the five-digit code, it was automatically assumed that business would get "incentive assistance" from the government to make the transition. "Incentive assistance"—an imaginative name—is, of course, a subsidy. When distribution formulas are designed, there is often a tendency to develop the criteria in such a way as to spread eligibility. By 1980, for example, the accretion of formulas that had collected around the Economic Development Administration since its creation in 1965 (its direct predecessor was created in 1961) made geographical areas containing 85 percent of the population of the entire United States eligible for "special aid" (Rich, 1980), even though the program was supposed to help only areas that were chronically depressed economically.

Subsidy—distributive policy—expands so as to submerge and blur class lines. Politically, if the numerous and active variants of the middle class get "their share," the policy makers are given some extra latitude and support in policy making in general.

In any given year the structure of interests, bureaus, and subcommittees within a subgovernment looks only marginally different from the preceding year. Substantive change is gradual, and the cast of characters—both individual and institutional—varies only a little bit from year to year.

Ronald Reagan and some of his supporters, advisors, and appointees issued rhetorical statements that they would attack the "iron triangles" (their favorite name for subgovernments) in their policy decisions. They portrayed the recent past of the 1960s and especially the 1970s as a period of unrestrained feeding at the public trough by a plethora of interest groups. By implication, they excoriated the administrations of both Republicans (Nixon, Ford) and Democrats (Johnson, Carter) for caving in to (or even encouraging) this development. They promised an end to it.

The claim and the performance of the Reagan administration need to be assessed because, at one level, there seemed to be a promise to change the basic character of policy formulation in the United States. When analyzed, the Reagan claim need not be taken too seriously, for two reasons.

First, the Reagan folks tended to define any program that resulted in federal spending and that they did not favor as the result of "iron triangles." This meant that they focused much of their attack on programs for the less advantaged classes and groups in society—programs such as welfare and food stamps, for example. In our analysis, these programs are redistributive and are surrounded by political relationships quite different from those typical of distributive policies and programs. For the most part, the Reagan people engaged in the standard effort of any administration to punish programmatically those in the opposing political coalition and reward those perceived to be in the supportive political coalition. The rhetoric the Reagan spokespersons chose stressing "iron triangles" did not change the reality that their main targets were programs redistributive to the less well-off. Only a few of their targets were genuine distributive or subsidy programs as we have conceived of them in the present analysis.

What happened even in those few areas in which the Reagan administration took direct aim at genuine distributive policies and programs? Some very modest changes were effected, but these changes certainly amounted to no revolution in the nature of policy formulation in the United States. Incremental change—nothing extraordinary or unexpected—occurred.

In 1981 *Congressional Quarterly* singled out eight programs that, in its view, were individuals in what Budget Director David Stockman once called "the thundering herd of sacred cows." We eliminated two of those programs because one seems to us to be more redistributive than distributive and one is clearly in the realm of structural foreign and defense policy. The other six were clearly distributive and were the targets of attacks by Reagan, Stockman, and others in and around the White House. What happened to these items? How resilient were they in the face of administration attack, with the membership of Congress considerably altered by the election returns? At the end of 1981 only one of the six—Public Health Service hospitals—had apparently been led to slaughter. The other five survived, some unscathed, and others with some modest cuts (Keller, 1981c, 1982). These programs included federal aid to schools in areas "impacted" by federal establishments, the Clinch River breeder reactor, support for the Export-Import Bank, Amtrak passenger trains, and the peanut-allotment program. In short, the changes wrought by the "Reagan revolution" in domestic distributive policy were hardly revolutionary, but they were incremental. To be sure, Reagan took on—at least rhetorically—more distributive programs than his immediate predecessors, but he fared about the same—winning few battles completely, losing some completely, and settling for some sort of compromise on the rest.

In January of 1982 the *Washington Post* (January 24, 25, 26, and 27, 1982) surveyed what had happened to what they labeled "pork-barrel politics" in the first Reagan years. The label included a lot of distributive programs that had been targeted by Reagan for cuts or elimination in the name of fiscal sanity and retrenchment. The headlines of the stories summarize the results quite vividly: "Despite Budget Cuts, the Hill Finds Dollars to Spread Around at Home"; "Congress' Budget Cutters Protect the Home Folks"; "Budget Knife Only Nicks Road and Harbor Projects"; "Legislative Largesse Puts Energy Firms in a 'No-Lose' Situation."

As the second Reagan term opened in 1985 the level of subsidy for some programs was under challenge. Rates of program growth dropped and, in some cases, cuts were made. However, the general realization by a large number of members of both parties in Congress that a continuation of seemingly unchecked federal deficits could be political suicide for incumbents on election day in 1986 seems to have accounted for some limits on spending for subsidy. The Reagan assault itself did not have the impact the administration rhetoric suggested it would. The passage in December 1985 of the Gramm-Rudman bill requiring a balanced budget by 1991, and presumably setting up the machinery for achieving it, was a political response by Congress to a problem that was genuinely economic but even more pressingly and obviously political. Precisely what impact Gramm-Rudman will have is unclear. The most likely outcome is that defense spending—the major (perhaps only) Reagan priority in terms of increases—will be cut along with domestic spending and/or taxes will have to be raised.

The deficit has created a political climate for the late 1980s that has altered the assurance of virtually complete anonymity that most subgovernments could have expected in the 1960s and 1970s. Public attack is more frequent. However, it would be a mistake, in our view, to assert that the nature of distributive policy and the nature of the political patterns surrounding that policy have changed dramatically and unalterably. The changes are large and visible in a few areas, much more modest in other areas, and not very significant in others. In the substantive program examples in this chapter we will choose some of each type to illustrate what we mean. Even in 1985 a lot of politics as usual went on. The erosion of various tax reform proposals during the course of the year illustrates many interests successfully protecting various tax subsidies. The *New York Times* (March 17, 1985) ran an appropriate headline in discussing the salvation of the Urban Development Action Grant (UDAG) program in a Senate committee: "Why It's Easier to Scratch a Back Than Bite a Bullet." Lobbyists for real estate developers and cities—the interests directly served—were able to keep the program going (at a reduced dollar level) even though it was a major administration target for elimination. Despite rhetoric and some cuts, the UDAG situation was typical in many ways of the continued survival of many distributive programs.

THE CONGRESSIONAL-BUREAUCRATIC RELATIONSHIP IN DISTRIBUTIVE POLICY

Expectations about the Relationship

We expect the relationship between bureaucrats (at the bureau level) and individuals on Capitol Hill (both members and staff members at the subcommittee level) to be critically important in distributive policy. As indicated in Chapter 1, it is in this policy area that subgovernments often hold sway, and the bureau-subcommittee relationship is at the heart of subgovernments. The relationship is important in the sense that the actors deal with the full range of issues in the area, from the broadest items of general policy to the most detailed items involving a single subsidy for a single client. It is also important in that the actors usually make what amount to final decisions on the full range of issues. Only occasionally does a subgovernment lose control of part of its policy area and get overruled by some other authorities such as the full House or Senate, a conference committee, the Office of Management and Budget, the office of the secretary of an executive department, or the White House.

Ordinarily the relationship between the congressional actors and the bureaucratic actors is marked by a high degree of cooperation. All actors have a major stake in supporting and pleasing the interests of their clients because it is, in part, client satisfaction that can produce critical political support for both the bureau and the subcommittee as they seek to enhance their positions in their respective institutional settings.

Issues that involve differences of opinion are usually resolved by straightforward, face-to-face negotiations between the individuals directly involved in the relationship. There is usually no need to appeal to higher authority because agreement is usually relatively easy to reach. In fact, both parties have a stake in resolving conflict without involving other parties. If higher authority is invoked, then other matters on which there is agreement at the subgovernment level might also be called into question, and long-standing policies and programs might be changed in ways unsatisfactory to both the bureaucratic and congressional members of the subgovernment.

The normal resolution of disagreement within a subgovernment is a straightforward compromise somewhere in the middle of the two initial contending positions. This compromise is generally satisfying to both the bureaucratic and congressional parties, although it would be reasonable to expect that over time congressional interests and positions are likely to be more closely approximated than bureaucratic interests and positions.

Although the distributive arena in general follows the above patterns some further distinctions between different instances of subgovernment involvement are very important. As suggested in Chapter 1, subgovernments are not always immune to scrutiny from outsiders. The subgovernments' operations can be opened up by a number of factors—disagreement among members that cannot be resolved within the subgovernment; intrusion into subgovernment affairs by outsiders, such as an aggressive president; introduction of a new issue into the subgovernment's jurisdiction; or redefinition of a distributive issue into nondistributive terms. All of these factors increase the visibility of the subgovernment and of its functioning, and thereby broaden the number of participants who get involved.

There are four major variations in the congressional-bureaucratic relationships within the distributive policy arena. The most common is *subgovernment dominance.* Two important variations are major *subgovernment adaptation* and *competing subgovernments. Subgovernment disintegration* is the fourth variation, one that rarely occurs.

Subgovernment dominance is, in many senses, the "normal" situation in cases of distributive policy. Much of the time subgovernments make decisions affecting substantive matters within their purview basically without serious challenge from or involvement of anyone outside the subgovernment except in terms of formal ratification of subgovernment decisions. The subgovernments operate at a low level of visibility and at a high level of effectiveness from the point of view of the interests they champion. In those instances in which challenges are made to the subgovernment, it prevails with relative ease, thus retaining its dominance.

In a situation of subgovernment dominance, both short-run and long-run policy outcomes favor the interests of those in the subgovernment. No major redefinition of the policy positions by the members of the subgovernment is necessary because challenges can be met without such concessions. The domain in the subgovernment's fief is stable in content or, in the case of particularly strong subgovernments, may expand. Challenges are relatively infrequent and sporadic and do not pose much threat to the interests of the subgovernment.

Major subgovernment adaptation is required when challenges to a subgovernment become more persistent and powerful. If defeats begin to become frequent and if the subgovernment is being defeated on issues that are central to its interests, then often that subgovernment will adapt to adjust itself to new reality. If successful, the subgovernment will reestablish itself as dominant, although on the basis of a new definition of interests, issues, and positions. If either unsuccessful at adaptation or unwilling to make an adaptive effort, the subgovernment may disintegrate or may be supplanted by a competing set of interests represented in another subgovernment.

When a subgovernment undergoes major adaptation, short-run policy outcomes are likely to be a mix of favorable and unfavorable from the perspective of the subgovernment. But, if the adaptation is successful, long-run policy outcomes will be favorable. Obviously, policy positions will be redefined by the members of the subgovernment during the process of adaptation. During this process the domain under subgovernment dominance is also likely to change. Before and during the process, challenges to the subgovernment will be at least moderately strong and relatively frequent.

Competing subgovernments can develop when an issue area is lodged in the governmental decision-making apparatus in a way that allows or even promotes the development of institutionalized competition for dominance. The competition may result in the eventual redefinition of jurisdictions so one subgovernment becomes dominant, or it may result in the competing subgovernments being replaced by some other mode of decision making, or it may simply result in continued sharing of the issue-area space with sufficient adjustments to mute conflict and allow decisions to be made.

In a situation of competing subgovernments, both short-run and long-run policy outcomes typically are mixed from the point of view of either subgovernment. Each of the competitors prevails some of the time. If one of the competitors begins to prevail an overwhelming proportion of the time, the element of competition will evaporate. In most competitive situations, members of the competing groups do little redefining of their policy positions. Stability of the domain influenced by each of the competitors is relatively low to moderate because competition will ordinarily breed changing patterns of dominance. Challenges to the dominance of any one subgovernment are, by definition, relatively strong and frequent.

Subgovernment disintegration occurs only rarely, but that it occurs at all suggests that some significant change—both procedural and substantive—is at least possible in national policy making. Disintegration may occur because the subgovernment loses jurisdiction over its issues (either because of a reshuffling of congressional or bureaucratic boundaries or because of a redefinition of the issue as nondistributive), because it has been weakened by repeated losses on a series of individually minor challenges, because it has collapsed in the face of a major challenge, or because of key personnel changes in the critical units of the subgovernment.

As a subgovernment approaches disintegration, both short-run and long-run policy outcomes become unfavorable. The subgovernment is not likely to redefine its policy positions (if it would do so it might be able to adapt to changed circumstances and survive). The domain in the purview of the subgovernment shrinks until it vanishes. Challenges are strong and frequent and, ultimately, fatal.

Table 4–2 summarizes the four major variations in the situations or contexts in which subgovernments find themselves as they participate in distributive policy making.

TABLE 4-2
Four Major Subgovernment Situations In Distributive Policy Making

Major Attributes of Situation	Overall Subgovernment Position			
	Dominance	Major Adaptation	Competing Subgovernments	Disintegration
Short-run policy outcomes	Favorable	Mixed	Mixed	Unfavorable
Long-run policy outcomes	Favorable	Favorable	Mixed	Unfavorable
Degree of redefinition of policy positions by subgovernment	Low	Moderate to high	Low	Low
Stability of subgovernment domain	High; may expand	Low	Low to moderate	Low; then vanishes
Strength and frequency of challenges	Low; sporadic	Moderate to high; frequent	Moderate to high; frequent	High; frequent (ultimately fatal)

Subgovernment Dominance

Water Resources: The Classic Period.   Water resource policy has evolved piecemeal. Like many distributive areas, there is no single comprehensive policy, but rather an aggregation of separate decisions made over time. Administrative responsibility for water policy has been split since 1902 between the Army Corps of Engineers, whose fiefdom was concentrated in the eastern United States, and the Bureau of Reclamation, charged with water development in the western states. For decades legislating for water projects represented classic pork-barrel politics. Generous benefits were distributed to states and localities and controversy was limited.

The smooth operation of the subgovernment was shaken in the 1970s, and disruptions continued into the 1980s. In what follows in this section we describe the traditional, smoothly functioning subgovernment surrounding the Corps of Engineers water projects in its golden era (before the mid-1970s). We continue our discussion of water resources over the last ten to fifteen years in the section on subgovernment adaptation.

Rivers and harbors projects have been a traditional form of subsidy throughout our national history, and the principal agency involved in rivers and harbors projects has been the Corps of Engineers (see Drew, 1970; Maass, 1950). The corps's responsibility for developing the nation's water resources is greater than that of such potentially competing agencies as the Bureau of Reclamation, the Tennessee Valley Authority, and the Soil Conservation Service. The corps's projects, which have been described by some as a federal giveaway to local communities, include building of dams, levees, and reservoirs; straightening and otherwise rearranging rivers; and building harbors and canals. The purposes served by the projects include flood prevention; creation and improvement of waterways; and provision of hydroelectric power, water supplies, and recreation opportunities.

The corps's water resource programs operated through a well-established network of ties between individual members of Congress seeking projects for their districts, congressional committees (the House and Senate public works committees and the House Public Works Appropriations Subcommittee), officials of the Corps of Engineers, and representatives of affected local interests and national lobbying organizations (such as the National Rivers and Harbors Congress, the Florida Waterways Association, and the Mississippi Valley Association). A description of how a project becomes a reality illustrates the ties within the subgovernment (Drew, 1970).

A project originates at the local level, when representatives of concerns that can see profit in a corps project (industrialists, real estate developers, barge companies) get together with the corps district engineer and draw up a proposal for a dam, canal, reservoir, or other project. They then proceed to enlist the aid of their senators and representative(s) to sponsor legislation to authorize a feasibility study by the corps. Many proposals never advance beyond this stage, but this is a cheap favor for legislators to do for their local constituents.

The proposals are referred to the House and Senate public works committees. These committees make decisions about which of the projects receive feasibility studies by the corps and also about which of the projects that have received the corps's approval will be authorized for funding and construction. The appropriations committees provide the funds for the feasibility studies and for the construction of authorized projects. Once a proposal has received authorization for a feasibility study, the corps's engineers in the district conduct the study (this may entail many years and volumes of technical reports) and report their recommendations for or against a proposal based on determinations of whether the economic benefits to be derived from the project would be equal to or greater than the costs of the project. (At congressional insistence, the criteria used to evaluate the economic benefits are extremely flexible.) Every two years, in an authorization bill, the public works committees identify the projects authorized for feasibility studies and those authorized for construction.

The process of making decisions about whose projects in which districts receive funding is characterized by political negotiation, bargaining, and compromise by the committee members, with a large dose of interest-group lobbying. In general the projects are distributed to all parts of the country, but the South, West, and Southwest have the largest proportion of water projects. Former Senator Paul Douglas, a Democrat from Illinois, offered an assessment of the pork-barrel flavor of the negotiations that characterize water resources decision making (Drew, 1970: 55): "The [public works] bill is built up out of a whole system of mutual accommodations, in which the favors are widely distributed, with the implicit promise that no one will kick over the applecart; that if senators do not object to the bill as a whole, they will 'get theirs.' It is a process, if I may use an inelegant expression, of mutual backscratching and mutual logrolling."

By and large, the subgovernment operated quietly and efficiently, with the corps supervising the construction of projects that benefit legislators' local interests, and Congress authorizing and funding projects that continued the corps's dominance in water resource development.

Agricultural Policy: The Classic Period.   Farm policy has long been synonymous with the presence and dominance of subgovernments (Lowi, 1973a; Talbot and Hadwiger, 1968). This is not to say that the policies are not controversial; they often are, and victories of agriculture subgovernments are, for example, often ratified by narrow votes on the floor of

Congress. Furthermore, it is often necessary for those dominating the agricultural policy area to trade their support to others for other issues in return for building majority coalitions for their own favored farm policies. The major farm bill passed in late 1985 represented significant adaptive behavior on the part of the agriculture subgovernments and will be treated separately in the next section. What follows presents the general picture of agricultural policy making for many decades before the mid-1980s.

Agricultural policy is, of course, complex and made up of many pieces, and subgovernments typically form around each of the separate pieces. Although on some occasions members of these separate subgovernments may form temporary alliances to promote a broader policy, ordinarily they work independently and focus on narrower policy concerns. A few examples will demonstrate how strong subgovernments work. First, we will look at two broad areas in which success has been fairly consistent over long periods: price supports and soil conservation. Then we will observe a subgovernment, in effect, expanding its domain by opening the federal Treasury in a major way to new "disaster" claims by farmers.

Price Supports.   The price-support program is a highly complex set of laws administered at the national level by the Agricultural Stabilization and Conservation Service and the Commodity Credit Corporation (both part of the U.S. Department of Agriculture) and at the state and local levels by delegated state, county, and local committees. The price-support program is designed to protect the incomes of growers and producers of commodities through a combination of acreage allotments (crop quotas), target prices on commodities, government loans and payments to growers, and government purchases of crops.

Subgovernments have developed around each major crop or supported item. The basic participants are relevant specialists in the Agricultural Stabilization and Conservation Service, the members of the various commodity subcommittees of the House Agriculture Committee, and representatives of the interest groups for the various crops and commodities (such as the National Association of Wheat Growers, the National Wool Growers Association, the Soybean Council of America, and the National Milk Producers Federation). Table 4–3 illustrates some of the commodity subgovernments by giving a partial listing of the institutional locations of some of the principal members.

The House Agriculture Committee divided into commodity subcommittees in 1955. The subcommittees drafted the various commodity provisions that were then stapled together by the full committee and sent to the floor for ratification. A similar scenario played out in the Senate; in the words of the press secretary for the Senate Agriculture Committee, "Chairman [Herman E.] Talmadge [Democrat from Georgia] would ask every Senator what he wanted for his commodity" (Stokes, 1985: 633).

TABLE 4-3
Composition of Illustrative Commodity Subgovernments

| Commodity | Institutional Location of Subgovernment Members | | |
	Congress	Bureaucracy	Interest Groups
Cotton	House Cotton Subcommittee	Agricultural Stabilization and Conservation Service (ASCS) cotton program	National Cotton Council
Oilseeds and rice	House Oilseeds and Rice Subcommittee	ASCS programs for peanuts, rice, tungnuts, flaxseed, soybeans, dry edible beans, and crude pinegum	Soybean Council of America
Tobacco	House Tobacco Subcommittee	ASCS tobacco program	Tobacco Institute
Dairy and poultry products	House Dairy and Poultry Subcommittee	ASCS milk program	National Milk Producers Federation; National Broiler Council
Livestock and grains	House Livestock and Grains Subcommittee	ASCS programs for wheat, corn, barley, oats, grain sorghum, rye, wool, and mohair	National Association of Wheat Growers; National Wool Growers Association

Each commodity subgovernment worked to obtain the most favorable support possible for the producers of the commodity, both in terms of acreage allotments and target prices. In general, these subgovernments operated without successful challenge in setting the levels of commodity supports, which were ratified by Congress and announced by the secretary of agriculture. Agriculture policy was thus built from the bottom up, the result of horsetrading and cooperation among a close-knit group of subgovernment members, many of whom met socially. Only in the 1980s did this way of making the nation's agriculture policy begin to alter.

Soil Conservation.   The basic program (or "mission") of the Soil Conservation Service (SCS) is development of a national soil and water conservation program (although the SCS has never had the only program in this area). This responsibility takes the form of building small dams to help conserve soil, prevent floods, and increase recreational opportunities in rural areas. In addition, the SCS provides a variety of technical assistance to land owners, land users, and land developers located in approximately 3,000 soil conservation districts to assist in carrying out locally adopted programs.

The local districts have a good deal of muscle and are directly involved in the operations of the soil conservation subgovernment. For example, the watershed projects of the SCS are the result of requests made at the local level, usually by the conservation districts, to the SCS. The SCS then obtains the necessary authorizations and appropriations from Congress to carry out the requests. The subgovernment that emerges from this process includes SCS watershed bureau officials, members of the House and Senate agriculture committees (who must make the authorizations), and members of the House Appropriations Subcommittee on Agriculture. Relevant nongovernmental participants include representatives of the National Association of Soil Conservation Districts and the Izaak Walton League of America. The decisions of this subgovernment are quiet and continuous.

Crop Disaster and the Small Business Administration: Subgovernment Expansion.   In 1977 farmers in Georgia and other southeastern states suffered crop losses because of drought. This triggered events that cost the Treasury of the United States billions of dollars more than it expected to spend (Havemann, 1977; Meisol, 1978).

The crop problems in Georgia prompted action by Sam Nunn, one of the senators from the state and a member of the Senate Select Committee on Small Business. He pointed out to both farmers and the Small Business Administration (SBA) that a little-noted provision of a 1975 statute affecting the SBA had made farmers eligible for SBA disaster loans. That amendment had been offered by two senior senators, one of them from a rural state and chairman of the Senate Small Business Committee.

Once Nunn had pushed the SBA into admitting that it could not exclude farmers from disaster loans, the chairman of the House Small Business Committee, Neal Smith, an Iowan (Iowa farmers had also suffered crop problems in 1977), joined in urging farmers to apply and the SBA to respond favorably.

The results were costly. In fiscal year 1976 the SBA allowed no disaster loans to farmers. In fiscal year 1977 the SBA made only 798 loans to farmers (4 percent of all its disaster loans) for a total of about $40 million. All of these came late in the year as Nunn and Smith pried open the public coffers for the benefit of their constituents and other farmers. In the first three quarters of fiscal 1978 disaster loans to farmers increased to $1.7 billion—44 percent of the number of SBA disaster loans and more than 75 percent of the total money in the program.

Even though the usual members of agriculture subgovernments had not instituted this action, they now rallied to the cause of preserving this gain, despite the existence of a parallel program in the Farmers Home Administration. (Because the parallel program had tighter eligibility requirements and a higher interest rate, the SBA loans looked particularly attractive.)

Challenges came from two locations: the White House and the Senate Budget Committee. The challenge from within Congress was to no avail as Congress passed an SBA authorization bill extending the disaster loan program, keeping it open to farmers, and putting no dollar limit on expenditures ("such sums as are necessary" were authorized).

White House opposition was only partially effective. After Congress had left town in October 1978 (and therefore could not vote on overriding a veto), President Carter vetoed the bill for a number of reasons, including the budget connotations of the treatment of disaster loans for farmers. He objected to the duplication of the program with the Farmers Home Administration loan program, the very low interest rate (3 percent), and the lack of a limit on the amount spent. This veto had the effect of raising the interest rate (to 6.625 percent) but, because of earlier legislation, still left the Treasury unguarded. The new interest rate was still low by commercial standards.

In 1980 Congress moved the program to the Farmers Home Administration but made no serious effort to control the cost of the program. In 1981 it was operating at its highest levels ever, with more than $4 billion in loans granted for the first half of the year alone.

The Reagan administration proposed severe cuts and limits on the program, including raising the interest rate to 14 percent. The administration achieved only limited success by raising interest rates to no more than 8 percent for borrowers without other sources of credit (by far the most common status and relatively easy to establish) and market rates for others. During years in which regular credit was about 20 percent, 8 percent loans were, of course, enormously attractive. Massive amounts of federal money kept going for this program. Agricultural supporters continued to have good reason to smile.

Veterans' Benefits.   Over many decades, the veterans' subgovernment has become quite powerful, tapping the public purse for enormous benefits (Keisling, 1982; Keller, 1980; Scott, 1977). The natural appeal for helping those who have served their country, sometimes in combat, has produced the third-largest bureaucracy in the government—the Veterans Administration, with 238,000 employees, is surpassed in size only by the Defense Department and the Postal Service. The budget of the VA in the mid-1980s was more than $26 billion and headed higher. This made the VA one of the largest spenders in the entire federal establishment as well as one of the largest employers. The VA's budget purchases a range of benefits and programs for veterans (and their dependents and survivors) that include:

The largest single hospital and medical care system in the country.
Educational assistance.
Compensation to injured veterans, regardless of their income.
Pensions for needy veterans, whose needs do not stem from their time in service.
A life insurance program covering more than five million veterans.
Mortgage insurance loans on more than nine million homes.

Both the cost of benefits and the nature of benefits have expanded over time. Naturally, the number of veterans and eligible relatives also helps determine the actual dollar outlay in any given year.

Critical in determining that these benefits continue to grow is a subgovernment involving the VA; veterans' groups such as the American Legion, Veterans of Foreign Wars, and Disabled American Veterans; and the veterans' affairs committees of both the House and the Senate (the House committee has been the congressional bulwark of the subgovernment; the Senate committee was created only in 1970—perhaps in itself a sign of the strength of the rest of the subgovernment).

In 1978 the veterans' subgovernment demonstrated its power by successfully increasing veterans' benefits in three areas: (1) The nonservice-connected disability pension program was amended in three major ways: benefits were increased by as much as 50 percent in some cases, a cost-of-living factor was added to keep pensions increasing, and veterans on these pensions were guaranteed what amounted to a minimum annual income; (2) VA housing programs were liberalized in several important ways; and (3) a special employment and training program for veterans was created in the Department of Labor largely as a response to pressure from veterans' groups. Furthermore, an attempt by the Carter administration to eliminate "veterans' preference" points added to civil-service examination results, in connection with general civil-service reform, was unceremoniously dumped in both houses of Congress.

In 1981 and the following years, the Reagan budget-cutters basically left the VA alone, unwilling to tackle such a well-entrenched set of interests whose organizations also happened to be in the president's corner politically on most issues.

Regardless of the ultimate impact of the Gramm-Rudman bill that mandated a balanced budget by 1991 (passed in late 1985), it is worth noting that veterans' pensions were exempted from *any* mandatory cuts and the allowable cuts in veterans' health care programs were severely restricted—to 1 percent in 1986 and no more than 2 percent in any year after that, regardless of the size of the total deficit to be pared. Clearly, Congress, supported by the Veterans Administration and powerful veterans lobbies, was in a position to keep this subgovernment's preferences protected. Under Gramm-Rudman the subgovernment basically exempted its programs from the bruising political debate that could encompass most programs.

In short, the veterans' subgovernment has continuously been very effective, powerful, and successful in securing extensive and expensive benefits (subsidies) for veterans. The subgovernment has operated with relatively low visibility and limited intrusion by outsiders, and it is rarely challenged.

Merchant Shipping. The structure of subgovernments in the merchant shipping policy area is very fluid. This field is even more fragmented than most distributive policy areas. It is itself composed of sub-subgovernments, and disaggregation of subsidies to recipients is virtually complete. The participants and subsidies are numerous, but the supporters of any given subsidy are not concerned with the existence of other subsidies as long as their own subsidy is continued.

Lawrence (1966) estimates that between fifty and one hundred federal government components in both the executive branch and Congress are involved in some way with merchant shipping. Given this fragmentation, it is hardly surprising that a single subgovernment has failed to emerge. The resulting fragmented structure has produced a situation in which industry wishes have dominated policy. Subsidy along familiar lines is thoroughly entrenched, and there seems to be no locus in which sufficient interest or energy for change can be generated. Congress as a whole shows no interest in supervising the various subcommittees dealing with pieces of maritime policy. Likewise, the upper echelons of the executive branch show virtually no interest in supervising a variety of executive agencies dealing with pieces of the policy. Consequently, each issue tends to develop its own very small subgovernment made up of a very few people from an obscure subcommittee, an obscure executive agency, the subsidized company or companies, and—as appropriate—the subsidized and/or affected labor union or unions.

The companies are given a particularly strong role to play in instances in which there is tension between the relevant portions of Congress and the executive branch. This situation has allowed the retention of existing policies, most of which are generally favored by the shippers.

Lawrence's summary (1966: 331–33) describes a classic case of multiple subgovernments that logically should compete but that, in effect, avoid competition by simply increasing the amount of subsidy indiscriminately:

> Because responsibility is diffused and widely dispersed, no single government agency has sufficient power to seize the initiative to overcome the status quo. Operating at the periphery of government, the administrative agencies and congressional subcommittees concerned with maritime affairs have attempted to resolve problems through negotiation rather than referring them to the President or the Congress as a whole. Frequently they have been forced to compromise on the industry's terms. Higher political echelons, when they have become involved, usually have acted as peacemaker between dissident groups. They have often allowed the cost of the government's program to increase rather than risk alienating any immediately affected group. In effect, creeping liberalization of government aids has substituted for hard decisions and real innovation. . . .
>
> Political support of the merchant shipping industry . . . depends on a very narrow base of informed persons. This small core of trade association, executive, and congressional officials who are friends of the industry has been able to use its friendships and position to safeguard the industry's prerogatives, but it has not been strong enough to introduce any real innovations in established programs. This situation immobilizes the political process. Those favored by the subsidy program have reason to avoid any action which will disturb the equilibrium. Those not so favored tend to be so disorganized that they cannot act effectively to win a larger share. Furthermore, the fragmentation of power within the U.S. political system relieves the shipping industry of any sustained external pressure to introduce innovations.

Nothing important has changed in the maritime situation since Lawrence's analysis in the mid-1960s. The variety of subsidies available is incredibly large and complex and makes little economic sense (Congressional Budget Office, 1984; Jantscher, 1975.) No existing subsidies are rescinded, and the whole package is never rationalized.

A member of Congress, Elliott Levitas, a Democrat from Georgia, summarized the situation well in 1978 at a hearing on the relationships between the maritime industry and the Maritime Administration: "The symbiotic relationship between private industry and a government agency is spelled out so clearly here. Here you actually had a marriage formalized with documents. Government and business are right in bed together" (*Washington Post*, July 21, 1978). The congressman should have added that many key members of Congress are in that same bed.

Tobacco and Smoking.   Before 1964 the tobacco industry in the United States—including growers and manufacturers of cigarettes—was protected by an effective subgovernment that subsidized the growers and let the manufacturers alone to advertise their product as they saw fit (see Fritschler, 1983, for a full discussion of this area; see also Friedman, 1975). Fritschler (1983: 4-5) summarizes the composition of the subgovernment and its quiet functioning in the normal pre-1964 situation:

> The tobacco subsystem included the paid representatives of tobacco grow-ers, marketing organizations, and cigarette manufacturers; congressmen repre-senting tobacco constituencies; the leading members of four subcommittees in Congress—two appropriations subcommittees and two substantive legislative committees in each house—that handle tobacco legislation and related appro-priations; and certain officials within the Department of Agriculture who were involved with the various tobacco programs of that department. This was a small group of people well-known to each other and knowledgeable about all aspects of the tobacco industry and its relationship with the government.
>
> As long as no one objected too loudly, the important and complex tobacco programs, like price supports and export promotion, were conducted without interference from those not included in this subsystem.

But there were objections to the tobacco subgovernment from outsid-ers, specifically the "health lobby" and the Federal Trade Commission. Scientific evidence linking smoking and human diseases had been accu-mulating at least since 1857, accompanied by a very gradual increase in public awareness of the dangers of smoking; this culminated in the United States with the publication of the 1964 report of the U.S. surgeon general (head of the Public Health Service) that placed an official government seal of approval on assertions about dangers of smoking. Aware of the accu-mulating body of scientific evidence on smoking, the Federal Trade Com-mission (FTC) had been engaged in trying to discourage advertising and sales of cigarettes, but without much effect. The tobacco subgovernment would have preferred to leave the whole issue of governmental treatment of tobacco and cigarettes as a distributive matter. But the challengers—the "health lobby" and the Federal Trade Commission rule makers—obviously wished to shift the issue into the regulatory arena.

The objections of the outsiders got loud enough to be disruptive to the subgovernment when the FTC, following the surgeon general's report on smoking and health, published proposed rules in the *Federal Register* that would have severely restricted advertising for smoking and would have required strict health warnings for cigarettes. These regulations were viewed as very detrimental by the tobacco growers and manufacturers, and the reaction from Congress, led by the strong tobacco subgovern-ment, was swift. The immediate upshot was the Cigarette Labeling and Advertising Act of 1965, which represented a greater victory for tobacco than for health interests. The bill had two main features. First, the tobacco interests realized that public awareness about the dangers of smoking had reached a sufficient level that some government regulation would probably be inevitable. Allied with advertisers and broadcasters, they lobbied for the weakest regulation possible and succeeded in including a very weak labeling requirement in the law (the warning was limited to packages and was not required in advertising). Second, the tobacco interests were also successful in cutting the hamstrings of the outsider that had caused the disruption in the first place—the FTC. The 1965 legislation placed a four-year ban on FTC rule-making activity in the cigarette-advertising field, and it also foreclosed other regulatory agencies, as well as state and local agencies, from taking action in the field. The tobacco interests had beaten back the challenge, at least for the time being.

In 1970 Congress passed a law that extended the ban on FTC activities for two more years, weakened the wording of the health warning, and required that the FTC give Congress six months' notice of any future rule-making proposals, thus ensuring that the subgovernment would have ample time to rally its forces.

Subsequently, more government restrictions on advertising for smoking have emerged. But these additions have come over a number of years, and their implementation has always been gradual and milder than it could have been. Many of the changes forced on the subgovernment have been largely symbolic. The challenge from the FTC and health lobby failed to produce anything resembling a full-scale government attack on smoking. And, critically, the tobacco subgovernment's crown jewel, tobacco crop subsidies, remained secure.

By the mid-1980s the tobacco industry had several new worries. Cigarette manufacturers thought they could get the federal tax on cigarettes cut in half in 1985. Opponents of smoking and those concerned about the negative health impacts of cigarettes were eager to double the tax. The final outcome was an unchanged tax. High subsidies for tobacco growers were also the focus of public attention. Some members of Congress from tobacco-growing areas were leaders in the effort to reduce the level of subsidy in ways that would both preserve economic viability for tobacco farmers and increase the competitiveness of American tobacco on world markets.

The tobacco subgovernment had achieved unwanted levels of visibility by the 1980s. However, the core of public policy was still favorable to the subgovernment: generous federal price supports for tobacco as an agricultural commodity and a stable federal excise tax on cigarettes. Above all, per capita U.S. cigarette consumption was only slightly dented despite incontrovertible proof of the detrimental health effects of smoking and aggressive campaigns by health lobbies. A rosy future was not guaranteed, as it had been in the days of a truly anonymous subgovernment. But skilled lobbyists working with important allies, especially in Congress, were surely not going to lose the privileged position enjoyed by tobacco farmers and tobacco manufacturers overnight.

Major Subgovernment Adaptation

Water Resources: Adaptation in the 1970s and 1980s.   No major omnibus water project authorization bill has gotten through Congress since 1972 (a small one emerged in 1976). Construction has continued on previously authorized projects, but at a slower rate. Fewer dollars have been appropriated for water projects, and the share for new construction has declined relative to the amount for upkeep of existing facilities. Agreements reached in subcommittee have been reopened to heated debate on the floor.

Why the alteration in operations? The tides of change have swirled around the water subgovernment since the mid-1970s, interrupting smooth routines and injecting the scrutiny of outsiders into water project decisions. In essence, both the rules of the game and the context of subgovernment operations were changing because of forces beyond the control of subgovernment participants. Each of the factors below interacted to raise the level of visibility of subgovernment operations and to make agreement more difficult to reach:

Growing federal budget deficits loomed over all domestic policy decision making, reducing the amount of funds available for discretionary spending and heightening a sense of fiscal conservatism in Congress.

The finite limits of water as a national resource came to be recognized in this period as population and farming in arid areas increased and water tables were depleted.

Environmentalists stimulated debate about and attention to the value of unquestioned development and raised alarms about pollution dangers from some water projects, such as saline runoffs from irrigation projects.

Both Carter and Reagan challenged the subgovernment, Carter much less effectively than Reagan. Both insisted that decision making had to change to take into account cost-benefit calculations, cost sharing on project construction, and outside review. The Office of Management and Budget joined the fray as an important actor, reviewing congressional proposals for water funding. Congressional reaction to these trespasses into their prerogatives was predictably negative.

Changes within Congress itself precipitated some alterations as committee chairmanships changed hands, many going to westerners. Newer members and fiscal conservatives were more willing to question old-fashioned pork-barrel politics.

As resources (both fiscal and physical) began to contract, competition increased between rich states and poor states and between eastern states and western states. Bureaucratic units fought for influence (the Army Corps of Engineers versus the Bureau of Reclamation); congressional committees argued among themselves (authorization versus appropriations), and water users battled for priority (agricultural versus industrial versus recreational).

President Carter's challenge to the subgovernment in 1977 was simultaneously vivid and inept. Carter's goals were to eliminate an array of needless and expensive projects from a congressional wish list and to make sure that local beneficiaries would begin to pay a fair share of the cost of federally subsidized water. But Carter's staff lacked political sense, and the "hit list" confrontational style with Congress was needlessly maladroit, causing permanent damage to executive-legislative relations during Carter's term as president. His efforts increased the level of outside attention to water projects in the 1970s, but failed to affect the outcomes very much. The subgovernment successfully resisted most of the Carter incursions.

President Reagan, a westerner, was welcomed as being more sympathetic to western water interests. In fact, Reagan continued to promote many of the same changes that Carter had advocated, especially cost sharing by localities. But Reagan's style and approach were less abrasive and more flexible than Carter's. In addition, states and localities and members of Congress had had time to grow accustomed to the idea of cost sharing.

Cost sharing has stalled the activities of the subgovernment in the first half of the 1980s. The president personally, the secretary of the interior, the assistant secretary of the Army responsible for the corps, and the head of the OMB have stated repeatedly that authorization of new projects would be contingent on state and local beneficiaries providing nonfederal financing for the projects. Administration officials did not always agree among themselves about whether the cost sharing was to be applied as a fixed formula or on a sliding scale, case-by-case basis (a tiff between the head of the corps and the secretary of the interior in 1983 over this issue resulted in the resignation of the corps's chief), and the cost-sharing principle has been applied flexibly. But the general stance of the administration has been fairly consistently supportive of the "no cost share, no project" philosophy.

The Reagan administration has let some water legislation go by without cost sharing when it was politically expedient to do so. Thus, in a 1985 supplemental appropriations bill, the administration allowed funding for forty-five new projects, even though twenty-one of them did not have previous authorization and lacked the cost-sharing provisions (the funding was tied to a Foreign aid bill that the administration wanted badly). In 1984, the administration let election-year politics dictate that a dam safety bill would be entirely federally funded in order not to jeopardize reelection prospects of western Republicans.

But the Reagan message on cost sharing has penetrated subgovernment consciousness. The major 1984 omnibus authorization bill failed to clear Congress because of internal disputes between fiscally conservative proponents of cost sharing who opposed traditional pork barrelists trying to circumvent cost sharing. The participants could not reach agreement on financing and the bill sank. A presidential veto had been promised if cost sharing were not included.

Even without a comprehensive authorization bill, both the corps and the Bureau of Reclamation have moved on their own to include cost sharing in new projects they recommend—localities that can produce nonfederal financing get preference. Gradually the new reality is being accepted by the subgovernment members. Cost sharing is viewed as inevitable by the states and localities and, increasingly, by members of Congress. The water development area is maturing—there will be fewer big projects and federal financing will fund a smaller share of them. Emphasis will continue to shift from new construction to maintaining existing projects. Western water interests, especially agribusiness, and the Bureau of Reclamation have gradually displaced the Corps of Engineers from water supremacy. The liquid pork barrel is not dead, but it leaks a lot and is harder to carry through the legislative process without spilling a drop. But a water subgovernment—with some different members and attitudes—will still be in a strong position to engineer a lucrative future. Billions of federal dollars will continue to be spent on water development.

Adaptation in Agricultural Subgovernments: the 1985 Farm Bill. In 1985 American agricultural policy stood at a crossroads. Existing legislation was expiring, and the renewal debate ground on all year over the direction farm policy should take. The Reagan administration and agribusiness organizations favored a sharp departure from the policies of the preceding fifty years. They wanted to turn to a free market economy for agriculture, take the federal government out of the business of subsidizing farmers, make American produce more competitive internationally, and help trim the burgeoning federal deficit.

Traditional farm groups and farm state legislators of both parties hesitated over making any change that would reduce farm income in a period when nearly a quarter million farmers were threatened with insolvency. Agricultural subgovernments were under heavy fire throughout the year. But the bill that emerged, the Food Security Act of 1985, while giving some concessions to both sides, demonstrated convincingly that the subgovernments were secure.

In this section we shall look at why agricultural decision making was disrupted and at how the subgovernments adapted to accommodate the disruptions.

A Changed Context. Since the implementation of the Agricultural Adjustment Act of 1933, the federal government has become an active partner in nearly all decisions made by farmers (when to plant, when to harvest, how much to plant, and what kind of crops to plant) through its extensive direct and indirect subsidies: price support loans (mandated loan rates for commodities grown by farmers who can use their crops as collateral and default if the market price is lower than the loan rate); acreage and production controls; mandated target price levels (these generate deficiency income support payments to farmers when market prices fall below target levels); and other mechanisms such as marketing orders, storage facilities, tax breaks, agricultural research and development, and low-interest loans. The normal cloak of anonymity that veiled decision making and implementation of farm policy was shredded in the 1980s as the external environment began to undergo uncontrollable changes. Some of the factors contributing to the new atmosphere for decision making included:

Escalating international competition (declining U.S. exports, overval-ued U.S. dollar, cheap imports).

Overproduction creating surpluses and lowering market prices.

Mounting farm debt (increasing numbers of farm foreclosures as farmers failed to meet loan payments and operating costs exceeded farm income).

Hemorrhaging federal expenditures on farm subsidies between 1981 and 1985 that exceeded estimates by more than $50 billion.

Increased pressures to trim the soaring federal budget deficit, and agriculture bore some of those pressures.

Making a Choice.   In 1981 the Reagan administration had tried and failed to reduce the power of agricultural lobbies by trimming price support loan rates and target price levels. Congress and affected interest groups rejected these attempts. In early 1985, the administration tried again, presenting a package of reforms that nearly every observer agreed was too drastic to stand a chance of adoption. The Reagan package would have quickly removed the crutch of federal subsidies from farmers and forced American agriculture to deal with market forces and international competition. The plan was so significant a change from the status quo that even administration loyalists considered it dead on departure from the White House. Its fate was sealed by contention within the administration (the OMB director versus the secretary of agriculture) and by the lack of the president's personal involvement during the year.

Traditionalists, especially in the House, favored continuing existing programs of price supports and income supplements, with increased aid for fiscally ailing farms. Moderates, particularly in the Senate, looked for some way to bridge the distance between both views. The struggle was often portrayed in emotional terms as preserving rural culture ("saving the family farm") versus going to a free market economy where government would not interfere and only the largest operators could survive. The debate was muddied because participants perceived (although did not usually articulate) multiple goals for agricultural policy: for example, increasing sales overseas versus ensuring high prices to farmers versus providing low prices to consumers versus elimination of market fluctuations. The goals, and the means to achieve them, conflict with each other. Agriculture policy in the preceding fifty years had not attempted to clarify or prioritize goals, and thus farmers received federal payments to produce surplus crops that lowered market prices and depressed farm income.

So Many Cooks. The large number of participants in agricultural decision making was increased by the heightened interest from many lobbyists not previously active. Stokes (1985: 634) identified more than 200 agricultural lobbyists in Washington. Traditional broad-spectrum farm organizations, such as the American Farm Bureau Federation and the National Farmers Organization and groups representing specific commodities were joined by environmental groups concerned about soil erosion, consumer groups anxious about food prices, and representatives of agriculture-related businesses such as fertilizer, farm equipment, and supermarkets. Unanimity of opinion about the direction of farm policy was notably absent among these diverse groups. In the absence of consensus, the influence of the commodity groups was greatest. Their aims were narrow and focused, and they worked with each other through informal solidarity. The chief lobbyist for the American Soybean Association obviously wasn't worried about the outcome of the 1985 agriculture bill near the end of the legislative process when he commented: "They [Members of Congress] pretty much do what each commodity wants" (Rauch, 1985: 2535).

The Outcome. The final bill, hammered out in the closing days of the congressional session in 1985, was a compromise between the House and Senate bills developed by the respective agriculture committees, which were working with a rigid budget ceiling set in the congressional budget process. Floor debate was lengthy and controversial. Both bills were anchored in the status quo policies, the House version more so than the Senate. Neither bill came very close to the administration's original proposal. The compromise exceeded the president's budget target by $2 billion, but he signed it anyway on Christmas Eve, perhaps a fitting date.

The major coup for the subgovernments was the retention of the existing structure of price supports and income payments to farmers. The victory for the president was that over the five-year life of the bill, the level of price support loans would be reduced (a modest savings of 10 percent), the level of export activity would be enhanced, and compulsory reduction in corn and wheat acreage and voluntary dairy herd buyout would help reduce overproduction. Both sides had a victory pennant to fly, and both claimed victory. The commodity subgovernments, which had the best reason to cheer, were diplomatically jubilant—they just sat and smiled quietly at the result of the legislative process they had helped to fashion. They gave up some things (hence the treatment of this story as "adaptation"), but they preserved a lot more.

Competing Subgovernments

Health Research and Cancer.   During the post–World War II period up until the late 1960s, the biomedical and health research community created an enviably strong and, from its point of view, productive subgovernment (Greenberg, 1967; Strickland, 1972). There were tensions in the development of the subgovernment, but for the last decade or more of its dominance (from roughly the mid-1950s to the late 1960s) it routinely could count on virtually all of the funds it could use profitably (usually more than the Bureau of the Budget and the president requested). There were dominant individuals in the subgovernment in particularly critical institutional positions: the director of the National Institutes of Health, Dr. James Shannon; the chairman of the Senate appropriations subcommittee responsible for funding in this broad area, Lister Hill; the chairman of the House appropriations subcommittee with parallel jurisdiction, John Fogarty; and a persistent and skillful lobbyist for more and more health-related biomedical research, Mary Lasker.

The subgovernment was formed in response to perceptions of the need to increase federal support for health and medical research as a means to improve the nation's health. The success of the subgovernment in creating a federal health-related, biomedical research system is clear in the existence of the extensive National Institutes of Health (NIH) structure with its separate research institutes, which "at its peak in 1967–68 [supported] more than 67,000 senior research investigators; it sustains academic science progams and research projects in more than 2,000 universities and medical schools, and helps provide advanced science training in basic science and various clinical specialties for more than 35,000 individuals" (Strickland, 1972: 236).

Support for the programs of this single subgovernment began to lag in the late 1960s in large part because of the economic demands of the Vietnam War during the Johnson and Nixon presidencies and also because of greater fiscal conservatism during the Nixon and Ford administrations. As one way of resuscitating the flagging fortunes of biomedical research, a new coalition assembled in the early 1970s, stressing the single goal of conquering cancer. Although the new cancer subgovernment drew some of its key members from the broader and older subgovernment, it also challenged the hegemony of that subgovernment and competed for the same resources. Not surprisingly, real issues developed between the two competitors. Specifically, the cancer group sought autonomy from other layers of the bureaucracy and wanted direct access to the president, in addition to a concentration of funds, to spur its research effort. Also, there were warnings from scientists within the older subgovernment that a special emphasis on one disease would lead to diminished attention to other health-research programs.

The cancer group's positions were adopted in the Senate, but supporters for the broader biomedical research position prevailed in the House. When the 1971 Cancer Act emerged in final form, both subgovernments got part of what they wanted, and of necessity they had to maintain an uneasy alliance. The government-sponsored drive against a single disease, cancer (a particular pet of President Nixon's), was officially endorsed with special organizational and budgetary recognition, but the National Cancer Institute was to remain within the structure of the NIH.

In the years following the 1971 act, the broader biomedical subgovernment has seen its fears realized as budgets for the cancer program have grown while resources for other NIH research programs have remained stable or shrunk. In an effort to correct the imbalance, the biomedical subgovernment pushed successfully in 1974 for inclusion in the bill renewing the Cancer Act of a provision creating a special presidential panel to monitor and advise on all federal health-research programs. Top-level officials in Health, Education, and Welfare (HEW) opposed the panel (the president had not requested it), but otherwise the administration supported the bill, which authorized $2.8 billion for cancer programs over three years. The inclusion of the clause creating the special monitoring panel met no resistance in either the House or the Senate, where the bill was passed nearly unanimously. Only one member of the House committee (but not the subcommittee) with jurisdiction over the bill opposed the bill, objecting to special legislation for separate diseases. Thus the Cancer Act was renewed for three more years, and the subgovernments were again required to resume their competing stances.

Action in late 1978 by Congress suggested the continued existence of a competitive situation. Congress passed a single bill reauthorizing the programs of both the National Cancer Institute and the National Heart, Lung and Blood Institute (the two largest institutes) for two years. The reauthorization was for a total of about $4.2 billion, about half of which went to cancer, about $1.1 billion to heart, lung, and blood control and research, and the rest to a variety of other purposes. Congress also instructed the Cancer Institute to expand its research beyond looking for single "causes" of cancer (a glamorous possibility, but one that has produced limited results) to a preventive focus based on controllable factors: personal habits such as smoking, occupational exposure to cancer-causing agents such as asbestos, and environmental exposure to cancer-causing agents such as certain air or water pollutants.

When the budgets for all of the National Institutes of Health are examined, the picture of competition also emerges. The Cancer Institute part of the total National Institutes of Health budget was 32 percent in 1977 and shrank gradually to 30 percent in the next two years. By 1985 it was about one-quarter of the total NIH budget. It had grown more slowly than the other institutes. But, on the other hand, its budget still remained much larger than that of any of the other eleven institutes.

Patents versus Antitrust.   An almost invisible and highly technical continuing conflict exists between a distributive subgovernment centered around the Patent and Trademark Office and a subgovernment centered around the Antitrust Division in the Department of Justice that is essentially regulatory (although it has distributive elements, too). Although resolution of the conflict between the two subgovernments has been sought over the past twenty years, no settlement has emerged. The competition between the two subgovernments has produced a policy stalemate that results in patent policy that favors monopoly but also has low credibility when challenged in the courts. The detailed technical disputes over the nature of patent policy do not concern us here, but the shape and membership of the competing subgovernments illustrate how two such entities can coexist over a long period of time within the same governmental institutions and produce the erratic and bifurcated policy that characterizes the combination of patent and antitrust policy most of the time.

The patent subgovernment is made up of key individuals from the Patent and Trademark Office, the patent bar (lawyers seeking patents for clients or challenging other patents), corporations seeking and receiving patents, and the Senate Judiciary Committee's Subcommittee on Patents, Trademarks, and Copyrights (Cohen, 1974). The mission of the Patent and Trademark Office is to promote business growth by granting limited monopolies through patents. It is located in the Commerce Department, which is generally expected to be the administration's supporter of business regardless of which party controls the White House. The lawyers of the patent bar and their clients have an obvious interest in having the Patent and Trademark Office proceed quietly and privately to grant as many patents as possible (although there are, of course, conflicts between companies over specific patents).

The antitrust subgovernment that relates to patent policy is composed of key individuals from the Antitrust Division and members of the Senate Judiciary Committee's Subcommittee on Antitrust. This subgovernment seeks to reform and open up the patent-granting subgovernment, and it points to the Patent and Trademark Office's poor record in the courts—when its decisions are challenged, they are often overturned by the judges.

Relationships between the two subgovernments are anything but cordial. The Commissioner of Patents from 1971 to 1973 stated a common view among members of the patent subgovernment when he labeled the Antitrust Division as "the enemy" and spoke of mutual hostility between the Patent and Trademark Office and the Antitrust Division. In Congress the chief counsel to the Senate patent subcommittee represented the view of the congressional members of the subgovernment when he criticized a reform proposal made by the Antitrust Division because it had been drafted by people "who have no patent experience" and because "the recommendations of the Commerce Department were not generally accepted" (Cohen, 1974: 480). The chairman of the Senate patent subcommittee opposed a bill introduced by the chairman of the Senate antitrust subcommittee that would have made the Patent and Trademark Office independent and presumably more visible and more subject to scrutiny by its congressional critics. The patent chairman favored the existing organizational arrangement, which kept the Patent and Trademark Office tied to his subcommittee. The Patent and Trademark Office and the administration also favored retention of the existing institutional arrangements.

Despite a presidential commission in 1966 and major legislative activity (but no law) in 1974, the conflict between the patent and antitrust subgovernments continues. Unless major change can be imposed, the patent subgovernment will continue to prevail until it gets to the courts—then, in effect, a number of judges become operative members of the antitrust government. So stalemate continues. Both subgovernments partially check the wishes of the other, but consistent policy that will stand up under judicial review is lost in the process.

Employment and Training Policy: CETA versus JTPA.   The composition of the employment and training subgovernment has fluctuated since the entry of the federal government into employment and training policy in the early 1960s. (Employment and training policy combines aspects of both distributive and redistributive policy, but in this discussion we focus on the former.) But the changes in the subgovernment from 1960 to 1982 had been primarily in the direction of expanding participation by enlarging the number of programs authorized (Baumer and Van Horn, 1984; Franklin and Ripley, 1984). The transition from the categorical programs of the 1960s to a decentralized form of special manpower revenue sharing known as CETA (the Comprehensive Employment and Training Act) in 1973 shook the subgovernment but did not end it. Instead, the transition was the occasion for a major enlargement when the representatives of the local governments responsible for administration of the CETA program were added. This expansion did not reduce the influence of other key members of the subgovernment. And between 1973 and 1982, other groups were accommodated into the subgovernment. Members coexisted more or less harmoniously as long as the major operating principle—that CETA could provide something for everyone—was not challenged.

This principle and the subgovernment itself were challenged, disrupted, and dethroned in 1982 when CETA reauthorization was debated. The old employment and training subgovernment was upset for a number of reasons: (1) the intrusion of nonmembers into the subgovernment's proceedings (these included the president and the secretary and assistant secretary for labor); (2) the very high visibility of CETA's reauthorization (CETA has become a very public program with a significant name recognition and a negative reputation); (3) the redefinition of administrative responsibility proposed by the Reagan administration (an increased role for state governments and the private sector and a greatly decreased role for the federal government and municipalities); (4) the inability of members of the old subgovernment to coalesce and agree on how to fight off external challenges; and (5) a strongly organized opposition to the traditional allocation of CETA benefits.

The states and the private sector wanted a greater share of the action, and with the conservative Reagan administration and the newly Republican and conservative Senate, there was a supportive ideological context in which they could advance their interests. The traditional subgovernment centered on the House Subcommittee on Education and Labor and included representatives of community-based organizations, service deliverers, participants, local governments, and liberal Democrats. This group was in disarray during the 1982 reauthorization and was unable to make more than incremental compromises with the new group, which centered on the Senate Committee for Labor and Human Resources and included newly influential representatives of state governments and private-sector groups. The decisions of the conference committee on the Jobs Training Partnership Act (JTPA) favored the new coalition.

Subgovernment Disintegration

Occasionally a subgovernment will lose such a major battle that it will disintegrate or change character drastically. For example, if the cancer lobby had succeeded in creating a new subgovernment completely at the expense of the broader biomedical research subgovernment, that might well have been the beginning of the breakup of the broad group into a series of specialized, ailment-specific subgovernments. Biomedical research might have, under such conditions, come to resemble the merchant shipping situation described above.

Another way for a subgovernment to disintegrate is for the issue to be redefined out of the distributive arena into either the regulatory or redistributive arena. This is rare because the natural tendencies for redefinition run in the other direction, but it can happen. The tobacco subgovernment lost some hegemony over antismoking activity by the government because the issue was no longer solely one of subsidy but had become one of regulation for public health. Likewise, the rise of ecological concerns in the regulatory arena caused even such a venerable subgovernment as that focused around the programs of the Army Corps of Engineers to lose an occasional decision.

Sugar.   A case of temporary collapse followed by what appears to be fairly rapid rehabilitation occurred in one of the most venerable of sub-governments—in fact, the example that Cater (1964) used when he coined the term *subgovernments.* In 1974 the world of the sugar subgovernment was turned upside down when the House of Representatives defeated an extension of the Sugar Act by a vote of 209 to 175: the basic structure of a series of subsidies to sugar growers and processors that had been in place since 1934 dissolved.

There were several reasons for the defeat of the Sugar Act in 1974, but the basic reason was the soaring retail price of sugar in a time of high national inflation made sugar subsidies visible to consumer groups. The visibility was heightened because the timing of the price increases coincided with the renewal of the act in Congress. Pressure from consumer groups redefined the traditional subsidy issue into one of regulation to protect consumers. The high prices also provoked the opposition of industrial users of sugar (manufacturers of candy, soft drinks, and other refined foods) who believed the price increases reflected profit motive more than market necessities. An additional element helping to defeat the bill was the inclusion in the House of some prolabor amendments that diluted the distributive character of the act by introducing redistributive tones that were jarring to the normal supportive coalition.

The act had many features, central of which was the detailed division of the U.S. sugar market between domestic and foreign producers. Producers were given a guaranteed market and, in effect, guaranteed profits. An excise tax on the production went to support the income of the growers in the United States. Thus, U.S. growers and processors alike worked in a completely managed economy—with set quotas for growers on the amount that could be grown and marketed to processors and with quotas for processors on the amount that could be produced and sold to both industrial and, ultimately, individual users. The payoff was a price usually higher than the world market (despite the availability of less expensive foreign sugar) and profits for growers and producers that were stable, high, and virtually guaranteed for domestic interests and foreign processors who lobbied frantically for increased shares of the foreign allotment.

The authorization hearings to extend the Sugar Act beyond 1974 began normally. The House Agriculture Committee—a key institution in the subgovernment—held hearings at which leading members of the committee, representatives from the industry, and officials from the Department of Agriculture praised the bill. The department did suggest some major modifications that would have moved the sugar price system toward a freer market, but the secretary assured the committee of his general support, and the department was probably not much surprised or dismayed when its modest initiatives were largely rejected by the committee.

When the bill came to the House floor in June, the subgovernment was presumably confident of victory. However, it had not counted on the impact that escalating sugar prices were having on groups such as the National Consumers Congress, the National Consumers League, Consumer Action for Improved Food and Drugs, and the Corporate Accountability Research Group, all of which lobbied against the bill and found members of the House willing to listen rather than routinely approve the work of the committee as they had been doing for almost forty years.

The world economy and, some would assert, the greed of U.S. processors had redefined the political context of sugar, and the subgovernment had not had the foresight to prepare for the redefinition.

The private-sector members of the former sugar subgovernment did not suffer economically in 1975 and 1976, although the record prices of late 1974 dropped modestly. However, as world production of sugar increased enormously, world prices began to fall substantially—for example, raw sugar had sold for 57.3 cents a pound in November 1974; in January 1977 it sold for 11.5 cents. Domestic producers of sugar began to lose business and profits because the big users of sugar in the country—soft-drink producers, candy makers, and bakeries—naturally bought cheap foreign sugar. Many of the subsidies, including the high tariffs and quotas for foreign imports, were no longer in place to protect those U.S. concerns with direct economic interests.

Under these conditions, the subgovernment began to revive and reassemble itself both in terms of identifying important members and agreeing on programmatic requests to the new Carter administration and to Congress. A complicated set of subsidies won the support of the president and almost came out of Congress in the closing days of the Ninety-Fifth Congress in 1978. However, the smoothness with which the pre-1974 subgovernment had worked had not been fully recaptured; the final conference-committee compromise still left enough interests dissatisfied that the compromise was killed on the House floor.

In 1979 the sugar lobby again did not get what it wanted. It helped write the bill in the House committee but then lost on the floor in October 1979 on a lopsided vote of 249 to 158. The consumer lobbies remained vigilant and persuasive with some members of the House in opposing the producer lobby. Sugar interests from Hawaii also joined opposition to the bill because of limits on payments to individual producers unfavorable to the very large producers in that state. Turnover in congressional members had also removed some reliable sugar allies. The industry also found it difficult to get together as more and more differences in regional interests (not just limited to Hawaii) emerged.

In 1981, with President Reagan agreeing to support sugar price supports as part of an omnibus farm bill in connection with his bargaining for potential votes for his tax and budget packages, the lobby first suffered a narrow defeat on the House floor. But the Senate had inserted a new sugar price-support program. The conference committee, making the numerous compromises required to get a final bill before the two chambers, accepted a new price-support program. House conferees kept the pressure on the Senate conferees to make the sugar program less lucrative. But, ultimately, sugar producers again were in a position to get a good part of what they wanted. The sugar subsidy remained constant and protected for five years in the 1985 omnibus farm bill. The support price was more than four times the world market price. Life for the sugar subgovernment was, however, not as sweet as during the four decades before 1974.

CONCLUSIONS

The material presented in this chapter supports two general conclusions: first, the general picture of the distributive arena drawn at the outset of this chapter is largely accurate; and second, subgovernments are not static (as the literature would seem to suggest) but change and adapt to changing conditions in a number of ways. Subgovernments are important in relation to distributive policy, but they are a more complex phenomenon than some descriptions portray.

The cases of subgovernment dominance lend support to the overview of the distributive arena summarized in the first six columns of Table 4–1. In these cases virtually all aspects of the issues were decided within the confines of the subgovernment: rarely was there intervention by "outsiders." Normally the degree of cooperation was very high, but when there were conflicts they were resolved within the confines of the relationship on the basis of face-to-face negotiations, resulting in a rather straightforward compromise that left everyone reasonably happy.

In the last column of Table 4–1 it is asserted that, if conflict persists, the congressional position taken by the subcommittee is more likely to prevail than the bureaucratic position (or at least the compromise will be weighted in that direction). In the cases of conflict this generally seems to hold true. When Congress and the Corps of Engineers disagreed over the nature of the proper cost-benefit ratio for the corps to use, the congressional position prevailed. In 1974 when the Department of Agriculture attempted to modify the sugar bill in the direction of a freer market, its suggestions were rejected by the House committee, and the committee position went to the floor.

One exception to the generalization appears in the mechant shipping area. Here when Congress and the bureaucracy disagree, it appears that the usual resolution is a role larger than normal for industry spokespersons and their position. This seems to be an artifact of the superfragmented structure of the policy area.

Only rarely do outsiders have much impact on the business of a subgovernment, as in the cases of the victory for large commercial users of sugar in 1974 and the limited, but cumulatively important impact of Presidents Carter and Reagan on the water resources area.

The ways in which subgovernments can change are numerous. A "smart" subgovernment—one intent on preserving its dominance without serious diminution—will adjust to potentially threatening developments ahead of time, perhaps by finding a way of defusing them. Sometimes a challenge that is defeated will provide the cues for the subgovernment about marginal policy change it would be wise to make. Often a successful challenge will force marginal adjustments that still preserve the substance of policy and the reality of subgovernment dominance.

Continuing competition among several subgovernments can also stimulate one or more of them to make adjustments that will preserve their importance and dominant positions. The biomedical lobby has not given in to the challenge of the cancer lobby but has continued to generate support for broad health research.

Only rarely does a subgovernment fold altogether and, as the sugar case demonstrates, a defeated subgovernment may well possess some Lazarus-like qualities.

Subgovernments change, even in the distributive arena. They are, however, remarkably persistent and tenacious. Consequently, most distributive policy is usually under the control or strong influence of subgovernments.

5

Protective Regulatory Policy

THE NATURE OF PROTECTIVE REGULATORY POLICY

Regulation of private activities for the presumed protection of the general public or major parts of it has been undertaken by the federal government in a major way for a century. The general pattern has been for Congress to legislate broad policy goals and perhaps a few details and then establish a regulatory commission or other agency in the bureaucracy to develop and administer all or most of the details necessary for achieving the goals.

There is considerable variation in the types and operations of regulatory agencies. A few are concerned much of the time with competitive regulation. Thus the Federal Communications Commission (FCC) decides who gets what television channels and what radio frequencies. Before major deregulation action in the late 1970s the Interstate Commerce Commission (ICC) decided what trucking companies, barge lines, pipelines, and railroads got what routes for what goods. And the Civil Aeronautics Board (CAB) decided what airlines got what routes. But even these agencies have protective duties to perform: the FCC is supposed to make sure that broadcasters serve the public interest by not broadcasting offensive material (either program content or advertisements); the ICC has rules designed to protect the consumer who hires a moving company; and the CAB made rules designed to protect the lungs of nonsmokers from the pollution created by their fire-breathing brothers and sisters on airplanes.

Most regulatory agencies are concerned primarily with protective regulation. Public debate over deregulation often confuses the protective and competitive modes of regulation. Economic and political pros and cons in relation to both kinds of regulatory policy are often debated in a jumble, both by academics and by officials.[1] In this chapter we focus on the politics of the formulation and legitimation of protective regulatory policy.

Beginning in the late nineteenth century a number of agencies were created that were primarily concerned with regulation of the conditions under which different kinds of private activity could and could not take place. At least four major waves of such regulatory activity have been identified, and each wave has left us its residue of bureaucracies that have become permanent (Wilson, 1975).

The first wave occurred between 1887 and 1890 and produced the Interstate Commerce Act (aimed at regulating railroads) and the Sherman Antitrust Act (aimed at regulating trusts that had been created to achieve monopolies in the provision of various goods). The second wave came between 1906 and 1915 and produced the Pure Food and Drug Act, the Meat Inspection Act, the Federal Trade Commission Act (aimed at preventing unfair business practices such as deceptive advertising), and the Clayton Act (aimed at strengthening the antitrust law). The third wave came during the 1930s and produced the Food, Drug, and Cosmetic Act; the Public Utility Holding Company Act (aimed at preventing the concentration of economic power in the public utility field); the Securities Exchange Act (aimed at regulating the stock market); the Natural Gas Act; and the National Labor Relations Act (aimed primarily at preventing unfair labor practices by business). The fourth wave began in the late 1960s and was aimed at protecting consumers and the environment. It produced such legislation as the Water Quality Act, the Clean Air Act, the Truth in Lending Act, the National Traffic and Motor Vehicle Safety Act, amendments to the drug control laws, and the Motor Vehicle Pollution Control Act.

By the late 1970s the regulatory impetus had waned. The Reagan administration opened its period in power by calling for wide-ranging "deregulation" in a variety of protective regulatory areas. They garnered both support and opposition. The tensions that led to the shake-up in the Environmental Protection Agency in the spring of 1983 symbolized the debate over the meaning of enforcement of protective regulatory

---

[1]Recall that protective regulatory policy is quite different from competitive regulatory policy, as we explained in Chapter 1. Competitive regulatory policy is found almost exclusively at the implementation stage of policy making; it is rarely formulated at the general level, from scratch, but instead involves application of regulations by the agency to individual participants on a case-by-case basis. The main actors in its implementation are generally members of the agency, representatives of the regulated interests, and individual members of Congress (but not the institution of Congress—the subcommittees, committees, or either house). Protective regulatory policy, on the other hand, is frequently the object of formulation and legitimation, with the actors including representatives from the agency and the regulated interests as well as institutional parts of Congress.

legislation that their beliefs and attitudes engendered. By early 1986, however, Congress had passed no deregulating statutes in the protective area and seemed unlikely to do so. Businesses themselves were, in some instances, much happier contemplating regulation from a single federal agency than from fifty different state agencies. The Reagan administration, in effect, shifted its attack on protective regulation strictness to the realm of implementation, where the administration had the latitude to pursue much less vigorous enforcement than in previous years.

Throughout the nineteenth century Congress oversaw the activities of regulatory agencies with considerable care, and thus the agencies did not develop a great deal of independent political weight. However, as agencies increased in size and number, they began to develop independent political power. At the same time, Congress began to delegate more power to them and to pay less attention to the exercise of that power. Thus, the foundations were laid for what has been called "the bureaucratic state" (Wilson, 1975). When government vastly increased its scope of activity in the 1930s, Congress increased the amount of latitude it gave regulatory bureaucracy through rather vague delegations of power, increasing the basis for almost independent bureaucratic influence (Lowi, 1979).

Decisions about protective regulatory policy are characterized by considerable visibility. As policies are debated, those entities targeted for regulation are very conscious of what they think is at stake. In general, most of those vulnerable to regulation—mining companies, petroleum producers, and pharmaceutical companies, for example—would prefer to avoid government regulation. But where regulation seems inevitable, they pursue options designed to make the regulation as light as possible or to acquire governmentally conferred benefits simultaneously as a form of compensation for being regulated. When new areas of regulatory activity or major changes in existing activity are under debate, however, quiet functioning of subgovernments is not possible. In fact, given shifting interests, subgovernments may not even be a feature of the policy landscape in a given area. When implementation of existing regulation occurs, subgovernments may be more likely to form and have an impact (Ripley and Franklin, 1986: chapter 6).

Coalitions of groups involved in regulatory decisions are unstable, depending on what is at stake. Groups contend for the favor of Congress, but usually at the level of the full House and Senate (and conference committees) rather than only at the subcommittee or committee level. Subcommittees and committees certainly get involved in decisions, but their preferences often get altered by other decision makers. Similarly, in the executive branch, when regulatory policy is implemented, there is more central direction of that implementation and far less autonomy for individual bureaus within a department or other large agency.

THE CONGRESSIONAL–BUREAUCRATIC RELATIONSHIP IN PROTECTIVE REGULATORY POLICY

We expect the relationship between bureaucrats (at the bureau level) and individuals in Congress (members and staff members in Senate and House subcommittees) to be only sporadically central in protective regulatory policy. Only some of the issues of regulation get full consideration within the confines of the relationship itself. Major decisions on new areas for regulation or on changes in existing regulations typically get made by the full Congress interacting with a high level of bureaucratic actor, such as individuals from the office of a departmental secretary or the White House. Only in the stable regulatory areas does the relationship become important in the sense of allowing the participants to make what amounts to final decisions. And even then the chances of review by higher authorities are greater than in the distributive area.

Conflict is much more frequent in this area than in distributive policy. When conflict occurs at the bureau-subcommittee level, it often arises because the congressional actors who are seeking exceptions to regulations for favored constituents or clients meet resistance from bureaucrats who oppose those exceptions. Less often, the congressional actors are pushing the bureaucrats for more rigorous enforcement of regulations. Conflict over regulatory policy also occurs at a higher level than the bureau-subcommittee relationship because participants who are dissatisfied with the decisions made at the subcommittee level can appeal those decisions to the full committee, the House or Senate floor, and the conference committee.

Disagreements between subcommittee members and bureaucrats may get resolved within the relationship, but usually the conflict gets transferred to a higher level, either because the participants appeal to the higher levels or because higher levels intervene on their own initiative.

If resolution of disagreement occurs within the subcommittee-bureau relationship, it is likely to be a compromise between initial specific positions. Some disagreements may also go unresolved for some time. Still others may be made part of a broader compromise (not necessarily at some midpoint) reached at a higher level of institutional actor.

In cases of disputes between the two branches, the congressional position probably prevails more often—especially when the full Congress gets involved.

The regulatory arena is not undifferentiated in terms of what is at stake and how the actors behave, however. There are at least two major kinds of situations in which behavior might be expected to vary. Both of these situations will be investigated by looking at several instances of regulatory action or proposed action in recent years.

The first kind of situation is one in which the focus of debate is over the creation of federal regulatory power that had not previously existed or had existed in only sporadic and scattered form.

The second kind of situation is one in which major alteration of existing federal regulatory power is the focus of debate. These alterations can be in the direction of either more federal power or less federal power.

The Creation of Regulatory Power

Strip Mining.   The strip mining process is an efficient (in a narrow economic sense) means of removing coal from the earth—layers of earth are scraped away to expose veins of coal that lie relatively close to the surface. However, the aftermath of this process can be aesthetically devastating and economically debilitating, because unless care is taken in the selection of the site and in the use of reclamation procedures the land can be permanently scarred, eroded, and made barren, and water can be severely polluted. Most states where strip mining occurs have enacted legislation to prevent this negative aftermath, but this legislation varies greatly in restrictiveness and enforcement.

The need for coal, both in the short run and in the long-range future, was dramatically underscored in 1973 by the Arab oil embargo and the energy crisis. Coal was thrust suddenly into the forefront as a desirable source of energy for the United States both because the deposits are extensive and because the technology of strip mining is present for extracting it. It was assumed that coal would play a major role in helping the United States meet its officially announced goal of energy self-sufficiency, a policy designed to make the country less dependent on foreign sources of fuel, especially oil.

Congress has been involved in the question of whether the federal government should regulate strip mining since 1968, when the Senate first held hearings on specific bills on the subject. In 1971 President Nixon proposed legislation, and in 1972 the House passed a bill but the Senate did not act. In 1973 the Senate passed a bill. In 1974 the House passed a bill and went to conference with the Senate on its 1973 bill. After a long conference that almost collapsed at several points, Congress passed a bill, only to have President Ford pocket veto it, thus preventing an attempt to override the veto. By mid-March 1975 both the Senate and House had again passed bills similar to the vetoed bill, and again the president vetoed the bill. The attempt to override was delayed because of weakening support in the House, and when the attempt was made in July 1975 it failed by three votes.

In late 1975 attempts were made in the House Interior Committee to revive the bill, but they failed, largely because the pro-bill forces calculated that President Ford could again prevent what they wanted by a veto they could not override. Similarly, in 1976 the House Rules Committee forestalled a veto by twice preventing strip mining bills from reaching the House floor. (Also in 1976 the Department of the Interior promulgated regulations that allowed increased strip mining of coal on federal land in the West.)

In 1977 the basic political situation for the proponents of federal strip mining legislation changed dramatically because of the election of Jimmy Carter, who pledged support for a bill in this area. By mid-1977 such a bill became law.

What follows tells two selected parts of the complicated story sketched above. The first part focuses on the debate and decision making in 1974. The second part concentrates on 1977.

1974.   The basic controversy in this area since at least 1971 had been whether there should be a federal law and, if so, how strong it should be. The administration bills introduced in both 1971 and 1973 were regarded as weak by the environmentalists and leading Democratic supporters of strong legislation. The coal producers and most of the electric companies that burn vast quantities of coal to generate electricity wanted no bill at all. Their basic contention was that the coal companies were public-spirited about reclamation and that state regulation was sufficient anyway.

The general position of the "anti" coalition (those opposed to any regulation or at least to a strong bill) was that the controls proposed in the legislation would reduce output of coal drastically and would also raise its price. Either result would damage the energy self-sufficiency program endorsed by the administration. The general position of the "pro" coalition (those favoring a strong bill) was that strip mining had to be stringently regulated in order to avoid the risk that the entire country would emerge looking like the worst parts of Appalachia after strip mining. They argued that federal regulation was necessary because the states couldn't or wouldn't act with sufficient force to curb the problem. They disputed the estimates of the opposing coalition that strip mining regulations would cut the output of coal production significantly. Only a few members of the "pro" coalition favored banning strip mining.

A brief chronology of the 1974 process will help set the background. The Senate had passed a bill in October 1973 by a vote of 82 to 8 (the Senate Interior and Insular Affairs Committee had reported the bill to the full Senate without any dissenting votes). Two subcommittees of the House Interior and Insular Affairs Committee—one on environment and one on mines and mining—considered the bill jointly. The full House Interior Committee reported the bill favorably on May 30, 1974, by a vote of 26 to 15. The House held an unusually long debate on the bill—six days—before passing it with some amendments on July 25 by a vote of 298 to 81. The conference committee met off and on for eighty-seven hours between

August 7 and December 3 before reaching an agreement. Both houses approved the conference report by voice vote very late in the session, but President Ford refused to sign it and the bill died as a result.

Several features of the 1974 process deserve special mention. First, detailed drafting of the legislation was accomplished in subcommittees, committees, and the conference committee. However, unlike distributive policy, final decisions were not made at the committee level. Whichever interests believed they had "lost" by the decisions made in the various committee stages—particularly in the House—still had a chance to appeal their case to the full House or full Senate by getting a friendly member to introduce an amendment to redress their losses. Thus, the same battles tended to be fought before the committee and on the floor because the losers could come forward a second time. The same situation was at least potentially present with respect to the conference committee. The "losers" in conference could always appeal their case again to the full House or full Senate. This route was not fully used because the compromise in conference had taken so long to work out that Congress was very near adjournment, and the majorities of both houses were in a mood to pass the bill quickly and await presidential action.

Organized groups for all of the affected interests—environmentalist groups; coal, steel, and electric companies; the U.S. Chamber of Commerce; and the United Mine Workers union—and a large number of executive officials from the White House, Council on Environmental Quality, Environmental Protection Agency, Department of Commerce, Department of the Interior, and Federal Energy Administration approached both the House subcommittees and committee and the conference committee. Some of the interests—both private and bureaucratic—made some gains at the committee level. As Congressman Morris Udall, chairman of the House Subcommittee on the Environment, said, in speaking of the administration representatives, "We have done all the compromising we are going to do. We accepted a dozen of their amendments in committee, and they just come back for more. The demands are insatiable" (*Washington Post*, July 10, 1974).

Second, the coalitions supporting and opposing regulation of strip mining by the federal government were broad-based but unstable. The legislation was complex and contained numerous features that were separable in an analytical sense. Both coalitions included members who were interested only in narrow features of the bill that affected them directly. On other specific issues, these members would be relatively inactive or would even desert the coalition. For example, the United Mine Workers' executive board narrowly endorsed the bill, but the board's real concern was with an amendment to tax strip-mined coal more heavily than deep-mined coal. Such an amendment would have encouraged exploitation of coal reserves in the East, most of which are too deep to be strip mined, where most UMW strength exists. A rival union represents the workers engaged in strip mining in the West. The amendment, offered on the House floor, was defeated.

Another example is provided by Pennsylvanians who supported the bill, but whose real concern was that an amendment be added to exempt Pennsylvania's anthracite coal from the provisions of the bill on the grounds that Pennsylvania was already regulating such mining with sufficient laws and vigor. This amendment passed the House and was included in the final bill.

Yet another example: Once the conference report passed both houses, some coal companies broke previously united ranks engineered by the National Coal Association and urged the president to sign the bill as a better alternative than a possibly more restrictive bill in 1975. The same position was taken by the chairman of the board of Bethlehem Steel, a major consumer of coal and owner of "captive" mines.

Third, the executive branch agencies were badly split in their views of the bill as it progressed through the congressional process, and they kept changing their public stances. The Council on Environmental Quality and the Environmental Protection Agency supported both the legislation in general and the details that emerged from the conference committee. The Federal Energy Office, the Commerce Department, and the White House (with support from the OMB and the Treasury Department) supported only relatively weak legislation at most. The Interior Department was caught between the conflicting views and adopted a shifting attitude.

The administration was so divided that key administrators felt safe in making their disagreements public. While the bill was still awaiting floor action in the House, for example, the administrator of the Environmental Protection Agency publicly supported the bill, thereby contradicting the official administration position at the time that the bill was unacceptable because of its alleged impact on coal production and energy self-sufficiency.

Later in the process, when the head of the Federal Energy Administration said he had recommended that the president veto the bill, two other officials—one from the Environmental Protection Agency and one from the Interior Department—said they had urged him to sign it.

The Interior Department constantly changed and modified its position throughout the process. It was thought through the spring of 1974 that the department supported a reasonably strong bill. But after the House committee had agreed on a bill, the secretary of the interior attacked it on the grounds of diminished coal production. During the summer of 1974 both the Energy Administration and the Interior Department revised downward their estimates of how much production would be lost, and by the time the bill finally passed, the Interior Department counseled the president to sign it.

The administration was so indecisive at the end of the process that a somewhat unusual—or perhaps *bizarre* would be a better word—attempt was made to effect a last-minute compromise that would avoid a veto. While the president was still deciding whether to sign or veto the bill, communications between the chairman of the Senate Interior Committee and the administration led the administration to think that somehow Congress could pass another strip mining bill in the few days left in its session. This bill could be signed along with the original bill. Presumably this additional bill would contain amendments that would make the two bills together palatable enough to gain Ford's signature. Congress, of course, can rarely act with such speed short of a genuine national emergency. And the spectacle of a president signing a bill and amendments to weaken it before it had been law for more than a day or two made such a happening unlikely. Nothing emerged, except that the president used the amendments he had requested in late 1974 as the basis for the administration bill sent to Congress in early 1975.

Fourth, the critical decisions on the substance of the legislation were made on the House floor and in conference committee in the form of acceptance or rejection of amendments. Naturally, the House subcommittees and full committee had set the agenda for House floor action—as is the case for virtually every piece of legislation in all policy areas—but a broad range of options was presented, debated, and decided on the House floor. Likewise, enough differences remained between the House version passed in July 1974 and the Senate version passed in October 1973 that a range of options also received consideration in the lengthy conference committee proceedings.

The quiet, stable politics of distribution were nowhere to be seen in the maneuvering and decision making that marked this proposal for a major new federal regulatory endeavor. Instability and public proceedings were much more characteristic than were the stability, predictability, and privacy that usually are the hallmarks of a distributive issue. Furthermore, resolution of the conflicts was transferred all the way to the highest level —the president—where the "compromise," determined by a presidential veto, was a decision to have no regulation at all. This pattern of visibility, conflict, and presidential resolution was repeated again in consideration of the 1975 strip mining bill.

1977.   In 1977 the proponents of strong federal legislation had to retreat a bit further than even the 1974 and 1975 bills to get a bill through Congress. Unlike the previous years, however, getting the president's approval was no problem.

The first compromise decision made by the proponents was to limit the bill almost exclusively to coal mining. Earlier bills had covered other kinds of mining, such as that for copper, but the possibility of a powerful negative coalition being formed by a number of the interests targeted for regulation led to the focus on coal alone.

As in 1974, issues were not settled quietly and finally in subcommittee and committee. Rather, decisions made in those settings were reexamined, debated, and extensively amended on the floors of both the House and the Senate. And some issues remained to be resolved in the conference committee.

In general terms, the House committee produced a moderately strong bill in late April. It passed the House a week later and was strengthened even more on the House floor. In the Senate a different outcome occurred: the committee reported a moderately strong bill in early May, but a few weeks later the bill was weakened considerably on the Senate floor by expanding the allowable mining in alluvial valley floors in the West, withdrawing the requirement that the owners of the surface approve the mining of federally owned coal under their land, exempting small miners from some of the environmental standards set in the bill, and watering down the provision that the original contours of the land had to be restored at the conclusion of mining.

The conference committee bill, reported in July, was, predictably, somewhere between the two versions presented to it. The principal concessions to the mining interests were in the areas of mining alluvial valley floors, a 24-month exemption from environmental standards for smaller operators, variances allowed in restoring original contours, and allowance of mountaintop removal as an acceptable mining method. Both houses passed the bill, and the president signed it in early August.

As in 1974, the final decisions were made on the floor and in conference, and the regulated interests prevailed on some issues. The supporters of federal regulation made an early decision to focus only on coal in order to keep an opposing coalition from forming (copper mine owners and companies could not be expected to weep and work for coal mine owners and companies unless they too were threatened).

The coal companies did not give up their fight with the passage of the act. In a sequel typical of protective regulatory policy, the regulated interests simply shifted their pressure from Congress to the bureaucracy responsible for implementing the legislation and to the courts. The implementation stage now became the battle zone (Ripley and Franklin, 1986: 156–63). The Carter administration tried to administer the law with some vigor. The Reagan administration weakened and slowed implementation. No new legislation was forthcoming either to encourage or impede enforcement of the 1977 act.

Overall Energy Policy after 1977.   Energy policy is enormously complex. Some involves distribution, some involves competitive regulation, and some certainly involves protective regulation. Later in this chapter we will analyze one specific issue more closely—the partial deregulation of natural gas prices in 1977–78—when we deal with the alteration of existing regulatory policy.

In this short section, however, we want to characterize the politics surrounding the development (or nondevelopment, depending on one's point of view) of the protective regulatory features of "comprehensive" energy policy in the United States in the years since 1977, when President Carter first made a major attempt to get such policy established legislatively.

The politics of decision making in this area exhibit the major features we would expect in the protective regulatory arena. The whole debate had great visibility. The central bureaucratic and executive actors (for example, the president and people in the Department of Energy at the highest levels) interacted with many pieces of Congress and, ultimately, the whole of Congress in floor deliberations in the two houses. The regulated interests—represented by a rich array of active interest groups—were much in evidence. Some specific outcomes were the results of bargaining among these principal actors. Some issues simply went unresolved and, as of the mid-1980s, the United States still has no comprehensive energy policy or even any policy covering more than a few discrete areas of concern.

In 1977 President Carter put together his proposals with help only from his closest advisers. But once he made his package public, a large number of other actors had access to the formulation process. Lobbyists were assiduous early in the process in identifying the key actors on whom they should bring pressure.

Oil company lobbyists were particularly skillful in getting protective regulatory decisions made and defined in such a way as to minimize control and maximize profits. For example, Carter was first going to propose that exemptions from price control would be granted only for new wells drilled at least five miles from an old well. This would prevent new wells from tapping into the same oil pool as an old well, just to get the oil exempted from price control. Over the last weekend before the proposals were made public, the distance was reduced to two and a half miles. The lobbyists had done their work well.

In all of the debate that ensued over a range of protective regulatory proposals, a variety of individuals and groups played important roles. These included top environmental and consumer groups; major oil companies; leading oil, gas, and coal associations; law firms representing the oil industry; individual lobbyists for oil and gas companies and associations; a half dozen or so individual senators and representatives in such critical spots as the chairs of the Senate Finance Committee, the House Ways and Means Committee, and the Senate and House interior committees; key figures in the administration in addition to the president (people such as the chairman of the Council of Economic Advisers, the energy adviser, the secretary of the Treasury, the head of the Office of Management and Budget, the secretary of the Interior, and the secretary of the Department of Energy after the creation of that department); and representatives of the thirteen nations that made up membership of the Organization of Petroleum Exporting Countries (OPEC).

The Speaker of the House of Representatives in 1977 put together an unusual *ad hoc* committee to overcome the normal fragmentation of the House in dealing with energy matters. This was a procedural innovation and, in many ways, a procedural triumph. But even that coup did not result in anything approaching a comprehensive energy policy as envisioned by Carter or anybody else. The policy became disaggregated into many component parts. During the Carter years, some bills passed, some were defeated. No complete policy resulted, in part because so many actors had access to a wide-open process and apparatus in which the issues were highly conflictual. In addition, policy making was made much more difficult by quickly and constantly changing external events (such as the "oil shock" of 1979—another enormous price rise with far-reaching international consequences). The situation of many actors and quickly changing external events, coupled with Carter's personal style that seemed to inspire little confidence in anyone, meant the president ultimately became just one more actor in the process. Yet if major new protective regulatory efforts were to succeed in being established legislatively, the president had to have a widely recognized central role.

As a symbol of how reckless Carter had become in playing a leading role in the energy field, it is important to note that one of his worst congressional defeats came in 1980 and involved energy. Carter vetoed a bill that killed an import fee he had put on foreign oil to promote conservation. For the first time since 1952, a Democratic Congress overrode the veto of a Democratic president.

President Reagan came to office convinced the "market" should be unfettered and would provide the best solution to various energy problems. He proposed no new protective regulatory measures and sought to have some dismantled. His major proposal in the energy area was to deregulate natural gas completely and quickly. He also announced he wanted to scrap the new Energy Department. He did not achieve these goals, but no new protective regulatory efforts made much headway during the Reagan years, in large part because President Reagan did not want any.

The Alteration of Existing Regulatory Power

Deregulation of Natural Gas Prices, 1977–1978. In April 1977 President Carter declared the struggle with energy problems facing the United States to be "the moral equivalent of war," and he sent an extensive set of proposals to Congress dealing with many facets of the problems. Congress—after eighteen months of intense political debate—responded to the president's overall energy program by producing a bill that made numerous major changes in what had been requested. Despite the changes, the president signed the bill into law in 1978.

One area of change involved pricing for natural gas, an important source of energy. The president had proposed to continue the price controls on natural gas but to provide a higher ceiling on those controls. The law Congress passed had only the vaguest resemblance to the president's proposal in this area. Congress scheduled a phaseout of those controls by 1985 and set interim prices higher than the ceiling requested by the president. Natural gas producers did not get everything they wanted, but they had reason to feel satisfied with that section of the energy package. In addition, large industry users of natural gas had reason to feel content with this alteration of protective regulatory power. The president had wanted the bill to favor homeowners and businesses at the expense of large industry in terms of dividing the shrinking reserves of natural gas in the United States. The final bill was much more generous to industrial users and much stingier with residential and commercial users. (For details on the process and outcome involving natural gas pricing, see Corrigan, 1977a, 1977b, 1978; Corrigan and Kirschten, 1978; Greider, 1978; Pelham, 1978a, 1978b; and Rankin, 1977. For analysis of a complicated forty-year history, see Sanders, 1981. See also Nivola, 1980.)

Table 5-1 summarizes the chronological development of the natural gas section of the energy bill in 1977–78. The story is much too long and complicated to be told in detail here, but a few parts of the story illustrate an alteration of protective regulatory policy that, in this case, resulted in less regulation rather than in more regulation.

After the president's proposals were made to Congress in April 1977, the Speaker of the House moved quickly to take charge of the procedure for considering them—giving him and other staunch supporters of the president the whip hand in generating the substantive results. After different parts of the total program, including natural gas pricing, had gone to five committees, those committees were given a mid-July deadline for reporting. Then the five separate reports would be coordinated by a House Ad Hoc Select Committee on Energy, an invention of the speaker's to allow him to keep track of decisions and to make sure the final product came as close to what the president wanted as possible.

In the natural gas area, Carter asked that "old" gas (that coming from wells already in production) be priced according to existing regulations, that "new" gas (that from new wells) be sold at controlled prices—higher than existing prices but not dramatically so. The "old" gas (cheaper) would be allocated to residential and commercial users. The "new" gas (more expensive) would be allocated to industrial users. Regulation of prices would continue for the indefinite future.

The president's request got rough treatment in the subcommittee of the House Interstate and Foreign Commerce Committee to which it had been referred. This subcommittee voted narrowly to deregulate all natural-gas

TABLE 5-1
Natural Gas Pricing, 1977-1978

1977

April 20—President Carter appears before joint session of Congress to outline energy proposals, including continued price regulation for natural gas.

April 29—president sends draft legislation to Congress.

June 20—at conclusion of hearings and reports by five different House committees, the House Ad Hoc Select Committee on Energy reassembles the total package.

August 3—House rejects natural gas price deregulation on floor.

August 5—House passes entire bill, including continued regulation of natural gas prices.

October 4—full Senate adopts a gas-deregulation plan after stopping a filibuster against it.

December 22—conferees dealing with natural gas pricing give up for the year because they cannot reach agreement.

1978

March 22—conferees on natural gas pricing hold their first formal session of the year after working in private during the preceding weeks.

April 21—Senate and House conferees announce an agreement in principle on natural gas pricing.

May 24—both sets of conferees vote narrowly to approve the deregulation plan—still "in principle."

August 18—a bare majority of both sets of conferees (13 of 25 from the House and 9 of 17 from the Senate) sign conference report on natural gas pricing.

September 27—the Senate narrowly approves the conference report on natural gas.

October 13—the House agrees by one vote to consider all conference reports on energy (including natural gas) in a single yes or no vote.

October 15—the entire energy package, including natural gas price deregulation, is passed by the House.

November 9—president signs bill into law.

Source: Adapted from *National Journal*, November 4, 1978: 1762.

prices. However, the full Commerce Committee narrowly reversed this decision and stayed with the president's proposal. The ad hoc energy committee made one concession to the producer interests by expanding the definition of "new" gas to allow more to be priced at the higher level. That compromise was concession enough to help get the House to defeat a proposal for complete deregulation on the floor by a vote of 199 to 227.

The outcome in the Senate in 1977 was quite different. Here there was no forceful central leadership allied with the president. Instead, all of the energy issues were, in effect, up for grabs with the strongest temporary coalitions (which were constantly shifting as the issues changed) winning. A House staff member, commenting on the seemingly chaotic and random Senate performance, said, "I'll never try to interpret what the Senate is doing. For my own mental health, I'll never try to do that" (Corrigan, 1977a: 1489).

The natural gas issue was involved in the Senate chaos. The Committee on Energy and Natural Resources could not reach a decision. A vote deregulating all natural gas pricing in five years resulted in a tie that could not be broken. Thus, the question was passed on to the Senate floor unresolved. There, after a filibuster and other delaying tactics by the opponents of deregulation (who were supporting the president's original position, although the administration had abandoned that position at this critical point in the debate), a compromise form of deregulation passed fifty to forty-six.

The rest of 1977 and much of 1978 were taken up by the efforts of conferees from the House and Senate to reach agreements on a range of issues involved in the energy package. Lobbying was intense on these issues, including, of course, many aspects of natural gas pricing—whether to regulate prices or not, the maximum rates allowable, the differences between old and new gas, the treatment of gas sold in the same state in which it was produced, and the allocation of differently priced gas to different kinds of users. No stable coalitions on this complex welter of specifics emerged; rather, each lobbyist for each organization or company had his or her own self-interest to serve and defined it slightly differently than anyone else's.

By mid-1978 the administration, in the interests of getting an energy package before Congress adjourned in October, indicated its willingness to go along with phased priorities for minimizing costs to consumers by promoting lower prices for industrial users and passing the higher prices along to individual residential users and commercial establishments such as stores. The opponents of deregulation in the Senate again fought these moves but were finally defeated, after considerable delay, in late September by a vote of fifty-two to forty-seven. White House representatives in effect pressured lobbyists from a variety of other organizations to join them in their position that the deregulation of natural gas was an acceptable and necessary price to pay compared to the alternative of sacrificing the entire energy package. Thus, a temporary and fleeting coalition of unlikely elements was put together, at least on paper, and confronted the senators. The outcome in the Senate was widely hailed as a presidential victory, although it is not overly cynical to point out that the president's people wound up working hardest for provisions that seventeen months earlier they had flatly opposed. The symbol of victory had become more important than the content of the legislation.

When the House considered natural gas pricing for the last time, in October 1978, it agreed by only one vote to keep natural gas pricing as part of the entire energy package (rather than being broken out for separate consideration). The Rules Committee had at first, on a tie vote, been unable to keep the package together. But White House pressure apparently got a changed vote from one Democrat on the committee retiring from

Congress at the end of the session (literally in a few days), and the Rules Committee endorsed keeping the whole package together. The package, despite gas provisions unsatisfactory to many and quite different from what the House had passed in 1977, passed with relative ease, 231 to 168.

The final agreement that emerged from all of the foregoing activity (and our discussion covers only a few of the details) allowed the price of new gas to rise about 10 percent a year until 1985, when all price controls were scheduled to end. The allocations would make industrial users pay higher costs in earlier years, but the burden would gradually be shifted to residential and commercial consumers. The pressures coming from numerous (although not tightly coalesced) lobbyists and the gradual adoption by the White House of a "we must have a bill at any cost and no matter the content" philosophy helped produce this result.

A postscript to the 1977–78 story is worth adding. By the winter of 1982–83, natural gas was still very much on the public agenda, for two principal reasons. First, President Reagan called for complete and quite rapid decontrol of the prices of all natural gas as a replacement for the gradual decontrol and the elaborate system of twenty-three different price categories that had been created by the 1978 act. Second, because gas companies had entered into long-term, fixed-price contracts with gas suppliers (especially pipeline companies) when gas was in short supply, they were often stuck with higher-than-market prices for gas. These costs were passed on to consumers. The result was extraordinary increases in the price of natural gas to consumers in the winters of 1981–82 and 1982–83, with no particular predictable end to such increases in sight. Some industries could afford to convert to cheaper forms of fuel to avoid the drastically inflated prices. Homeowners, almost without exception, could not afford such conversion and were stuck with the bills. The demands of consumers and groups representing them put pressure on Congress to offer some relief, although no one had a formula that could attract the political support requisite for legislative success.

Legislative Limits on a Protective Regulatory Agency: The Case of the Federal Trade Commission. Congress created the Federal Trade Commission in 1914 and gave it a number of powers to prohibit unfair business practices and, in effect, to protect consumers. A complicated series of legislative amendments, regulations, and court decisions over the years expanded the power. However, in recent times the FTC has come under particularly careful scrutiny by business and has been subject to many business claims that it proceeds unfairly or without just cause. The period since 1977 provides a good case of a protective regulatory agency under attack. In this case the attack led to some congressional narrowing of the powers of the FTC. The whole of Congress got involved, as we would expect in a protective regulatory matter. Likewise, a great number of interest groups—both from different business areas and from the consumer view-point—got involved. Strong presidential involvement was missing, which helps explain why some limits could come through the legislative process. However, the limits were incremental and not fatal to the basic mission of the agency. Incrementalism and nonresolution of basic issues character-ized the outcomes in this period. Such outcomes are common in the highly charged atmosphere surrounding protective regulatory issues.

In the period leading up to 1977, the FTC kept a relatively low profile in choosing the cases it decided to prosecute. Thus, it did not anger a wide range of businesses (and their congressional supporters) at any one time (Katzmann, 1980). But in 1977 a new and aggressive FTC chairman was named. The agency initiated a series of actions that were widely interpreted to be proconsumer and antibusiness. The businesses affected complained vociferously. They and their representatives descended on Congress in droves and demanded restrictions.

A sizable portion of Congress responded to these complaints and be-gan to question the FTC's utility and performance and even its legitimacy. For four years, from 1977 through 1980, Congress did not renew the FTC's basic authorizing statute. The agency could not get regular funding through the appropriations process and ran on money provided through continuing resolutions. Symbolically, Congress forced the agency to close its doors for three days during the spring of 1980. When Congress finally did pass new authorizing legislation in the spring of 1980, it contained a major new instance of the legislative veto. Congress gave to itself a new formal role in overseeing the agency. It enacted a number of limits, the most important of which was the power to veto any FTC rules that dis-pleased it. Such a veto would come about if both the House and Senate passed a resolution of disapproval. The president played no role in this process and did not have to sign the disapproval resolution for it to have the force of law. Only some involvement by President Carter in 1980 kept the anti-FTC forces from enacting even stiffer restrictions. The howling of the business oxen who perceived that they were being gored beginning in 1977 produced a modification in the power of the FTC to act. And Con-gress put the agency on notice that it would be overseeing (and second-guessing) its work with close attention.

In 1981–83 congressional concern about the FTC continued. In 1982 Congress made its first use of the new legislative veto provisions it had en-acted in 1980. By lopsided votes the two houses disapproved an FTC rule—which had been ten years in the making—requiring used-car dealers to dis-close defects in the vehicles they sold. The used-car lobby prevailed. The president remained silent on the matter, although it was hardly secret that President Reagan's ideology would lead him to side with the car dealers.

In late 1982 Congress was struggling to provide the FTC with another new authorization bill. But a major fight broke out over the attempt of the

American Medical Association and some other professional associations to get a provision in the law exempting doctors, lawyers, and other professionals from FTC jurisdiction covering anticompetitive business practices. The House passed a bill with such an exemption favored by the professionals' lobbyists in December 1982. The Senate, however, did not act on an authorization bill. The compromise that saved this power for the FTC for at least a short-range future came by finessing the need for a final decision on the exemption by dropping the authorization bill, forgoing, therefore, regular appropriations for the agency, and once again reverting to a continuing resolution for providing funds to allow continued operations by the agency.

In 1983, both the House and Senate passed authorization bills for the agency, but failed to reach a final compromise.

Agitation surrounding the FTC subsided by 1984 and 1985, primarily because the external context was shifting. Business oxen were howling much less to Congress because the FTC was doing less goring. Reagan appointees dominated four to one; the new chairman, James Miller, was sympathetic to business interests, believing deregulation and the free market were a consumer's best safeguards (and a businessperson's best friends). As the FTC reined in its rule making, there was less reason for Congress to enact restrictions over the agency. Congress will remain vigilant, however, and an activist FTC can expect trouble from that quarter. Neither house acted on an authorization in 1984, although in passing the fiscal year 1985 appropriations, both houses agreed to curb FTC power to investigate monopolistic activities of municipalities (this artful compromise did not remove the FTC authority to investigate in this area, but it prohibited its exercise until an authorization bill specifically approved it).

By late 1985 both houses of Congress had passed versions of a three-year reauthorization bill and were awaiting a conference. The versions were not greatly different. They set similar levels of funding and contained a legislative veto (requiring passage of a joint resolution to be signed by the president; the FTC rule would go into effect if Congress did not act within ninety days). Both bills avoided the regulation of professionals that had been so visible in 1982 (as an indication of changed attitudes, a Senate amendment to delete FTC authority to regulate in this area was defeated three to one).

The sense of urgency present in 1982–83 has clearly dissipated as the FTC changed its course, steering away from the consumer activism of the Carter years. The agency had not totally sold out to business. In 1984 a rule went into effect requiring the funeral industry to make full disclosure of rates, and the FTC also issued a rule governing used-car sales (less stringent than the one Congress objected to in 1982). Without question congressional attention and interest have flagged because the regulated groups have complained less.

CONCLUSIONS

We can now enrich the very broad picture of the protective regulatory arena presented in the opening pages of this chapter and summarized in Table 4-1. In general the patterns described are accurate, especially in cases involving the creation of new regulatory powers. But the distinction between the creation of regulatory power and alteration of existing power also allows us to make some amendments and refinements to the initial statements. It should also be noted that creation and alteration of regulatory power are also interrelated. For example, the creation of powers usually is followed by continuing dispute over proposed alterations of powers, both by those who think the initial powers too broad and sweeping and by those who think them too pallid in comparison with the problems they are supposed to address.

In the cases discussed in the foregoing pages, the lowest organizational units—subcommittees in Congress and bureaus in the executive branch—discussed the full range of issues both internally and with each other. However, when dealing with broad questions such as the creation or alteration of regulatory powers, virtually no final decisions were made at these lower levels. Inevitably the issues were escalated to higher organizational levels for continuing discussion and, in some cases, resolution. Only in a few instances were final decisions made at lower levels. It should also be noted that escalation of issues to higher levels does not automatically mean final decision will necessarily be reached. Many regulatory issues are debated over and over in much the same terms for many years.

Protective regulatory issues all contain the seeds of considerable conflict. The conflict does not merely stem from aggressive agencies being challenged by legislators representing regulated clients. In some cases the senators and representatives involved are more aggressive in asking for regulatory action than the agencies themselves. And often the higher reaches of the executive branch are the most reluctant to pursue aggressive policies. There are certainly members of the House and the Senate who fight regulation. But there are also likely to be individuals such as Udall taking the lead in such areas as strip mine regulation.

The potential for conflict of a multifaceted nature in most regulatory areas also means that often the coalitions supportive of and opposed to some specific power or its use are not unified or stable. Members of Congress, executive branch agencies, and interest groups all have been shown to have varying degrees of commitment to general questions, depending on what specific, more focused question is at stake. Thus, in a sense, regulatory issues are also separable, just as are distributive issues. But the nature of the issues themselves means that instability and volatility will result in the regulatory arena instead of the relative stability and quiet of the distributive arena.

Conflict resolution generally occurs above the level of the bureau-subcommittee interaction when it occurs at all. But often resolution does not occur, and the conflict continues. Many important regulatory issues seem to be almost permanently on the agenda of the federal government before solutions are reached. Even when legislative solutions are reached, the conflict may continue, and the legislation may be amended later.

One way in which regulatory issues become less volatile is for them to begin to be turned into distributive issues. Arguments have been made that, over a long period, regulatory agencies will become "captured" by the presumably regulated interests. When such capture occurs—and there is good evidence that capture is not universal or inevitable—regulatory issues are treated as distributive. A good deal of the presumed regulation will be left in the hands of the interests themselves: self-regulation with governmental blessing.

Over time, if Congress is persistent, it probably will possess the potential to be more important in making protective regulatory decisions than the executive branch. However, the element of persistence is critical—particularly for the friends of regulation. The foes of regulation have an advantage in that they are more likely to have more powerful private interests supporting their position. The private interests supporting regulation (except for competitors) are usually not numerous or at least not very politically sophisticated or powerful.

6

Redistributive Policy

THE NATURE OF REDISTRIBUTIVE POLICY

Redistributive policy is characterized chiefly, in terms of process, by the amount of time required to reach agreement on an issue and by the ideological nature of the debate. In terms of outcome, redistributive policy is best characterized in terms of who wins what at whose expense.

Many groups get involved in the debate over redistributive issues, often whether or not they have a direct stake in the outcome of the issue being debated. Although there may be many different arguments on a redistributive issue, they always reduce to two sides—a pro (liberal) and a con (conservative) position—no matter how many middle positions there may logically be and no matter whether any final outcome represents some sort of middle way. These issues tend to produce similar coalitions on a number of specific matters. "Liberal" and "conservative" may not be highly pleasing labels to political theorists, but to participants in the political process dealing with redistributive issues, they have meaning in the sense that the same two coalitions usually emerge for any measure in dispute, whether it be medicare or aid to the disadvantaged in a variety of forms or civil rights or even procedural issues that have important implications for the handling and resolution of redistributive issues in the future.

The executive branch—particularly at the presidential level—is an important actor in the redistributive arena. The president and his closest advisors and appointees negotiate with representatives of the "peak associations" that get involved in the debate.

Controversy characterizes redistributive policy because the policy attempts to reallocate items and symbols of value among different groups in society. The intended beneficiaries also help distinguish redistributive policy from other types of policy—in redistributive policy, less privileged groups are the intended principal beneficiaries, at the perceived expense of more privileged groups. Some programs reallocate items of value from the less well-off to the more well-off, or from minorities to whites and Anglos, but such programs and policies are not perceived as redistributive and do not generate the same kinds of politics. In this chapter we examine the politics of redistributive policy, efforts in which the intended beneficiaries are the relatively disadvantaged in society and in which the relatively advantaged classes perceive themselves to be in danger of losing something they value.

The Reagan years saw a major shift in the treatment of redistributive issues in some ways and a major reaffirmation of the normal American way of perceiving and dealing with such issues in other ways.

The major reaffirmation was the reinforcement of the dominant perception that policy was redistributive only if it appeared to be aiming toward a redistribution in favor of the less well-off parts (classes, races) in society at the expense of the more well-off parts (classes, races). In 1981 President Reagan could say with a straight face that the tax system was not the proper vehicle to use for the achievement of redistribution. What he meant was he did not think the tax system should redistribute in favor of the disadvantaged. While denying that the tax system should be used in redistributive fashion, he was simultaneously proposing major changes in taxes that clearly redistributed in the other direction. Analytically, any tax system redistributes in some direction. But in American political parlance, most politicians and most of those engaged in public debate, and even most of those who are observant bystanders, accept the notion that "redistribution" occurs only if the less advantaged classes are perceived to be the beneficiaries and the more advantaged classes the "losers."

All kinds of policies constantly push in all kinds of redistributive directions. But, in the political perceptions of most Americans, policy perceived to be directed at aiding the disadvantaged was "redistributive," whereas policy that was aiding the already advantaged was largely perceived as "distributive," and its bias in favor of the already advantaged was probably not widely perceived.

These differences in perception mean efforts to aid the disadvantaged always set off major political rows. Efforts that add to the governmentally supported privileges of the already privileged classes often slip through without major controversy. Thus, "natural" political pressures often define issues that could, in principle, be redistributive as distributive.

The major change instituted by the Reagan administration had to do with the basic thrust of presidentially initiated and supported policy. Since the coming of Franklin Roosevelt to the presidency in 1933, the president—regardless of party—had taken the lead in at least some areas in pushing for redistribution in the classic sense of aiding the relatively disadvantaged. Different presidents had different priorities, commitments, and styles in making and supporting these initiatives. And, to be sure, Democratic presidents tended to be more supportive and active in this area than Republican presidents. But even Eisenhower, Nixon, and Ford all supported and even initiated some major redistributive efforts. And all presidents of both parties presided over the development of a federal bureaucracy in domestic areas that, with variations over time, developed considerable commitments to redistribution in favor of the more disadvantaged segments of society.

Ronald Reagan, however, dismissed the 1933–81 period of presidential and bureaucratic commitment and activity in the domestic sphere as wrongheaded and returned to a much different set of values, reminiscent both of the society of the 1920s and of the political commitments of the Republican leaders of the 1920s. He clearly wanted to halt the federal support of redistribution to the less well-off. He took major legislative and administrative initiatives to cut that support and to reverse the trend in some areas. Much of this activity was administrative in character. The legislative activity tended to be focused on major tax and budget bills. The effort to redistribute in the nondisadvantaged direction was consistent and began to have results, even though it was not labeled as redistribution, in keeping with the one-sided American definition of such policy (Palmer and Sawhill, 1982, 1984; Pechman, 1983).

In the early 1980s the presidentially led efforts working for at least some redistribution in favor of the disadvantaged came to a grinding halt. Presidential efforts ran in the other direction. Legislatively, the effort was limited to the comprehensive budget reconciliation and tax bills rather than bills targeted at individual programs. The president's limited initiatives to attack specific programs piecemeal did not get very far. Congressional support remained strong enough to prevent major changes. But through administrative changes—both in staff and in policies—and through the vehicles of major comprehensive budget and tax bills, he wrought major changes.

In terms of impact, Reagan's initiatives, when they succeeded, were particularly destructive to the interests of greater equality in society because, despite some popular perceptions, the impact of the federal government, even after five decades of effort, was only very mildly in favor of greater economic equality for the less well-off classes (see Page, 1983, for a major, persuasive analysis backing this generalization). The importance and access of a host of interest groups—structurally giving more influence to the relatively privileged classes and groups in society—and the nature of the widespread beliefs about our form of capitalism and "free enterprise" both militated in favor of only very modest movement in the direction of greater economic equality. This was true even after decades of New Deal, Fair Deal, New Frontier, and Great Society efforts reinforced by nonrepeal by Republican presidents and even a few equalizing initiatives on their parts.

REDISTRIBUTIVE POLICY AND THE
CONGRESSIONAL–BUREAUCRATIC RELATIONSHIP

We expect the importance of subgovernments to be minimal in terms of final decisions made regarding redistributive domestic policy. This is the case both because only parts of some redistributive issues are likely to be considered in the interactions of a subgovernment and because final decisions are almost always made at levels higher than a subgovernment.

The potential for conflict between various combinations of congressional and bureaucratic actors on redistributive issues is high because there are usually ideological and partisan differences present. If general agreement on these differences can be reached, the conflict potential can be reduced considerably. If these differences are not muted and if redistributive issues are not redefined in some way, then the debate and final decisions may take a long time. Four substantive areas—the war on poverty, medicare, civil rights, and voting rights—illustrate the congressional-bureaucratic relationship in reaching decisions on redistributive policy and also illustrate the factors that tend to impede and facilitate those decisions.

Even when there is conflict based on partisan and ideological differences, however, the contending parties in the two branches (and within each branch) may be able to reach agreement by casting the issue in distributive terms rather than continuing to debate it in redistributive terms. Three substantive areas—Model Cities, manpower revenue sharing, and aid to education—illustrate how redistributive policies can be redefined to emphasize distributive aspects.

When conflict exists, usually there is no resolution at the bureau-subcommittee level. If resolution is achieved, it comes at a higher level, usually in negotiations between the president, his top appointees and advisors, and the full Congress, often represented by the party leaders and relevant full-committee chairs. If conflict is resolved at this higher level, it is either in terms of a broad compromise or in terms of a redefinition of issues in distributive terms. Many times, however, resolution of the conflict evades the actors, sometimes for many years. When resolution of conflict does occur, the prevailing view depends largely on the relative strength of competing ideologies in Congress, the ties of those ideologies to the parties in Congress, and the relative strength of the parties and of the major ideological factions of the parties.

It is worth noting that many of the examples of redistributive policy we have chosen for this chapter occurred some years ago. We did not make this selection because we think the dim and distant past more informative than the recent past, however. Rather, the simple fact is that there have been few contemporary redistributive debates. Following an outburst of redistributive debate and legislation in the mid-1960s, interest and support for redistributive policies among government leaders and the public waned, and few redistributive issues made legislative headway in the 1970s and into the 1980s.

In the 1980s the almost total lack of political interest in redistributive thrusts (favoring the disadvantaged), together with major Reagan-supported actions running in the opposite direction, meant there were no cases with which to analyze the basic dynamics of redistributive decision making. The reauthorization of voting rights in 1982 is a notable exception. If debates occurred over efforts to cut specific programs rather than in the context of comprehensive budget bills, there would be raw material for analysis to see if the dynamics of "counterredistribution" are the same as the dynamics of redistribution. However, debates in the 1980s over eliminating even the mildly redistributive programs sponsored by the federal government rarely came down to analyzing them one by one.

Reaching Basic Decisions about Redistributive Issues

The War on Poverty.   The creation, alteration, and eventual dismemberment of the war on poverty between 1964 and 1974 exhibit a number of patterns common to redistributive policy. Individual members of the House and Senate, particularly those in strategic committee positions, were important in helping make decisions, as were individuals scattered throughout the administration and relevant executive branch agencies. However, these individuals could not make binding decisions by themselves: a much broader set of decision makers got involved, including all senators and representatives (through floor action), the president and his top advisors, and a variety of interest groups. Programs avowedly redistributive along class and/or racial lines (in favor of the poorer classes and minorities) once established were the center of constant debate and controversy and were gradually surrounded with restraints, both organizational and programmatic. The entire history of the war on poverty is too extensive to tell in compact form (for good discussions of its origins and early years, see Donovan, 1973; Levitan, 1969; Loftus, 1970; and Sundquist, 1968: chapter 4), but a look at a few individual programs and events in that history will illustrate the broader points we wish to make. These episodes include the 1967 Green amendment to the Economic Opportunity Act of 1964, the Job Corps, the Legal Services Corporation, and the end of the Office of Economic Opportunity as a separate organizational entity in the federal government.

The Green Amendment.   In 1967 the basic legislation authorizing the OEO and the poverty program was up for renewal after the first three years, and the war on poverty seemed to be in serious trouble (see Loftus, 1970, for a fuller account of what follows). There had been complaints about its administration and about its alleged involvement in stirring up the urban riots that had torn the country apart for the previous three summers. And in the 1966 congressional elections, liberal Democrats suffered in races for the House of Representatives. Thus, 1967 began with the expectation that the newly revived control of the House by the conservative coalition of Republicans and southern Democrats could kill the entire poverty program, which required a new authorization before the end of the year.

As it turned out, the program survived, largely because the House adopted an amendment sponsored by Representative Edith Green, an Oregon Democrat who had been critical of the Office of Economic Opportunity and its programs. The amendment was designed to mollify two groups: conservative southern Democrats and some northern urban Democrats from cities whose mayors had had poor relations with the OEO and its community action program. Basically the amendment gave the mayors and other locally elected officials the means to gain substantial control over the community action agencies.

The negotiations that produced the amendment were carried on by Green on the one hand and the director and staff of the OEO and members of the White House staff on the other hand, through the mediation of five Democratic supporters of the OEO who served with Green on the House Education and Labor Committee. Green did not want to admit she was willing to help save the program; the administration was not able to admit it was willing to pay the price of accepting the Green amendment in order to save the program. Therefore, their public stances remained conflictual, but through intermediaries—who wanted the program and realized the political necessity of acquiescing to the Green amendment—they negotiated a compromise. These relatively quiet third-person negotiations illustrate that even in the midst of loud public discord over redistributive policy, some features of subgovernment activity can appear and have an impact. This was not a consensual "poverty subgovernment" at work but rather a dissentious one in which private negotiations and compromises produced an outcome with which the disagreeing parties could live.

Job Corps.   (For a fuller discussion of the Job Corps from 1964 through 1971, see Ripley, 1972: chapter 3. Some of the following discussion is adapted from that chapter.) The Job Corps, one of the initial parts of the war on poverty, was aimed at preparing disadvantaged teenage youths for the labor market by offering them residential training and experience in centers both in cities and in rural areas. The central premise was that individuals from extremely deprived backgrounds needed to be removed from "the culture of poverty" in order to get basic skills (such as adequate reading), job-related skills, and appropriate attitudes about work and holding a job.

Controversy surrounded the Job Corps from the beginning. It received very negative press coverage during its first year of operation. Many incidents that reflected poorly on the program received national attention out of proportion to their importance. In addition, the program was expensive in terms of per enrollee cost. Even with the support of the Democratic Johnson administration, the Job Corps had trouble holding its own in Congress. Although the initial goal was for 100,000 enrollees, that target was soon revised downward, and the Job Corps leveled off at between 35,000 and 40,000 enrollees with an annual budget of about $280 million.

When the Nixon administration took over the executive branch in 1969, the Job Corps was quickly and severely cut. Nixon had promised such action in the 1968 presidential campaign and lost no time keeping his pledge. The Job Corps was taken away from the Office of Economic Opportunity and given to the more traditionally oriented Department of Labor (these two agencies had long been competing for the Job Corps) and the program was cut roughly in half in terms of enrollees and budget. The residential centers that remained open—all in or near urban areas—drew enrollees from the local labor markets rather than from a more national market.

The Job Corps survived, but only in a form that made it seem relatively nonthreatening and relatively minor in terms of its actual and potential redistributive impact. In this case—unlike the case of the Green amendment—no private negotiations saved the original concept and location of the Job Corps. It apparently was so vulnerable that continued existence— even under dramatically altered circumstances—was about the best it could hope for. It still retained enough Democratic supporters to be continued as a categorical manpower program in 1973, however, even though most other manpower programs were included under the Comprehensive Employment and Training Act, a form of special revenue sharing enacted by Congress. Its fortunes revived in the Carter administration.

The Job Corps was one of the few redistributive programs that caught the imagination and therefore the support of some conservative members of Congress. Thus, it survived—although its funding was quite modest—and received continuing support when CETA was reauthorized in 1978 and when the Job Training Partnership Act replaced CETA in 1982. The chairperson of the Labor and Human Resources Committee in the Republican-controlled Senate beginning in 1981, Orrin Hatch of Utah, was a particularly consistent and strong supporter. The Job Corps remained as a small categorical effort to aid the poor and seemed in no danger of disappearing in the Reaganite onslaught on other programs for the poor.

Legal Services Corporation.   The final form in which a Legal Services Corporation was permanently established in 1974 again illustrates compromise between individual senators and representatives (in this case, mostly the members of a conference committee) and representatives of the administration that resulted in the breaking of a three-year deadlock over a program with considerable redistributive potential, at least in the perceptions of those debating its fate, especially the opponents. This was a highly visible dispute. One side was committed to the federal government's providing legal services to the poor, arguing that such a program would redistribute the outcomes of the legal system in a more equal way. The other side opposed the proposed program for being disruptive of the social order. As with the Green amendment, final resolution of the conflict was achieved because some relatively private negotiations took place among the most concerned individuals at the last minute, which avoided the possibility of a direct confrontation with the president, whose veto could not have been overridden. Proponents were also motivated to negotiate by the awareness that the OEO was not likely to survive past 1974, and without resolution that year on the legal services issue, executive branch agency support in the future was extremely unlikely.

Congress passed a bill establishing a Legal Services Corporation in 1971, but President Nixon successfully vetoed it, primarily because it did not give him the power of appointing all of the directors of the corporation. In 1972 conferees eliminated an amendment to the bill reauthorizing all OEO programs that would have set up a Legal Services Corporation because they feared its inclusion would have provoked a presidential veto of the entire bill. In 1973 President Nixon sent his own proposal for a Legal Services Corporation to Congress. The House passed a version that was even more conservative and restrictive than what the president asked for in June 1973. Opponents of any Legal Services Corporation at all, no matter how restricted, filibustered against the bill in the Senate in 1973 and early 1974. The Senate stopped the filibuster on the third cloture vote and passed a bill that was far more liberal (less restrictive on the activities of the corporation and its professional staff) than the House or president's version.

The conference committee reached a series of agreements that both chambers approved in the spring of 1974. One provision of the bill continued to generate trouble, however. Conservatives in the House were opposed to a provision in the bill authorizing the creation of so-called backup centers (corporation-funded poverty-law research centers), and they narrowly missed (by seven votes) sending the bill back to the conference with instructions to delete the research centers. Even though the Senate was solidly in support of the research centers, the Senate supporters realized the president would probably veto a bill allowing them and the House would certainly sustain such a veto. Therefore, in a series of last-minute negotiations that avoided a more visible conference setting, the supporters met privately and agreed to delete the research centers from the bill as the price for having a Legal Services Corporation.

Other restrictions put into the bill also indicate the kind of price the liberals had to pay on this redistributive issue. The president was given the power of appointment for all of the directors of the corporation. Attorneys employed by the corporation were severely restricted in terms of their political activities, even on their own time. Legal Services lawsuits aimed at school desegregation or obtaining nontherapeutic abortions were forbidden. And lawyers for the corporation could not become involved in draft cases or criminal cases. Given this conservatively oriented bill, President Nixon signed it, although the staunchest opponents of any federally supported legal services for the poor urged him to veto it.

The Reagan administration launched an all-out assault on the Legal Services Corporation. It hoped for elimination. When that did not seem to be possible politically, the administration instead slashed both budget and staff. It also put new appointees on the board unsympathetic to the program. Some of the early appointees got into trouble by taking fat consulting fees and by declaring meetings to be secret even though such declarations were probably illegal (Drew, 1982; Kristof, 1982). The president and the Senate engaged in a long-running battle over board appointees in 1984 and 1985. The Legal Services Corporation had attained important symbolic status for both conservatives and liberals and future legislative-executive negotiations on its fate were sure to be visible and controversial.

The End of the OEO. The flagging fortunes of the Office of Economic Opportunity since 1969 and its eventual dismantling under Republican administrations suggest how critically important presidential support is to the success of redistributive policy and how devastating presidential opposition to redistributive policy can be. The OEO was established in the poverty-conscious political climate of the mid-1960s with President Johnson's strong support. Although its community action program had been amended in 1967, funding support did not begin to diminish until Nixon became president. Nixon had never been enthusiastic about the poverty program, and although he made no mention of the OEO during his campaign, his 1969 message to Congress expressed skepticism about the agency and its programs. In 1973 he began a full-scale attempt to kill the agency and cut off federal funding for its community action programs, which provided a variety of services to the poor.

The OEO had been created as an operating agency at the insistence of its first director, Sargent Shriver. When Nixon came into office, he began to whittle away these programs from the OEO and to cut its budget in order to reduce its operating role. In 1973 Nixon appointed an acting director of the OEO (with no Senate confirmation) specifically to dismantle the agency and to transfer certain of its programs to other agencies. At the same time, he sent his budget for fiscal year 1974 to Congress. In it no money was requested for the OEO as an agency (although it was authorized through June of 1974). The budget proposed placing OEO's legal services in a separate corporation, transferring certain OEO programs to other agencies (HEW, Department of Labor, Department of Commerce), and allowing the community action programs to expire with no request for any funding. This executive action sent threatened community action agencies and employee unions to the courts, where a judge ruled that no budget message could overrule a legislative authorization. The actions of the acting director were declared null and void, and he was declared to be illegally appointed.

The court decision forced Nixon to name another acting director, this time with Senate confirmation (the vote was eighty-eight to three because the nominee said he was in favor of continuing the OEO; later Nixon fired him for this very reason), but Nixon continued to move programs out of the OEO and into other agencies by administrative action (by declaring that a program was being "delegated" by the OEO to another agency, Nixon required no congressional approval). By the end of 1973, there were only three programs left in the OEO: legal services, community action, and community economic development. Moving any of these required congressional approval.

Despite Nixon's wish to let the community action programs expire in 1974, there was still strong liberal support in Congress for their continuation. In addition, support came from mayors and governors who in earlier years had opposed the poverty programs. They now came forward as supporters, declaring that loss of those services would place their communities in disastrous situations. The rising national unemployment rate gave sharp emphasis to the need for programs for the poor, and the less enthusiastic members of Congress realized that a bill passed in 1974 was bound to be less liberal than one that would emerge from the newly elected, more liberal Congress in 1975.

Given the support in and out of Congress for the community action program and the new president's (Gerald Ford) lack of opposition to the poverty program, a bill emerged in the late days of the 1974 congressional session. Again, as in the case of the Legal Services Corporation, conference committee members negotiating among themselves and presumably in touch with representatives of the Ford administration produced a winning compromise that reduced the redistributive potential of the poverty programs and of the successor agency to the OEO. But at least it kept many of the programs in existence (and even added two small new ones).

The Community Services Act was a victory in that the OEO's poverty programs were authorized through fiscal 1977, but the redistributive impact of those programs was considerably reduced. The OEO as an agency ceased to exist; its programs were lodged in a new independent agency (the Community Services Administration), but the president had the option of reorganizing this agency and its programs. The overall federal commitment was greatly reduced (Ford requested only $363 million for the CSA for fiscal 1976, a far cry from the $2 billion OEO budget of fiscal 1969), and the share of federal funding for community action programs was cut back to 60 percent over three years.

President Ford did not exercise the option to reorganize or transfer the CSA, but the redistributive impact of the agency and its antipoverty programs was seriously curtailed by the decreased funding level. Although Congress routinely provided much larger appropriations than the president requested between fiscal years 1975 and 1978 (for example, in fiscal year 1976, when President Ford requested only $363 million, Congress appropriated $496 million), the size of the appropriations was much lower than in pre-CSA days. The agency stayed alive and kept pace with inflation but did not expand.

In 1978 the CSA and other antipoverty programs were reauthorized through 1981. The CSA emerged from the authorization with no deletions from its programs but with no additions either. The federal sharing formula was once again altered, with the 60 percent figure increased to 80 percent, while the share that local communities were to provide was decreased from 40 percent to 20 percent to relieve the economic burden they were bearing. However, unless Congress significantly increased the amount of appropriations the change in the sharing formula still resulted in fewer dollars available at the local level. The mood of Congress as the 1970s ended was one of fiscal conservatism, and dramatic increases in appropriations for the CSA or any redistributive program were unlikely.

The CSA came to an end statutorily in 1981. It was eliminated in the comprehensive budget reconciliation bill passed in August of that year. This institutional effort to redistribute ceased altogether.

Medicare.   The notion of government-sponsored health insurance to assist citizens in meeting the cost of their medical care has been on the national agenda since 1935, as the chronology in Table 6–1 shows. But it was not until 1965, after years of debate, that a major piece of health insurance legislation emerged (the social security medicare program), and even then the scope and redistributive potential of the new program were reduced considerably from the initial proposal for comprehensive national health insurance. Medicare set up a federal medical care program for the aged under the social security system.

The central features of the story of medicare involve the emergence of two ideological positions used as the focal points by two large coalitions in direct opposition to each other. The debate between the two coalitions in rhetorical terms was largely static: the same arguments were repeated by the same actors year after year. The debate in procedural terms was also static: the opponents of action found the numerous levers in Congress that can be used to stymie action and, with relatively marginal exceptions, were successful in their endeavors for most of the period.

However, the deadlock broke with the emergence of an aggressive political majority in the presidency and in Congress (particularly in the

TABLE 6-1
National Medical Insurance, 1935-1965

1935	Roosevelt administration explores compulsory national health insurance as part of the Social Security Act, but no legislation is recommended to Congress.
1943	Three Democratic senators cosponsor a bill to broaden the Social Security Act to include compulsory national health insurance to be financed with a payroll tax. No legislative action.
1945	President Truman, in his health message, proposes a medical insurance plan for persons of all ages, to be financed through a social security tax.
1949	The Truman proposal is considered and hotly contested in congressional hearings. No legislative action results.
1954	President Eisenhower opposes the concept of national health insurance as "socialized medicine." He proposes the alternative of reimbursing private insurance companies for heavy losses on private health insurance claims. No action taken on this proposal.
1957	Representative Forand introduces the Forand bill, to provide hospital care for needy old-age social security beneficiaries to be financed through increased social security taxes. No action taken by Congress, but heavy AFL-CIO lobbying generates public interest.
1960	The Forand bill is defeated by the House Ways and Means Committee on a decisive vote (17-8). Chairman Wilbur Mills opposes the bill.
1960	As a substitute for the Forand bill, Congress enacts the Kerr-Mills bill, designed to encourage the states to help older, medically needy persons (those not poor enough to qualify for old age assistance but too poor to pay their medical bills).
1960	Health care is an issue in the presidential campaign; Kennedy vows support
1961-64	President Kennedy's version of the Forand bill is submitted annually in the House and Senate, but the House Ways and Means Committee defeats it.
1962	Senate defeats an amendment to a public-welfare bill embodying the Kennedy proposal (52-48).
1964	The Senate passes (49-44) a Medicare plan similar to the administration proposal as an amendment to the Social Security Act. The plan dies when House conferees (from the Ways and Means Committee) refuse to allow its inclusion.
Jan. 1965	The 1964 elections bring many new Democrats to Congress, and the composition of the Ways and Means Committee is finally changed to have a majority of medicare supporters.
Jan. 1965	President Johnson makes medical care his number-one legislative priority.
July 1965	Medicare bill is signed into law after passage in both houses by generous margins.

Source: Adapted from material in *Congressional Quarterly Almanac*, 1965: 236-47.

relevant committees) that allowed the passage of medicare in 1965. Even in 1965 the final decision floor votes in Congress could accurately be interpreted as logical outcomes of twenty years of conflict between a set cast of characters with set attitudes. The difference in 1965 was that the election of 1964 had produced more proponents than opponents. But the final success of the proponents was achieved only with considerable bargaining and compromise among members of the House and Senate with differing viewpoints and between members of the House and Senate and members of the administration at high levels. And given the unusual electoral results in 1964, which determined the balance of political forces in Congress in 1965, Congress played a more creative and shaping role in 1965 than might be expected in a redistributive issue.

The intensity of views held by proponents and opponents of medical care insurance remained high throughout the thirty-year debate. Two basic positions were taken by the broad coalitions on the general question concerning the federal government's proper role in this area. Proponents (AFL–CIO and other labor unions, a variety of public-welfare organizations, the National Medical Association [a group of black physicians], the National Council of Senior Citizens, and northern Democrats) supported full federal sponsorship of medical insurance and believed private insurance companies could not handle the job of national medical insurance, their high premiums would place too much burden on the elderly, and a state charity approach was unsatisfactory because state benefits were inadequate and because only the neediest could qualify.

Opponents of national medical insurance (the American Medical Association, the insurance industry, business groups like the U.S. Chamber of Commerce, Republicans, and southern Democrats) favored only a very narrow federal role, limited to encouraging private and state efforts and to providing federal health-care assistance only to the neediest (state charity) cases. (The Kerr-Mills bill was a response to this line of reasoning.) Opponents greatly feared government interference in private medical practice and warned against the dangers of "socialized medicine."

Marmor (1973: 108–9) reflects on the explicitly redistributive features of the medicare debate:

> Debate [was] . . . cast in terms of class conflict. . . . The leading adversaries . . . brought into the opposing camps a large number of groups whose interests were not directly affected by the Medicare outcome . . . ideological charges and counter-charges dominated public discussion, and each side seemed to regard compromise as unacceptable. In the end, the electoral changes of 1965 reallocated power in such a way that the opponents were overruled. Compromise was involved in the detailed features of the Medicare program, but the enactment itself did not constitute a compromise outcome for the adversaries.

As the chronology in Table 6–1 shows, the debate over medical insurance narrowed in 1957 to a focus on assistance for one group, the elderly.

The next eight years were spent trying to overcome stalemate on this nar-rower redistributive program. The lobbying efforts during this period were notable both for their intensity and because they were directed not only at Congress to sway votes, but also at the public to educate and in-crease consciousness. In the end, the static and largely unchanging debate was resolved with a compromise that included considerable conservative and Republican input into the final product to blur some of the redistribu-tive features. Republican contributions included coverage of almost three million people who were not covered by the Old Age and Survivors Insur-ance provisions of social security, the separation of medicare funds from old age funds, the authorization of the use of private nonprofit organiza-tions to deal with hospitals, and the addition of a subsidy to cover surgery and doctors' fees. The latter two features in particular introduced ele-ments of distribution into the program.

The issue of national health insurance for all Americans did not disap-pear with the passage of medicare in 1965. As the cost of health care soared in the late 1960s and into the 1970s and 1980s, some of the stigma of "socialized medicine" was reduced, replaced by a concern with distrib-uting relief to the many middle-class and upper-middle-class voters sad-dled with rising health-care costs. Many national health insurance bills were introduced in Congress during the 1970s with a variety of backers, including both Nixon and Ford, the American Medical Association, the American Hospital Association, the private insurance industry, and Democratic Senator Edward Kennedy of Massachusetts, the leading con-gressional proponent of health insurance. The features of the various pro-posals differed greatly, and divisive debate characteristic of earlier years recurred. The sharpest division of opinion focused on the role of the federal government versus the private sector in the administration of a health-insurance program; the degree of voluntary participation versus manda-tory participation; and the nature of financing (for example, payroll tax versus income tax credit).

None of the bills introduced in the 1970s met with success. Only in 1974 did compromise on a health-insurance program seem possible. The House Ways and Means Committee held lengthy hearings and came close to a compromise, but the committee was sharply divided on two issues and lacked strong leadership from the chairman, who was suffering from personal problems. The committee failed to report a bill, and since 1974 there has been little congressional activity other than ritualistic introduc-tion of bills.

Jimmy Carter made a campaign pledge in 1976 to produce a compre-hensive national health insurance program, but failed to redeem his pledge during his years as president. President Reagan showed little inter-est in the matter.

Medicare, like its older sibling social security, is not purely redistributive. The criteria for eligibility cut across class and income lines. Thus, the middle classes have a very large stake in making sure both systems—medicare and social security—are in sound health and future benefits will be forthcoming. The early Reagan years saw a crisis in providing for the future of social security. Congress followed the advice of a bipartisan commission, whose recommendations were supported by the president and most Republicans in Congress as well as by most Democrats, and passed major new social security legislation in early 1983. If and as a perceived crisis in medicare develops in the 1980s, there seems to be a high likelihood that the same processes might well produce a similar kind of broad compromise formula for "saving" medicare. Thus, the marginal redistributive impact of the program would be preserved, but, politically, it would be supported because of its universal character. Entitlements to medicare payments for people who really could afford to do without or at least to pay part of their own expenses are not likely to be challenged. Universal benefits generate universal political support.

The Civil Rights Act of 1964. Civil rights for racial and ethnic minorities (understood and debated almost exclusively in terms of blacks from the 1930s through the 1960s) had a long and complex, and often heartbreaking, history from the end of the Civil War up to the passage of the first postreconstruction civil rights legislation of much substance in 1964. This history was both legislative (characterized largely by nonaction) and judicial (characterized by sporadic, faltering, and often negative action until 1954 and then a quickening tempo of positive action after that). Recounting that history would take an entire book (see Kluger, 1976, for a superb summary of civil rights history). In this section we will focus on one important part of civil rights history, the passage of the Civil Rights Act of 1964, to illustrate the kinds of political forces that are generated when considering a redistributive policy measure that deals with questions of racial justice and injustice. As with other redistributive policies, there was a combination of highly visible and emotion-filled debate, both in Congress and in other public arenas, and private negotiating of compromises that allowed forward movement at critical points. The public debate was carried on by two large coalitions of groups and individuals that had opposed each other for years. The private negotiations were carried on by key individuals in both the executive branch and Congress (source material for this case is drawn from *Congressional Quarterly*, 1965: 1615–41; Kluger, 1976; Lytle, 1966; Sundquist, 1968: chapter 6).

When John Kennedy became president in 1961 he had raised the hopes of leaders in the civil rights movement that some federal civil rights legislation might be forthcoming if he chose to play a leadership role. Instead, he chose to proceed very cautiously in the area (critics said he was not proceeding at all), primarily to protect other parts of his domestic program from being defeated because of the actions of angry southerners well placed in the House and Senate. However, as the pace of the civil rights movement at the local level increased, with a variety of demonstrations, protests, boycotts, and some violence, the administration at last felt compelled to submit legislative proposals. The president announced in February 1963 that such proposals would be forthcoming, but in the absence of firm presidential commitment, only some bills of mild and minor character were introduced in May as a somewhat slow follow-up to his announcement. Major action still did not seem imminent.

However, in May and June the attention of the nation was directed to Birmingham, Alabama, where a particularly evil manifestation of officially supported and sanctioned violence in support of blatant racial discrimination was being challenged by dedicated civil rights leaders and large numbers of followers. Additional public drama was created when Governor George Wallace of Alabama took his stand in "the schoolhouse door" to prevent two blacks from registering at the University of Alabama. (He gave up in a few hours when the president put the Alabama National Guard into federal service.) The president, pushed by his own reading of these events, by supporters of civil rights in Congress, and by a host of interest groups and coalitions of groups supporting civil rights, submitted a civil rights bill of moderate strength to Congress in mid-June. More important, he committed his personal prestige to the fight to get the legislation passed. He immediately became involved personally in a number of meetings to work on strategy with groups supporting the legislation. These included a variety of black-led groups (for example, the National Association for the Advancement of Colored People, the National Urban League, the Congress of Racial Equality, and the Southern Christian Leadership Conference), a number of labor unions (particularly the industrial unions from the old Congress of Industrial Organizations), a large number of church groups, and the Leadership Conference on Civil Rights—a "holding company" of groups supporting civil rights, including all of the above plus many more (a total of seventy-nine groups in 1963). The president also began meetings with pro-civil rights Democrats and Republicans from Congress and with officials from the Justice Department (headed by his brother Robert as attorney general) and the White House.

A subcommittee of the House Judiciary Committee held hearings in the summer of 1963 and moved to strengthen the bill proposed by the president in a number of ways. The White House feared that the bill had been strengthened so much it would never pass the Senate. The administration calculated that the votes of a number of western Democrats and moderate Republicans were critical to passage, particularly in the Senate, and that only a bill of moderate strength could gain their support. In order to gauge what could pass even the House, Attorney General Kennedy now entered directly into negotiations with two key Republicans—the ranking Republican on the Judiciary Committee and the minority leader. When the bill went into full committee, the southern Democrats worked to obtain the strongest possible bill because they believed a strong bill was more likely to be defeated on the floor than a bill of moderate strength. The administration intervened both publicly and privately to get the majority Democrats to weaken the bill so it could pass the full House. The attorney general asked for weakening amendments in full committee hearings and was also active in private negotiations. The administration was successful, and the House Judiciary Committee reported a bill most agreed would pass the House relatively easily.

In 1963 in the Senate not a great deal occurred. The Senate Judiciary Committee, chaired by one of the most reactionary of the southern Democrats, had, predictably, buried the parts of the bill referred to it. One major part of the package—that guaranteeing nondiscriminatory access to public accommodations such as hotels and restaurants—had gone to the Senate Commerce Committee and had been approved, although not formally reported (for strategic reasons), by the end of the session.

Nineteen sixty-four dawned with a new president, Lyndon Johnson, in office because John Kennedy had been assassinated in November 1963. Johnson quickly made his total commitment to a strong law in the civil rights area quite evident and worked closely with friendly lobbyists and members of Congress and individuals in the White House and Justice Department to develop a strategy and generate compromises that would attract enough moderate votes to pass the package.

Pressured by northern Democratic and Republican support, the House Rules Committee, although chaired by an archconservative Virginian, proved to be no major stumbling block for the progress of the bill in early 1964. The full House debated the bill for ten days and passed it by a large margin (290 to 130) on February 10. The bill's managers acquiesced in accepting a few amendments on the floor restricting the scope of the bill, but, on the whole, the bill the House passed was very close in nature to the bill that had been hammered out in the multiparty negotiations in the autumn of 1963 in the Judiciary Committee. Two amendments even strengthened the bill a bit.

The first critical action in the Senate occurred when the whole Senate voted simply to place the House-passed bill on its calendar for floor consideration rather than referring it to the Judiciary Committee, where it no doubt would have died. The Senate then debated the bill from early March until mid-June 1964 (one year to the day after President Kennedy had submitted his legislative request). The key figure in the Senate soon turned out to be the minority leader, Everett Dirksen of Illinois. If he could be convinced of the fairness of the bill, he would vote for closing off a filibuster the southern opposition had mounted and would also vote for the bill. More important, he would bring along a number of moderate Republicans with him on both votes. The vote on the filibuster would clearly be the most important, because two-thirds of those present and voting must vote yea (67 votes were required because all 100 senators were present—a rare event—for the vote on cloture and also for the vote on final passage of the bill). The attorney general and the Senate Democrat taking the lead in floor debate, Hubert Humphrey of Minnesota, negotiated extensively over several months with Dirksen. Eventually they reached some compromises that weakened the bill somewhat but brought victory— 71 to 29 on cloture and 73 to 27 on the bill itself.

The majority of the House Rules Committee again overrode its chair to guarantee that the House could vote directly on the Senate-passed bill without sending the bill to a conference committee, where again it might die (the chances for death in Congress are extraordinarily high for any single bill). The House easily approved the Senate bill 289 to 126 on July 2, and later the same day President Johnson signed it into law on national television.

Despite the numerous compromises that had been necessary to get the new law through several sticky points in both houses, it was not toothless legislation and, in fact, the contributions of the negotiations and discussions among the White House, Justice Department, supportive interest groups and organizations, and supportive senators and representatives had strengthened the bill beyond what President Kennedy had initially requested. It was a broad bill and had titles dealing with voting rights, public accommodations, desegregation of public facilities, desegregation of public education, extending the life of the Civil Rights Commission, nondiscrimination in programs assisted with federal dollars, equal employment opportunity, registration and voting statistics, and the creation of a Community Relations Service in the Commerce Department.

The passage of the 1964 Civil Rights Act was characterized by lengthy debate that was highly emotional and highly visible. There was no quiet subgovernment at work in this policy area. The benefits to be conferred by the legislation—equal treatment under the law—created distinct classes of peceived winners and losers. Successful passage of the legislation required the forceful personal involvement of many key actors, most notably the president, and a willingness of the supporters to compromise. The passage of the act alone did not guarantee implementation of its provisions, but it was an important step in the country's history of providing simple justice to its citizens.

Voting Rights Act Renewal, 1982.   In 1965 Congress continued its civil rights activity by passing the Voting Rights Act. This law has brought about a remarkable increase in the number of minorities registering and voting in elections at state, local, and federal levels and is generally held to be the most effective of the nation's civil rights laws. Certain sections of the 1965 law were made permanent, but the enforcement provisions in Section 5 (these require affected states to obtain federal permission or "preclearance" before making election law changes) require periodic legislative action or they will expire. The most recent renewal—for twenty-five years—occurred in 1982, before the expiration deadline in that year.

Congressional passage of the Voting Rights Act in 1982 contrasted sharply with the turbulence surrounding enactment of the 1964 Civil Rights Act. In 1982 the redistributive effects of the legislation enjoyed widespread and bipartisan support in both houses of Congress. The law's effectiveness in increasing registration and voter participation was undisputed. Even among southerners, support for passage grew significantly between 1965 and 1982, as the number of black voters increased.

The enactment of the 1982 law was not entirely free from controversy, although there was really no challenge to the premise that the law would be extended—the issue was how long and under what conditions. A widespread network of interest groups coordinated a lobbying campaign during 1981 and 1982, and there was no organized opposition to the extension.

Two significant issues were debated during House and Senate consideration. The first addressed the standard of proof to be used in settling suits alleging voter discrimination brought under Section 2 of the act. Senate conservatives and the Department of Justice wanted to insert a narrower interpretation requiring that the *intent* to discriminate must be proved, rather than proving that the effect or *result* of a voting law was discriminatory. The second issue affected the preclearance requirement of Section 5 and addressed how states could be released for good behavior if they complied consistently with federal rules and did not discriminate in their election laws. The bailout issue concerned how stringent the test must be and what criteria would be used to release a state from preclearance requirements.

The only tarnish dimming the Voting Rights Act renewal was caused by the lusterless role of the president and the Department of Justice. Despite criticism and encouragement from civil rights groups, the president withheld his endorsement of the bill and took no personal role in promoting its passage. The attorney general and the head of the Civil Rights Division of the Department of Justice favored the narrow "intent" standard of proof and a limited period of extension. No one from the administration testified at the House hearings in 1981.

Passage in the House was overwhelming, 389 to 24; debate and the final vote took only one day. The House Judiciary Committee had worked for many months to find a reasonable compromise on the bailout issue; all diluting amendments offered on the floor were defeated by wide margins.

The Senate was a somewhat tougher nut to crack, although the bill had sixty-five cosponsors when it was introduced in January. The chairman of the Judiciary Committee, Republican Strom Thurmond of South Carolina, was a longtime opponent of the act, and the subcommittee chairman, Republican Orrin G. Hatch of Utah, opposed use of the "results" standard of proof and wanted extension of the act limited to ten years. The committee divided on the standard of proof issue, but after two months compromised by accepting the broader "results" criterion that the House had used. Opponents were somewhat mollified by a clause that proportional representation for minorities on local governing bodies was not guaranteed or intended. Senator Jesse Helms of North Carolina waged a dispirited filibuster for nine days before withdrawing his opposition, allowing the bill to be brought to a successful eighty-five to eight vote. Supporters easily defeated diluting floor amendments.

Redistributive Issues Redefined as Distributive

The redefinition of redistributive issues may occur as the price for allowing any redistribution to emerge. Reaching accord is easier if the participants in a redistributive debate choose to emphasize the distributive aspects and mute the redistributive aspects. This approach was used in some of the cases already discussed. The retention of community action programs and the retention of legal services for the poor were bought at the cost of severe limitations on the redistributive potential of these programs—a very small budget in the case of community action and strict limitations on the services that could be provided in the case of legal services. In the case of medicare, success was achieved in part because subsidies went to hospitals and doctors. Procedural safeguards were added to mute the redistributive potential of the 1964 Civil Rights Act.

The redefinition of redistributive issues may also occur following initial legislation. Subsequent amendments are made that gradually whittle away the redistributive emphasis. The examples that follow illustrate how distributive aspects of redistributive policy were stressed in order to secure both initial passage and continuation.

Model Cities.   The history of Model Cities—from its germination in a presidentially appointed Task Force on Urban Problems in 1965 and its initial statutory authorization in 1966 until its replacement by a special revenue-sharing program in 1974 and its organizational programmatic termination in 1975—is one characterized by a short initial period of redistributive rhetoric followed by the reality of a distributive program. It was basically oriented toward distributing federal dollars to cities. The cities were also given increasing autonomy in making decisions about the purposes for which the money was spent. Improving relations between the federal government and cities was another goal of the program. (This discussion of Model Cities is based on Ripley, 1972; chapter 5.) The central reason for this important shift from redistributive ends to primarily distributive ends lies in the nature of congressional attitudes and reactions to administration initiatives. Through informal contacts with high-ranking officials in the Model Cities Administration, the Department of Housing and Urban Development, and the White House, and through formal actions taken on authorizing legislation and appropriations, members of the House and Senate helped set the direction that Model Cities took in practice—a direction altered from the early reasons given for the passage of the act by President Johnson and the liberal Democratic supporters of the program.

The original formulators saw Model Cities as a program that would consciously manipulate social conditions in favor of the poorest residents of city slums. They sold the program to others—especially those in Congress—in two ways: in speaking to liberals, they advocated it as a program of social redistribution; but in speaking to conservatives, they portrayed it as a program of subsidy for city governments.

Achieving congressional legitimation of the Johnson administration's program of redistribution was a difficult task from the outset. Significant opposition to the program developed in Congress, especially among Republicans, including members of the authorizing committees in both houses. Compromises were required to pass the initial authorizing statute in 1966. These compromises—like those in other programs we have already discussed—muted the redistributive potential of the program. For example, provisions requiring Model Cities to have racial integration as a goal of their plans were dropped. Subsidy to cities and the autonomy of cities were stressed in changes in the administration's proposal that increased the number of eligible cities, dropped the requirement that cities establish a separate agency specifically designed to administer the program, and eliminated a federal coordinator who was to be stationed in each model city.

Under congressional pressure and then by administrative preference, the stress in Model Cities implementation came to rest more on the process of administration than on outcomes. The shift began in the Johnson administration. Action in 1967 and 1968 mixed a concern for subsidizing increasingly autonomous city enterprises with other themes such as viewing Model Cities as the ultimate federal tool for eradicating urban blight and poverty, concentrating the planning and implementation efforts on limited areas of selected cities, using citizen participation in the planning and implementation of the program (but not at the expense of the established local government's role), fostering the centrality of the mayors' role in the program, bolstering local government in general, improving the "delivery systems" for existing federal programs for the cities, and according states a place in the program.

In the Nixon administration in 1969 and 1970, the dominant themes became almost exclusively devoted to a concern with creating strength and autonomy in local governments and to creating a distributive rather than a redistributive image for the program. The emphases now changed to making the program more responsive to local needs and less susceptible to federal management; to supporting mayoral authority; to deemphasizing citizen participation in the program, especially in administration; to expanding the scope of the program to include entire cities rather than just target neighborhoods (while cutting total funding); to toning down the promises of social results; and to stressing the need for a more unified interpretation of administrative policies at all levels of administration. From 1971 on, the emphasis changed even more strongly in this direction as HUD officials announced their desire to give cities almost complete control of mobilizing and coordinating resources, to reduce federal monitoring to simple auditing rather than setting national program standards against which performance would be measured, and to make block grants to cities rather than categorical grants. Beginning in 1971 President Nixon made evident his desire to do away with the Model Cities program in favor of a broader special revenue-sharing program for housing and community development. He was stymied for several years by liberals in Congress reluctant to see another Great Society program succumb, but in 1974—shortly after Nixon had resigned the presidency—Congress passed the Housing and Community Development Act that spelled the end of Model Cities and numerous other programs as separate entities.

At its inception the Model Cities program was envisioned by its formulators and most liberal supporters as a vehicle for the manipulation of social conditions and the redistribution of economic rewards. It was to be a demonstration project for a small, limited number of cities that would eradicate blight and create monuments of true urban renewal. But the realities were that the environment in Congress from 1966 onward was not hospitable to such goals, and the administrations of both Johnson and Nixon used the program as a device for regulating intergovernmental relations (through strengthening city halls) and intragovernmental relations (through coordinating federal delivery systems) and for creating the appearance of subsidizing a lot of cities (although with severely diminished funds).

Special Revenue Sharing: The Case of Employment and Training. Special revenue sharing passes federal funds to states and localities for a particular use (for example, education or transportation) with relatively few federal strings attached. Commonly, special revenue-sharing money comes in the form of a block grant that replaces a variety of federal categorical grant programs in the issue area. Between 1966 and 1975 five major block grant special revenue-sharing programs were created: the Partnership for Health Act of 1966, the Omnibus Crime and Safe Streets Act of 1968, the Comprehensive Employment and Training Act of 1973 (CETA), the Housing and Community Development Act of 1974, and Title XX (social services) of the Social Security Act of 1975. The most significant that have survived into the late 1980s are the Community Development Block Grant program (CDBG) created by the Housing and Community Development Act, and the replacement for CETA, the Job Training Partnership Act (JTPA), passed in 1982.

In general, special revenue-sharing programs replaced programs with considerable redistributive potential with programs that emphasize distributive potential. The clients receiving special revenue-sharing benefits are governmental units—states, cities, counties—rather than a class of persons—the economically disadvantaged. The choices about who gets what at the expense of whom (the essence of a redistributive program) are fuzzed over by the use of a formula to allocate funds and by the stress on local control. To the extent that redistributive questions get discussed directly, that discussion may take place either in the parts of the federal bureaucracy that supervise revenue-sharing programs (the Employment and Training Administration in the case of CETA and JTPA and the Department of Housing and Urban Development in the case of CDBG) or at the local level (presumably through some mandated mechanism for citizen input).

But neither the federal bureaucracy nor local government is accustomed to confronting redistributive questions head-on, and both are generally inexpert at it. Both are also severely hampered even if the desire is present. The federal bureaucracy is hampered because its role in revenue sharing is formally limited primarily to "technical assistance," and the local-citizen input mechanism is hampered because it is usually defined explicitly as being only "advisory." Given the absence of a national mandate to emphasize redistributive benefits, and the inexperience and/or unwillingness of city and county governments to engage in redistributive activity, special revenue-sharing programs get defined and implemented as distributive programs, and the conflicts that arise focus on questions of jurisdiction and dollar allocations to geographically defined units rather than on who benefits to what effect in a broader social sense.

The initial replacement of categorical employment and training programs with a revenue-sharing block grant involved a lengthy battle. (For excellent summaries, see Davidson, 1972, 1975.) It took five years for the Nixon administration to get a comprehensive manpower bill and the resulting package was less than it had wanted but more than the supporters of categorical programs had wanted to give. The debate over comprehensive employment and training revenue sharing focused on three major aspects of the Nixon proposal: decategorization, decentralization, and public-service employment.

The categorical programs represented a piecemeal approach to redistributive manpower policy. Although they were established for their redistributive potential (training unemployed and disadvantaged workers to improve job skills and standard of living), the categorical approach emphasized distributive features, and numerous subgovernments sprang up around each grant program, its congressional committees, and relevant bureaucrats. These groups fought the hardest to resist revenue sharing because they feared it would mean the end of their categorical programs and their privileged access to resources. The proposals being considered from 1969 to 1973 gave discretion to local governmental units to decide which categorical programs might be continued—none of them (except the Job Corps, as it turned out) had any guarantees about their future. This fact had implications not only for the continuation of the subgovernments, but also for the redistributive potential of the programs themselves, because the prime sponsors (the local elected officials) could shift clientele orientation as they saw fit, and those served would not necessarily be among the most needy.

Decentralization was also an issue, and there was competition among states, cities, and counties with large populations for chief administrative responsibility under the comprehensive bill. Cities especially feared that they and their urban problems (where those most in need of redistributive policies tend to reside) would be slighted if responsibility were lodged with the states, which historically had not been sensitive to urban problems. Likewise, the bulk of the populous counties' population is suburban, typically not the most needy.

Debate on the consolidation of employment and training programs was complicated by the inclusion of the public employment issue. This issue aroused the historically divisive, ideologically based question of the proper role of the federal government in creating and subsidizing jobs for the unemployed. Liberals were traditionally in favor of a strong federal role, while conservatives opposed it. President Nixon strongly resisted the inclusion of a public employment title in a comprehensive manpower bill. Ultimately he was unsuccessful. Public service employment was included in the consolidation debate because its supporters argued it was pointless for manpower programs to focus on training workers if there were not enough jobs. The concept of public service employment has been around since the New Deal, and supporters were eager to have an existing employment program continued.

The essence of the final compromise in 1973 was that the administration got its basic mandate for decentralization and decategorization and a much diminished federal role in making program choices, and the liberals got the retention of a few categorical programs (notably the Job Corps) and some categorical references in the statute and a sizable permanent public service employment program. Public service employment was expanded in late 1974 by a large emergency public service program designed to combat the employment problems facing the nation because of a recession.

The central features of CETA were:

1. Basic responsibility for deciding how to spend money for manpower purposes was given to "prime sponsors," which were with only a few exceptions, cities or counties with more than 100,000 population, consortia of cities and counties, and states.
2. The great bulk of manpower money was allocated to the prime sponsorships by formulas based on various weightings for unemployment, number of low-income people, and previous federal manpower spending.
3. Several forms of advisory council were mandated by the statute and the regulations issued by the Department of Labor. Most important were the planning councils that were required in each prime sponsorship.
4. The regional offices of the Department of Labor retained a variety of supervisory duties and responsibilities, although in general they were to offer primarily "technical assistance" to prime sponsors.
5. In pre-CETA manpower operations, the standard model of service delivery to clients was for the regional or national office of the Manpower Administration to contract directly with deliverers. Under CETA the prime sponsors wrote and monitored the performance of those contracts.

The experience under CETA underscores the generalizations made earlier about the implications of revenue sharing for redistributive policy impacts (for a lengthy analysis of the CETA experience see Franklin and Ripley, 1984). For example, a greater stress on white clients compared to black clients and other minorities and on near-poor clients compared to the poorest clients quickly developed. Community action agencies— which were among the more redistributively oriented of local institutions—lost their role as service deliverers in a number of jurisdictions. "Work experience" for youth—including large numbers of black youths— was given greater stress under CETA than in pre-CETA programs. This was a relatively cheap way of "serving" large numbers of clients who were both black and among the most disadvantaged. This could be used by prime sponsors to offset charges from politically hostile groups that the program was short-changing such clients. The advisory councils were generally not meaningful bodies for representing clients. In some jurisdictions they were relatively effective in representing officials, service deliverers, or high-status individuals, but as representatives of actual and potential clients they were not structured to serve as effective access channels.

When CETA was reauthorized in 1978, Congress attempted to insert a bit more redistributive potential into the program by tightening some of the eligibility requirements. But a good deal more effort was spent on considering the public service employment program—both its size and how to prevent abuses. Questions of size primarily had to do with how much subsidy CETA should generate for units of local government—an essentially distributive question.

In 1982, when Congress replaced CETA with JTPA, there was a mixture of elements of distribution and redistribution. The new modes of funneling money through states and to and through the private sector (that is, local businesses) were clearly distributive elements to the program that made it salable, ultimately, even to a conservative Congress and a very conservative president. But the program remained nominally redistributive in class terms in that 90 percent of the individual trainees had to come from economically disadvantaged groups, with standards that did not change from the 1978 definitions. This emphasis was muted because allowances to trainees (some minimal income during the period of training) were, for the most part, prohibited. Thus, it was unclear that the genuinely disadvantaged could really afford to sign up for training unless they were receiving welfare. During the transition period from CETA to JTPA in 1982–83, the scramble in terms of implementation focused almost exclusively on the distributive features of the act—the details of state and private-sector control and basic structural decisions about which portions of state government and the private sector would have what kinds of influence.

Aid to Education.   The history of federal aid to education in the United States since World War II is complex and tangled (Bendiner, 1964; Eidenberg and Morey, 1969; Munger and Fenno, 1962; Sundquist, 1968: chapter 5). In broad terms it can be asserted that the federal government began to give increasing amounts of special purpose aid to both elementary and secondary education and to higher education during the early parts of the period, but a logjam developed on the question of broad general aid—especially to elementary and secondary schools—and the logjam was broken only by shifting the form and purpose of general purpose aid. In more analytic terms it can be asserted that educational aid measures that were perceived as providing benefits to many special segments of the population or to specially defined geographic areas (measures that were distributive) were much easier to enact than broad general purpose aid measures that were perceived as shifting benefits from one racial or religious group to another racial or religious group. The final breakthrough on a form of general purpose aid in 1965 was possible only because the redistributive focus was shifted away from race and religion to poverty and because distributive features were emphasized. Redistribution was still perceived to be taking place, but given the heat of the philosophical, racial, and religious controversies that had raged for the preceding years, it was a muted form of redistribution.

Throughout all the debates, members of the House and Senate and a few individuals in the hierarchy of both the Department of Health, Education, and Welfare (HEW) and the White House were important in framing initiatives, attempting compromises, and—usually—shifting the grounds of debate until the most threatening aspects of redistribution were removed. Generally these individuals were subcommittee chairs and ranking members in the House and Senate and individuals in HEW at the level of assistant secretary or above. However, given the broad involvement of many groups and interests, agreement at this level was never sufficient to generate policy decisions. Inevitably, large associations and groups such as the National Education Association, civil rights groups, and both Catholic and Protestant religious organizations also got involved. The highest echelons of the executive branch—usually including the president personally—also participated. Consequently, most members of the House and Senate felt a personal stake in outcomes, even though their own committee assignments might be quite remote from education, and congressional decision making tended to get escalated out of quiet committee settings onto the floors of the two chambers. Perceived redistribution—coupled with philosophical and some partisan differences—increases the likelihood that more participants and participants in higher formal positions will become more important than the normal subgovernment members. The aid-to-education case illustrates this generalization. Committee members and HEW and Office of Education bureaucrats even up to the level of assistant secretary and commissioner of education were only moderately important actors rather than dominant actors in reaching final decisions.

The tenor of the federal aid to education provided between 1940 and 1965 was distributive, and that alone explains the relative ease of establishing those aid programs. Table 6–2 summarizes the most important programs. In all cases except the 1965 Elementary and Secondary Education Act, subsidies for students or institutions (colleges, school districts) are provided in a nonredistributive way.

General aid to school districts foundered throughout the same period because of hostility to federal "control" of a traditionally local function, because of the perception after 1954 that aid would be used as a lever to force public-school integration, and because of the issue of whether private schools, especially those run by the Roman Catholic Church, would or would not receive benefits. Various combinations of these issues—with the racial question being explicitly redistributive in nature—repeatedly killed general aid in Congress. Presidents—especially Eisenhower and Kennedy—were unable or unwilling to find a winning solution. Eidenberg and Morey (1969: 23–24) summarize the history of failure to achieve compromise:

> In searching for school aid stumbling blocks, one is quickly led to the House of Representatives. Starting in 1948 the Senate passed each bill that reached the

TABLE 6–2
Federal Aid to Education, 1940–1965

Program	Benefits	Recipients
Higher education		
1944 G.I. Bill of Rights	Living expenses, books, tuition	World War II veterans (later Korean, cold war, and Vietnam veterans)
1950 National Science Foundation	Support for science research and education	Colleges, universities
1950 Housing Act of 1950	Low-interest loans for dormitory construction	Colleges, universities
1958 National Defense Education Act	Loans; training in science, math, languages; equipment purchases	Students; teachers; colleges; universities
1963 Classroom construction	Grants for classroom construction	Public and private colleges
1965 Higher Education Act	Scholarships, library support, construction grants	Colleges, universities
Elementary and secondary education		
1940 Lanham Act	Financial aid	School districts impacted by war-related personnel dislocation
1946 National School Lunch Act	Aid for providing school lunches	School districts
1950 Impacted areas aid	Financial aid	School districts impacted with federal personnel
1954 Agricultural Act	Aid for providing school milk	School districts
1958 National Defense Education Act	Matching grants for equipment and classrooms; aid for foreign-language training institutes, testing, guidance, counseling	States

TABLE 6–2 *(concluded)*		
Program	Benefits	Recipients
1965 Elementary and Secondary Education Act	Aid for equipment, classrooms, staff, construction; aid for library resources; matching aid for supplemental education centers; aid for education research; aid for state departments of education	School districts with concentrations of poor and unemployed persons; state departments of education; local education agencies; colleges, universities, states

Source: Adapted from E. Eidenberg and R. D. Morey, *An Act of Congress*, (New York: W. W. Norton, 1969), 16–18, 247–48.

floor—1948, 1949, 1960, and 1961. On the other hand, in the House three bills were killed on the floor (1956, 1957, and 1961) and another (1960) was passed but subsequently held in the Rules Committee on the way to conference.

From 1943 to 1955 the prime obstacle in the House was the Education and Labor Committee. During this period, hearings were held on seven bills, but not one was reported. In 1955 the opposition bloc finally crumbled when 15 non-Southern Democrats aligned with 7 Republicans to approve a bill for the first time in recent history. By 1959 federal aid supporters had a solid majority on the committee. . . .

As the complexion of the Education and Labor Committee changed in the mid-1950s, the antifederal aid bloc in the Rules Committee was solidified. This committee was the principal obstacle to school aid bills in 1955, 1959, 1960, and 1961 through 1964.

The breaking of the logjam in 1965 came for several reasons. One was that liberal Democrats made sweeping gains in the House of Representatives in the 1964 election as a result of President Johnson's landslide victory. But, even more important, the effort to achieve general purpose aid essentially was compromised in favor of a special purpose approach. As Sundquist (1968: 206) describes it, both proponents and opponents of general purpose aid finally decided that some benefits were better than none.

The sudden turnabout reflects, perhaps most of all, a simple fact: people *do* learn from experience. First, both sides of the religious controversy had learned. The NEA and its public school allies now knew that an all-or-nothing attitude would mean, for the public schools, nothing. Likewise, Catholic leaders now understood that an equal-treatment-or-nothing position would mean, for the Catholic schools, nothing. For each side the question was whether it preferred to maintain the purity of its ideological position or receive some tangible benefits for its schools. The Washington representatives of organizations on both sides were, with a few exceptions, cautiously on the side of accommodation. . . . Accommodation was supported by public opinion polls, which showed that a majority of Americans no longer opposed aid to parochial schools. Second, the tacticians had learned. The National Defense Education Act had shown that special-purpose aid, carefully designed, could be enacted at a time when general-purpose aid could not be.

Basically the breakthrough came because the proponents of a redistributive aid policy packaged their program in a way that emphasized special purpose, distributive features (which had been succeeding since 1940) and combined it in a bill with other special purpose aid. The new special purpose was "the education of children of needy families and children living in areas of substantial unemployment." As Sundquist (1968: 210) points out, "Congress had, after all, acknowledged a federal responsibility for assistance to families on welfare and for aid to depressed areas. Assistance to school districts 'impacted' by federal activities was also long-established; would not it be as logical to assist 'poverty-impacted' districts?"

A change in the general political climate was also important in establishing the partially redistributive emphasis on disadvantaged children in the 1965 aid-to-education bill. The changed climate included the rediscovery of poverty by the federal government a few years earlier, a commitment by the liberal portion of the Democratic party to attack poverty in a number of ways, and the dominance of the government by an aggressive liberal Democratic president and large, liberal Democratic majorities in the House and Senate.

CONCLUSIONS

The general shape of the redistributive arena and the specific characterization of congressional-bureaucratic relations in that arena outlined at the beginning of this chapter and in Table 4–1 are generally confirmed by the material we have analyzed. However, several important additions to that general picture can now be made.

First, it seems clear that initiative for redistributive policy can come from within Congress and, occasionally, from the higher levels of the career bureaucracy. But more often the initiative comes from the White House, and presidential participation in an active way is helpful and usually essential for those wanting to achieve redistribution—at least on behalf of the poorer segments of society.

To the extent that the president is either opposed to the proposed redistribution or active only verbally, sporadically, unenthusiastically, or ineffectively, the chances increase that either nothing will happen and a long-standing stalemate will persist or that the issue will be redefined, at least in part, as distributive. There are always strong natural tendencies in Congress to seek compromise through such redefinition. Lack of presidential initiative or, even more dramatically, presidential initiatives against redistribution to the less well-off, almost foreordain that redistribution—even of a mild variety—will not be ratified legislatively. And, in some cases, past redistributive decisions will be undone and repealed, or at least severely altered.

Another recurring pattern also gives a particularly important role to Congress. At those critical moments in the history of debate over a redistributive proposal when the political situation seems to allow movement rather than repetition of previous positions resulting in continued stalemate, important congressional figures—often working with technical experts from the bureaucracy—engage in relatively quiet bargaining and negotiation that are essential to success. Usually these negotiations result in limits on the original redistributive potential of the proposal, but some such potential often still remains.

The attainment of redistributive policy is achieved at a cost of diluting its impact by adding or emphasizing distributive elements. Programs that are purely redistributive are virtually impossible to enact. Programs that have distributive elements broaden the base of support and both camouflage and reduce the redistributive elements. The pressures to redefine controversial redistributive proposals as distributive continue after original passage is secured. Both implementation and subsequent reauthorizations are often the occasions for attempts to broaden the number or type of beneficiaries beyond the most disadvantaged. These pressures mean the actual cumulative impact of redistributive federal policies is mild, because the latitude for redistribution is constrained as part of the bargain for having any redistribution.

7

Foreign and Defense Policy

THE NATURE OF FOREIGN AND DEFENSE POLICY

Congress has the potential to be heavily involved in many aspects of foreign and defense policies. It actively used this power during the 1970s and 1980s. The quiescent position of Congress in the late 1950s and early 1960s in many of these areas was deceptively atypical (on the changing role of Congress in foreign and defense policies in general see Carroll, 1966; Franck and Weisband, 1979; Frey, 1975; Kolodziej, 1975; Lanouette, 1978; Manley, 1971; Moe and Teel, 1970; Pastor, 1980).

Unfortunately, most of the literature on the involvement of Congress in foreign policy—and on the relationship between Congress, the president, military and foreign-policy bureaucracy, and interest groups—treats foreign and defense policy as a single, undifferentiated area. We argue, however, that there are three different kinds of foreign and defense policy, distinguishable by the kinds of politics surrounding each. Tables 1–3 and 4–1 and the discussion of those tables have previously laid out the shape of these three areas in summary fashion.

The characteristics of *structural policy* (which occurs in noncrisis situations) are virtually the same as in domestic distributive policy: subgovernments composed of actors from bureaus, subcommittees, and small units in the private sector (individuals, corporations, small interest groups) dominate policy making on the basis of mutual noninterference and logrolling. The relationship among the actors in these subgovernments is stable, and their decisions are implemented in a decentralized fashion, usually at the bureau level.

In *strategic policy* (which also occurs in noncrisis situations), the pattern is somewhat similar to domestic protective regulatory policy, with the major difference being that interest groups and especially bureaus and subcommittees have a reduced role. The major decisional locus is central-ized in portions of the executive branch, especially the presidency, which deals basically with the whole Congress.

In *crisis policy*, the basic decision-making structure is very simple: it is the president and whomever he chooses to consult. Usually he will consult only a few of his top advisors; sometimes he will bring in leading individ-ual members of Congress or occasionally "peak association" leaders. The issues are defined quickly, debated in private, and responded to quickly in a highly centralized fashion through executive (presidential) action. Of course, the decisions may provoke considerable public debate after they are announced.

As in the case of domestic policies, the different policy types are inter-woven in two senses. First, some policy areas do not fall neatly into just one category, and/or their central thrust may move between strategic and structural. (Or, what began as a crisis may last long enough to take on at-tributes of strategic policy.) Second, decisions in one area clearly have im-plications for decisions in one or both of the other areas. Decisions made in a crisis help determine the options identified and the final choices in later strategic decision making. Decisions made on strategic matters to some extent help limit the options on subsequent structural decisions. Thus, the perceived need for certain kinds of weapons in trying to put pressure on the Soviet Union or in trying to be ready for certain kinds of "brushfire" actions will presumably help determine the kinds of requirements and specifications that go into later procurement decisions. By the same to-ken, however, the necessities of domestic politics that help determine structural policy may push certain kinds of strategic options forward. A decision to help get rid of American agricultural surpluses makes decision makers look for programs such as Public Law 480 ("Food for Peace") or ex-panded grain sales to the Soviet Union. These latter programs have im-portant strategic implications for general foreign relations between the United States and other nations.

In the pages that follow, we discuss examples of all three types of policy. We think it important to note that both defense decisions and broader foreign-policy decisions—for example, foreign economic policy or immigration policy or recognition policy—provide some of the exam-ples. Both broad types of decisions fall into the analytical scheme that helps identify recognizably different political patterns surrounding policy formulation and legitimation. It is probably true that defense decisions tend to be most frequent in the structural area, and broader foreign policy decisions tend to be most frequent in the strategic area. But it is equally true that both types of substantive policy also have numerous instances that fall clearly into both the structural and strategic categories. And, of course, crisis situations almost all have both military and broader foreign-policy dimensions.

THE CONGRESSIONAL–BUREAUCRATIC RELATIONSHIP IN FOREIGN AND DEFENSE POLICY

The relationship between members of the executive branch at the bureau level and individuals in Congress at the subcommittee level vary depending on the kind of foreign and defense policy. In the case of structural policy, we expect the subgovernment relationship will be the most important source of decisions that emerge, and those decisions will not be altered in subsequent stages of the formal legislative process. The subgovernments will deal with many aspects of the issues within their jurisdiction. There is a high degree of cooperation between bureaucrats and legislators because each is motivated to serve clients. If there are differences of opinion, they will generally be resolved by the members of the subgovernment, without involving a large number of other participants. Subgovernment members have a high degree of motivation to reach some form of compromise between their initial positions so as to prevent "outsiders" such as the secretary of defense or the president or a congressional party leader from intervening. The compromises they reach are likely to contain more subcommittee preferences than bureaucratic preferences, although the interests of neither (nor those of their clients) will be badly treated.

In strategic policy, we expect the importance of the subgovernment relationship to be greatly reduced. Only a few narrow aspects of an issue will be dealt with at the bureau-subcommittee level, and very few final decisions will be made there. Most will instead be made in the higher reaches of the executive branch, where strategic policy usually originates. Conflict based on ideological differences between congressional and executive branch actors may occur. Such conflict is not usually resolved at a subgovernment level but is passed along to a higher level for final decisions. At that higher level, conflict is either resolved by a broad compromise between contending positions or it may remain unresolved. Executive branch views typically dominate final decisions. Congress may, in some instances, push for redefinition of issues as structural rather than strategic because the former is the area in which members of Congress feel most comfortable and in which, in many cases, they prevail if there is disagreement.

In the case of crisis policy we expect that the subcommittee-bureau level of interaction will not be a factor in the decision-making process. Major decisions are made within the confines of the presidency with the participation of those few individuals the president chooses to include. There is little chance for either cooperation or conflict, except in the confines of the small group summoned by the president. Conflict between the president and Congress may develop after an event, of course. Formal statements after the event usually take the form of either congressional resolutions disagreeing with or supporting presidential action or executive orders that either formalize a course already being followed or impose a solution despite congressional dissent. Genuine compromise on controversial actions is generally not reached, largely because it is irrelevant since decisions have already been made and actions have already been taken. Sometimes sham compromise is effected in the name of "national unity." Some differences of opinion are, in effect, eliminated through an imposed solution (either a congressional action with teeth or an executive order). Generally, the presidential view of issues left in controversy prevails.

STRUCTURAL POLICY

The Defense Budget

Many aspects of the defense budget, especially those related to ongoing procurement decisions, provide good examples of structural policy. Of course, the defense budget contains items with strategic impact—for example, the choice of a major new weapons systems—and these items represent decisions that get made in the executive branch and sometimes get debated in Congress, usually on the floor of the House or Senate. The items of a more purely distributive nature, such as decisions to fund existing procurement contracts, typically get decided in the interaction between relevant subcommittees and parts of the Pentagon, with more perfunctory ratification by the entire House and Senate.

A great deal is, of course, at stake when defense decisions are made. The requests made by President Reagan in early 1985 for the defense budgets for fiscal years 1986, 1987, and 1988 give a good sense of the amounts of money involved by major function, including procurement. Table 7–1 summarizes these requests. In each of these three years, procurement represented about one-third of total requests. It was, by a sizable margin, the largest request in both dollar terms and relative shares each year.

We will investigate congressional-bureaucratic interactions in defense budgeting by examining a number of patterns of interaction that both enhance subgovernments' domination of many decisions and reflect that dominance.

Procurement Subgovernments.   Very close links exist between Pentagon procurement officials, private sector contractors, and members of the House and Senate whose states and districts benefit from defense contracting. The close ties and shared benefits reinforce the attitudes of other participants to proceed quietly to disburse the many billions of dollars spent each year to procure military hardware. Contractors are approached by defense procurement officials, and jointly they work out the

TABLE 7-1
National Defense Budget Requests by President Reagan, Early 1985 ($millions)

Mission/Program Category	FY 1986	FY 1987	FY 1988
Miltary personnal	73,425	75,762	77,719
Operation and maintenance	82,450	95,834	108,754
Procurement	106,813	122,432	141,223
Research, development, evaluation	39,280	42,607	49,289
Military construction, housing and other	20,237	26,624	34,478
Total	322,205	363,259	411,463

Source: *Budget of the United States Government, Fiscal Year 1986,* (Washington, D.C.: U.S. Government Printing Office 1985), 5–5.

specifications to be met. Members of Congress are kept abreast of the progress of such negotiations and are given the privilege of announcing awards of contracts in their districts and states. A recent study of "the Government relations practices of military contractors" reaches the following general conclusion: "decisions on defense policy and weapons procurement rest almost entirely in the hands of insiders and policy experts, walled off from outsiders and alternative perspectives. The policy-makers, whose expertise is real and necessary, are also people and organizations with interests to protect and promote: (1) defense contractors whose success is measured by weapon sales, (2) the defense department, with positions and a future to protect and, (3) members of Congress who share in making military policy and are prime targets of industry-Government relations" (Adams, 1982: 207).

In early 1985 Georgetown University's Center for Strategic and International Studies released a major report that severely criticized the Defense Department's procurement system. It pointed out that the individual services are allowed to develop weapons systems "independently, each according to its own sense of national priorities." Likewise, it pointed out that individual contractors can "buy into" a weapons program by keeping the initial cost estimates low. Once they are in the program the Pentagon and the affected senators and representatives happily fund cost overruns more accurately reflecting what the contractors should have bid in the first place, plus a healthy profit (*Washington Post,* February 26, 1985).

When two weapons systems are put into competition, rival subgovernments sometimes will spring up. Typically each of the competing systems will have a Pentagon sponsor (usually one service favoring one system and a different service favoring a competing system), favored contractors as allies, and members of the House and Senate linked with given contractors for geographical reasons as additional allies. The Pentagon rivals will deliberately seek to mobilize the largest group of allies, even though such mobilization involves nonexperts in decisions that have strategic impact (Armacost, 1969).

When a system has been decided on, there may still be competing contractors with their respective congressional supporters giving them at least ritualistic support. Once the basic decision is made about what kind of system is going to be developed, however, the Pentagon has a relatively free hand in making the final choice of contractors. Although, over time, these decisions are made to build as large a constituency for military programs as possible (Smith, 1973).

The decentralized nature of governmental procurement, especially within the Department of Defense (DOD), enhances the latitude of groups of interacting DOD officials, contractors, and senators and representatives. In the absence of a central clearinghouse, defense procurement subgovernments operate with a high degree of autonomy. The federal procurement structure (of which defense procurement expenditures represent two-thirds) was described by a former head of the General Services Administration as a "garage sale," with no one in charge.

The procurement subgovernments aim to keep companies profitable and stable. In such an arrangement everyone in the subgovernment—companies, the military services, and members of Congress with large defense contractor payrolls—benefits. Only the general taxpayer foots the bill. A study released in 1985 shows that the ten largest defense contractors were about twice as profitable as American corporations in general (measured in terms of profits as a percent of equity). The absolute size of the profits in 1984 was staggering (*New York Times*, April 9, 1985). They ranged from a low of $108 million to a high of $787 million. In 1985 the least profitable of the ten largest contractors (Grumman) was given an extra infusion of support from DOD to help keep it healthy economically (*New York Times*, August 5, 1985). Two planes manufactured by Grumman for the Navy were no longer providing much work (the A-6, with production almost halted, and the F-14, with shrinking sales). New Navy contracts provided more than $1 billion to upgrade both planes, even though defense experts questioned the military wisdom of the decision.

It is hardly coincidental that spending by the largest defense contractors on political campaigns soared during the 1980s, doubling from $1.8 million in 1980 to $3.6 million in 1984 (*New York Times*, April 9, 1985). Naturally, the spending was concentrated on friends of defense spending in the House and Senate.

Congressional Priorities within the Defense Budget.   Congressional activity on the defense budget tends to concentrate on procurement and research and development items and to place much less emphasis on personnel and operations and maintenance categories. In the areas on which they concentrate, the input of congressional defense appropriations subcommittees is significant and has also been more in accord with the views of the individual services than with any differing views of the secretary of defense. The congressional focus on these areas is enhanced by the deliberate appeals of Pentagon officials for allies, even though they have to grant those allies some impact on strategic decisions. Kanter (1972) suggests that Congress is deliberately used by the military services to provide critical support so military preferences themselves will dominate, although because of interservice rivalries, any one service is likely to suffer some temporary setbacks.

The motivations of Pentagon officials, particularly the military services, to seek congressional support reflect the great importance they attach to procurement and research and development (Kanter, 1972: 135).

Members of Congress seek, with considerable success, to influence DOD decisions that are geographically specific—both in terms of the location of weapons contractors and the location of bases and other DOD facilities. The payrolls of contractors and of the Defense Department itself are important to senators and representatives trying to claim credit for aiding the economies in their states and districts.

DOD Congressional Liaison Structure.   The congressional liaison structure of the Department of Defense promotes the development and maintenance of independent subgovernments (Holtzman, 1970: 137–41 and 167–68; Pipe, 1966). Each service has its own very large liaison staff that works directly with relevant committees, subcommittees, and senators and representatives. In fiscal 1965, for example, the army had 92 individuals involved directly in congressional liaison, the air force had 144, and the navy had 70 (Pipe, 1966: 18). By contrast, the central DOD liaison operation in the Office of the Secretary had only 34 persons—hardly enough to compete with the services if they were pushing policy views and making alliances not in direct accord with policies favored by the secretary of defense. Holtzman (1970: 138) summarized the situation well:

> Each military department cooperated with the SOD [Secretary of Defense] in relation to the Congress when its interests coincided with his, but each attempted to play its own game when their interests conflicted. Control and coordination from the secretarial level were very difficult to impose, in large measure because key individuals in the Congress had long opposed such domination by the senior political executive within Defense. . . . when a military department was in rebellion against the policies of the SOD, that service's legislative liaison staff withdrew from the usual cooperative arrangements with the DOD liaison officer. Under such circumstances, the latter could not rely upon

the service's liaison staff as a resource for intelligence or as an aid in working with the Congress.

DOD-OMB Relations.   The relations between the Department of Defense and the Office of Management and Budget facilitate strong subgovernments. The OMB has deliberately (perhaps out of a sense of inevitability) structured its relations with the DOD so the latter has a freer hand in its budgeting decisions than the domestic agencies. OMB budget examiners work directly with Pentagon and service budget officers (usually working in the Pentagon) to arrive at a recommendation for the president. The secretary of defense and the White House still exercise some control, but the vastness of the military establishment lends itself to the official recognition of fragmentation.

In the Reagan years, the already weak national-security division in the OMB became even weaker in terms of losing more staff and more permanent positions than any other section of OMB. The pro-DOD stance by the Reagan administration reduced the already small efforts to control defense spending through OMB actions. Said one inside source: "The administration is kind of ignoring this small division, reducing a source of advice for reform. If we were stronger, not all the problems would be solved. But now that there's no one around to say to the emperor that he has no clothes, I don't think things are going to get any better" (*Washington Post*, March 9, 1983).

Conference Committee Procedures.   The practices of the House and Senate conferees on defense authorization and appropriations bills maximize congressional support for certain military policies that are highly valued by either the House or the Senate. Kanter (1972) analyzed 161 differences between House and Senate positions on DOD appropriations bills that were resolved by conference committees between fiscal 1966 and fiscal 1970. In examining the relative influence of the two houses, he found that only about 20 percent of the time did the conferees adopt a "split-the-difference" approach to resolve a disagreement. Rather, the usual approach was to give each house all of what it wanted on some issues, but none of what it wanted on other issues. In this way, both houses got what was most important to them without major compromises on those issues. Only the lower priorities were likely to suffer either in being compromised or in being cut. Thus, the highest priorities of the military services and their contractor allies were likely to emerge unscathed.[1]

[1]This same pattern of mutual deference was found in a study of congressional treatment of foreign aid in the period between 1951 and 1962 (Ripley, 1965). This similarity suggests that perhaps in foreign and defense policy, congressional committees may work—maybe unconsciously—to maximize their impact through this logrolling pattern of bargaining, which is quite different from the normal "split-the-difference" compromises characterizing many domestic policy areas.

Reprogramming Funds.   The Defense Department has considerable leeway to reprogram appropriated funds within appropriation accounts during a fiscal year. It can transfer money and use it for purposes other than those for which it was originally appropriated (Fisher, 1974). Reprogramming maximizes the ability of the military parts of defense subgovernments to make decisions that allow them to pursue their highest priorities despite competing priorities that might be articulated by the president, the secretary of defense, or the whole House or Senate. The relevant committees have to be informed about most reprogrammings—but that keeps the information within the subgovernment and does not involve "outsiders." Typically, reprogrammings for procurement have to obtain prior approval from the armed services and appropriations committees in both houses (and have to have at least nominal approval from either the secretary of defense or deputy secretary of defense before being sent to the committees). Research and development reprogramming has to have approval of the armed services committees or at least notification has to be given. This practice is not insignificant—between fiscal 1956 and fiscal 1972, for example, it involved between $1.7 billion and $4.7 billion annually. Between 1964 and 1972, an average of more than 100 separate reprogramming actions occurred annually.

Weapons Systems

Decisions about specific weapons systems have important strategic implications, and initial decisions and research are generally done within the Defense Department, usually by the services. Congress must approve or disapprove executive requests for new weapons, and interactions on these kinds of issues constitute strategic policy. But once a weapons system has been approved for "pilot testing" or prototype research, subsequent decisions regarding its continuation, expansion, or alterations take on patterns of structural policy.

The B-1 Bomber.   Since the 1960s the air force has lobbied for the development and production of the B-1 bomber to be the successor to the B-52 as the mainstay of the manned bomber fleet of the United States. Some critics a number of years ago began to suggest that manned bombers are superfluous in the age of missiles. But the air force continuously pushed the case for the B-1, consistently supported by the House of Representatives, the makers of the B-1 and their subcontractors, and Presidents Nixon, Ford, and Reagan. Only in 1978—with President Carter opposed—did the air force seemingly give up on the B-1. But a few short years later, in 1981, President Reagan resuscitated the B-1 after a short rest period and, with the same cast of supporters and a less dubious Congress, it resumed its course toward ultimate production. Even when seeming death (which proved to be temporary) came to the B-1, many in Congress (though not a majority again until 1981) remained loyal. Most important, the money did not vanish from the air force budget but was transferred to other projects such as the cruise missile. After 1981, production of 100 B-1s by 1988 was agreed on.

Three glimpses of decision making on the B-1 follow. In the first situation, in 1973–74, the supporters were basically in control and had the president on their side. In the second situation, in 1977 and 1978, the president chose to intervene in this structural matter by stressing its strategic aspects and claiming more presidential prerogatives. In the third situation, Ronald Reagan led a newly invigorated B-1 alliance in restoring the enterprise. The prime contractor, Rockwell International, began to push for purchases beyond the designated 100.

1973–1974.   In 1973 the air force requested an authorization of $473.5 million for the B-1 in order to continue funding the development of prototypes. The House Armed Services Committee recommended the entire amount, and an attempt on the floor to delete it was defeated easily by a vote of 96 to 313. The Senate Armed Services Committee recommended a reduction of $100 million, which was sustained on the Senate floor. However, an amendment adding $5 million to finance a study of alternatives to the B-1 was rejected. The Senate was willing to practice some economy but not at the expense of jeopardizing the whole project. The conference committee was even less inclined to economize, and the B-1 finally emerged with only $25 million less than had been requested—with the added stipulation that the money could not be saved by firing employees of the contractor.

In 1974 the air force asked for $499 million for continued prototype development in fiscal 1975. The House Armed Services Committee again recommended the full authorization. The supportive stance of Chairman F. Edward Hébert was unquestioning: "No matter what it costs, if that's what we need, we've got to pay for it" (*Congressional Quarterly Weekly Report,* May 2, 1974, p. 562). On the House floor, an amendment to delete all money for the B-1 was defeated 94–309, virtually the same vote as in 1973. The Senate Armed Services Committee recommended a cut of $44 million from the air force B-1 request but in the report made it clear the cut was not to be interpreted as showing lack of committee support for the project. Rather the members simply wanted to reduce the number of prototypes from four to three. A floor amendment to cut another $225 million from the B-1 authorization was rejected 31 to 59. The conference committee adopted the Senate figure of $455 million. However, the air force really didn't lose anything, as the remaining $44 million could be obtained by reprogramming as soon as the first prototype had been successfully flight tested. Congress gave the appearance of deferring slightly to the economizers and critics of the B-1, but in reality the support for the air force was almost total. The defense appropriations bill contained virtually full funding for the B-1 ($445 million of the $455 million authorized).

Rockwell took pains in its lobbying of members of Congress to emphasize the public works nature of the B-1. During a period of rising unemployment, Rockwell argued persuasively for the value of contracts and jobs, both nationally and in the individual states and districts containing subcontractors.

1977–1978.   One of President Ford's last acts (after his defeat in November 1976) was to order initial production of the B-1, even though incoming President Carter had already expressed opposition to the plane. Congress had stipulated that full-scale production would have to await the new president's review.

In his early months in office, Carter was subjected to the arguments of both supporters and opponents. By mid-1977 he had become firmly convinced the money would be better spent on a cruise missile, and he made his position public. He moved to rescind the $462 million appropriated in fiscal 1977 for building the first two planes. The Senate, which had been increasingly skeptical of the plane for several years, went along with the president. However, in December 1977 the House refused to accept the rescission by a vote of 191 to 166.

For the next several months after this vote, the administration orchestrated a concentrated campaign against the B-1. Gradually the administration won over the air force and then key prodefense establishment figures in Congress, especially on the Defense Appropriations Subcommittee and on the Armed Services Committee. The basic method of winning these key people was to stress that the defense subgovernment (air force branch) would not lose these resources but they would merely be shifted to other air force projects such as the cruise missile. Procedurally, the rescission was attached to an omnibus $7.8 billion supplemental appropriations bill that contained funding for an assortment of enterprises important to many House members. When the House voted on the rescission again in late February, it upheld the president by a vote of 234 to 182. However, supporters (except, perhaps, for the contractors themselves) had lost little. They had simply bowed to technological inevitability (the increasing obsolescence of the B-1) that had been seized on by the president and his supporters. He had been more than willing to pay the price of not removing the resources from the air force subgovernment sphere of influence.

The Reagan Years.   After Ronald Reagan became president in 1981 Congress rather quickly succumbed to his blandishments—with strong support from the air force and Rockwell International and its subcontractors—to put the B-1 into production. Death had been an illusion. Congress agreed to fund 100 planes, the last of which would be delivered in 1988. They would cost close to $30 billion (a late 1985 estimate).

Critics continued to claim the B-1 was obsolete before it was produced. They favored moving immediately to the Stealth bomber, designed and to be produced by Northrop. Leading congressional supporters of both companies—determined largely by location of company payrolls—sniped at each other. The administration and air force wanted both planes in sequence.

Rockwell and its allies by 1985 were planning a campaign to urge continued production of the B-1 beyond the initial limit of 100 (*The Wall Street Journal*, December 18, 1985). This is a customary ploy in the world of defense procurement (see the next section on the F-111 and the A-7D for successful cases of life support for weapons that no longer threatened a potential enemy much, but the loss of which threatened the economic and political interests of its supporters). As a prelude to its 1985–86 efforts Rockwell's Political Action Committee had given close to $350,000 to political campaigns in 1983–84. Rockwell had also spread its subcontracts around so many members of Congress had constituents with a tangible stake in the production of the aircraft. The fifth edition of this book will have to report on the outcome of the campaign for continued life for the B-1, but as of early 1986 no one was betting against Rockwell, whose lobbying skills for the B-1 had been honed through almost two decades of practice.

The F-111 and the A-7D.   The cases of the F-111 and the A-7D aircraft over recent years reinforce the point that subgovernment support for the procurement of a given weapons system does not die easily, even when the system in question has been purchased in sufficient quantities or becomes outmoded. In both 1973 and 1974 Congress added money to the defense appropriations bill for continued procurement of the F-111 (the controversial TFX of the 1960s) and the A-7D (an air force fighter plane), even though the Defense Department had not requested money for those planes.

The impetus behind congressional generosity to insert the unrequested money ($250 million in 1973 and $320 million in 1974) came from the Texas delegation. Their motivation was uncomplicated: both planes are manufactured in Texas, and the extra money would nearly all be spent in Texas. The Texans were aided by F-111 supporters in Congress who argued that as the only bomber being made until mass production of the B-1 began, the F-111 should not be allowed to go out of production.

The tenacity of the subgovernment was successful two years in a row and its work went largely unnoticed, except by one observer who labeled interaction between Congress and the Pentagon a "charade" (Getler,

1974). "The Pentagon . . . knows that the urge of the Texans in Congress to keep production going is so strong that if the Pentagon does not put the plans in its budget and allows production to slow or stop, then the Texans in Congress will put the money in. That is basically what has happened for the past two years."

President Ford, supported by the full House and Senate, put a partial and at least temporary stop to the charade in 1975 by requesting a rescission of appropriations that included funds for continued procurement of 12 F-111s. The House and Senate appropriations committees (the chairman of the House Appropriations Committee was a Texan), true to their air force allies and the supporters of the Texas contracts, rejected this part of the president's request. But the full House and Senate overrode the committees' decision and amended the rescission bill to disallow the F-111s.

The subgovernment supporters of both planes (and the contractors) showed their resilience and inventiveness by continuing to procure revised versions of both aircraft during the first few years of the Carter administration. The A-7D was produced as a trainer. The F-111 was altered into the FB-11H, a strategic bomber. The EF-111A, a plane loaded with electronic jamming equipment, was another version of the F-111.

Another reading on the status of the A-7 in 1981 captures the resiliency of this sort of pork-barrel procurement in the headline "Opponents Find Vought Corporation's A-7 Impossible to Shoot Down" (Wilson, 1981). The core of the pro-A-7 lobby was identified as the national guard, which uses the plane; Vought, the company that produces it; and the congressional delegation from Texas, where it is produced. President Reagan agreed with President Carter that the plane should not continue to be produced. But by mid-1981 the air force was able to confirm that a limited number of A-7s would continue to be produced as the A-7K, to be used for both "combat operations" and "transition training." Even Ronald Reagan could not shoot down this flying anachronism.

Reserve Forces

Since World War II the subgovernment surrounding the size, status, and prerequisites of the reserve military forces has operated in classic distributive fashion (Levantrosser, 1967). A close liaison has been forged between the chief interest group (the Reserve Officers Association), the armed services committees, other members of Congress who are either members of or have an interest in the reserves, and members of the executive branch—especially regular officers in the three military services. The concerns of this subgovernment have been to retain a large reserve force and give its members generous pay, retirement income, and other benefits. Both ends have been accomplished.

The Reserve Officers Association (ROA) is an interest group that functions directly as a policy maker. It initiates legislation in addition to monitoring legislation emerging from the executive branch or Congress. Its representatives participate directly in the "mark-up" sessions held by committees on bills pertaining to the reserve. It has a Legislative Advisory Committee made up of members of Congress who are reserve officers, and this committee both aids in the passage of favorable legislation and passes out awards to particularly important and supportive members of the House and Senate.

In the executive branch, the ROA actively builds allies in the services by seeking regular officers as associate members. The ROA also confers regularly with service officials following reserve legislation.

By the mid- and late-1980s the fortunes of the reserve forces were in fine shape. The proportion of all U.S. military strength in the reserves was growing. It stood at about one-third in 1985. Congress created a new post of assistant secretary of defense for reserve affairs in 1984, which provided a nice symbol of the strength of the reserve subgovernment. Members of Congress could claim they were motivated by concern for parsimony in putting more reliance on the reserves because reserve units are cheaper to maintain than regular units. Post-World War II history of the reserve subgovernment, however, suggests motivations of continuing mutual support were far more genuine.

Food for Peace

Since its passage in 1954, the history of the Food for Peace program (also known as Public Law 480) has been one of expansion in times of domestic crop surpluses and one of contraction when those surpluses have disappeared. P.L. 480 was designed as a means of disposing of surplus agricultural commodities abroad. The program has been used both for humanitarian purposes and for diplomatic and political purposes by the State Department and the administration. From the viewpoint of the subsidized producers of farm commodities in the United States, P.L. 480 represents a major subsidy in years of surplus.

The supportive subgovernment has been consistently successful in continuing and expanding the program. The major members of the subgovernment have been bureaucrats in the Foreign Agricultural Service of the Department of Agriculture, most members of the relevant subcommittees of the House and Senate agricultural committees, virtually all of the farmer interest groups, and the U.S. shipping interests, which get into the act by obtaining a guaranteed portion of the resulting shipping. Earl Butz, secretary of agriculture for Presidents Nixon and Ford, stated the viewpoint of the Department of Agriculture and the subsidized farmers succinctly when he referred to P.L. 480 as primarily a way of "getting rid of the stuff" ("stuff" refers to surplus food) (*National Journal*, November 23, 1974: 1761).

But the world of P.L. 480 is more complex than Secretary Butz's comment implies. P.L. 480 has both structural and strategic aspects, and a debate arose in late 1974 and 1975 over the purposes of the program. Commodity exports under the program were being increasingly used to reward political allies abroad (South Korea, South Vietnam, Pakistan) and to encourage desired behavior from other nations. Critics of the strategic uses of the program (who included Democratic Senator Hubert Humphrey of Minnesota, one of the original sponsors of the program) opposed what they viewed as the excessive use of food aid for political and diplomatic purposes. These critics combined a focus on humanitarianism with an implicit focus on stabilizing the subsidy aspects of the program at home— perhaps an unusual but certainly not an uncomfortable stance. Opponents of the revision (who included Secretary of State Henry Kissinger) were interested in more than just the U.S. image as a humanitarian nation and the stabilization of subsidies at home. They would have preferred to retain flexibility in the P.L. 480 program to use surplus commodities for diplomatic and political purposes.

P.L. 480 moved past its thirtieth birthday in 1984 healthier than ever. It continued to serve the twin purposes of buying agricultural surpluses and rewarding the foreign friends of the United States, such as South Korea, or at least trying to keep moderate governments in power in countries like Indonesia and Bangladesh. It seemed ill-suited to achieving these dual purposes simultaneously because of food-market fluctuations. The problems with the program seemed even more acute when judged by humanitarian standards of whether the surplus food actually reaches the poorest people in the aided countries in a timely fashion (Bird, 1978; Rothschild, 1977). But the subgovernment supporting P.L. 480 seemed to be in no danger of having its favored program altered in any major way. In fact, program spending grew in the Reagan administration.

STRATEGIC POLICY

In general, the congressional posture in dealing with strategic issues of foreign and defense policy has been either to support the administration's requests (as in the case of the strategic implications of defense procurement decisions about new weapons systems, including the B-1, discussed above) or to register a competing point of view in such a way as not to remove all administration flexibility. Congress usually gives either willing or at least grudging support to the administration's view of strategic matters. This does not mean that the congressional impact is missing, however.

Soviet Trade

In 1973 and 1974 the expansion of U.S. trade with the Soviet Union was a high priority on the executive branch's agenda—including the personal agendas of President Nixon, President Ford, and Secretary of State Kissinger. Leading figures in Congress, however, especially presidential aspirant Senator Henry Jackson, a Democrat from Washington, took the view that the United States should refrain from expanding trade until the Soviet Union altered its internal emigration policies to allow Jews to leave freely. The administration opposed linking trade and emigration, and a twenty-month deadlock ensued. In October of 1974 a compromise was reached that allowed passage of the administration's trade bill in the last days of the congressional session. Both the secretary of state and the president were personally involved in the negotiations with Jackson and other members of Congress in reaching the compromise.

The compromise was complex, but it illustrates both the eagerness of Congress to have an impact on this strategic issue and the unwillingness of Congress to bind the executive too tightly. The trade bill denied most-favored-nation trade status to countries that did not permit free emigration. But the restriction was not iron-clad. For eighteen months following enactment, the bill also allowed the president to request a waiver of the restriction if he received assurances from the country in question that its policies were leading to substantially free emigration, and if he informed Congress of those assurances. At the end of the eighteen months, the waiver right could be renewed for a year at a time by the president with the approval of Congress. The waiver procedure was embodied in an amendment offered by Senator Jackson and adopted on the Senate floor eighty-eight to zero. Kissinger and Jackson exchanged letters outlining the conditions that the Soviet Union would have to meet in order to qualify for the waiver provision.

The president did not request a waiver, and the congressional imposition of the Jackson amendment seemed, at least to the State Department, to inhibit the expansion of the Soviet-U.S. trade, although it had resulted in no reductions. The Soviet Union publicly took the position that its emigration policies were reasonable and were not the proper concern of the United States anyway, and it would certainly not give the kinds of assurances required by the legislation. The State Department and the Treasury Department—which has special responsibility for negotiating trade expansion—were reconciled to living with the Jackson amendment until after Jackson had completed his bid for the 1976 Democratic presidential nomination. Jewish voters in the United States were presumably impressed by Jackson's efforts on behalf of Soviet Jews, and few members of either party in either house were willing to risk appearing to be anti-Jewish by working actively for a modification or elimination of the Jackson amendment.

At about the same time that the Jackson amendment was being adopted, Congress extended the Export-Import Bank bill for four more years (this organization helps U.S. businesses sell their products overseas and finances U.S. export sales). The bill contained restrictions on the bank's activities in general and especially limited its activities in the Soviet Union. These limits seem to have been generated more by a desire to improve congressional oversight of the bank's activities than by specific complaints about Soviet behavior.

In this bill, however, Congress again shrank from reducing executive flexibility in a strategic field. The bill set a ceiling on the amount of credit to be extended to the Soviets, with a subceiling set on the amount to be used for energy research and development (apparently Congress hoped a restrictive ceiling would encourage energy development at home). However, the ceiling limits could be raised by the president if he found that an increase would be in the national interest and if both houses approved his request.

While thus allowing the president flexibility in regard to Soviet trade, the impact of the bank bill overall (which severely limits the amount of funds available to the bank) was to give Congress more opportunity to become involved in the bank's investment decisions before those decisions become policy commitments.

Troop Cuts

In recent years Congress has expressed considerable concern, for a variety of reasons, about the proportion and numbers of U.S. troops stationed overseas.

One of the leading critics of a large American military contingent in Europe was Senator Mike Mansfield, the Democratic floor leader until his retirement from Congress in 1976. Arguments for overseas troop reductions have focused on balance-of-payments problems, on the responsibility of allies for their own defense, and on the dangers of incidents that might lead to warfare. Despite efforts to reduce troops and to specify the locations of those reductions, Congress has ultimately contented itself with specifying overall troop levels (usually representing at most only modest cuts from existing levels) and has not specified location decisions. Congress has continued to leave the principal strategic decisions in the hands of the executive branch. Specific examples from the 1970s and 1980s support this general point.

In 1974 the defense appropriations bill contained a provision requiring a total troop withdrawal of 12,500 from overseas locations by May 31, 1975 (about eight months after the passage of the bill). This reduced the total authorized U.S. troop strength abroad to 452,000. (By early 1975 about 300,000 were in Europe, 125,000 were in East Asia—principally South Korea, Japan, the Philippines, and Thailand—and 27,000 were in a variety of other locations.) The decisions on locations for the 12,500 pull-back were left in the hands of the executive branch.

In reaching the decision to include a 12,500 mandated overseas troop cutback, the conference committee reconciled the Senate bill, which required a cut of 25,000, and a House bill that had specified no cut. The Senate Appropriations Committee indicated it would have preferred to mandate the cuts specifically in Europe. But the secretary of defense and his staff had worked very hard to convince the conference committee that such action was unwise.

The troop reduction issue had also been debated during the consideration of the 1974 authorization bill for procurement and research and development funds for the Defense Department. In the House, the majority leader, Thomas P. O'Neill, a Massachusetts Democrat, proposed an amendment reducing overseas troops by 100,000 by the end of 1975. This amendment was defeated 163 to 240. The House Armed Services Committee had recommended against unilateral troop withdrawal from Europe.

During Senate consideration of the defense procurement bill a large troop reduction (125,000) was defeated by a vote of fifty-four to thirty-five. The vote came on an amendment offered by Mansfield and was defeated in part because of the strenuous activities of high-ranking administration officials, including both Secretary of State Kissinger and Secretary of Defense James Schlesinger. The Senate barely defeated a second proposal—also made by Mansfield—to set the level of pullback at 76,000. The vote on this was forty-four to forty-six.

The one provision dealing with overseas troop strength in the defense procurement bill adopted in 1974 required a reduction of 18,000 support troops specifically from Europe—but at the same time allowed the secretary of defense to replace them with combat troops and gave him until June 30, 1976, to accomplish the reduction (6,000 would have to be removed by June 30, 1975). The Senate bill had set the reduction at about 23,000, but the conference committee reduced the figure. Again the twin urges of Congress are apparent: the desire to have an impact on a strategic issue and the desire not to bind the executive branch too tightly.

In 1977 and 1978 some members of the Congress exhibited an opposite concern when President Carter announced a phased withdrawal of U.S. ground troops from South Korea (scheduled to be completed by 1982). The opponents of this move did not generate any concrete activity, however (in part, because the joint chiefs of staff had been successful in getting the president to accept some conditions surrounding the withdrawal: withdrawal in a manner that would not "destabilize" the military situation between North and South Korea, a public renewal of American obligations under a mutual security treaty with South Korea, and a statement to the effect that the United States intended to remain a military power in the Pacific area). Thus, the congressional reaction was essentially symbolic.

In 1977 language was added to the bill authorizing funds for the State Department declaring that U.S. policy toward South Korea should "continue to be arrived at by joint decision of the President and Congress" and that implementation of the phased troop withdrawal plan should be "carried out in regular consultation with Congress." In 1978 the military aid appropriations bill contained a provision that it was the sense of Congress that additional withdrawal of U.S. troops from South Korea might upset the military balance in the region and that such moves require full consultation with Congress. But these provisions put no effective limits on the administration's power in this strategic area. Rather, they simply served notice on the president that Congress was watching this area carefully and might become troublesome if members did not receive appropriate stroking.

More important, in votes on concrete matters Congress supported the president. By a vote of almost two to one, the House rejected an amendment to the defense authorization bill that would have barred a reduction in U.S. troops in South Korea to a level lower than 26,000. The military aid bill contained provision allowing the president to give weapons of U.S. units in Korea to the Koreans as the U.S. units departed (about $800 million worth of weapons were covered).

In 1982, even under a very different kind of president and with an ideologically conservative Congress, the congressional interest in limiting the number of troops stationed abroad (and/or forcing foreign nations to increase their own defense efforts or perhaps their money contributions to maintaining our overseas garrisons) was once again made evident. But at the same time Congress made it clear it would not tie the hands of the president. Two specific issues were debated and finally resolved in this typical schizophrenic fashion by Congress in 1982. In both cases congressional anxieties and preferences were evident; in neither case was action taken that, ultimately, would force the president or Defense Department to do anything against their own best judgment.

The first issue focused on U.S. troop levels in Europe, a familiar topic in Congress over the years. The conferees on the appropriations bill (a continuing resolution in form, but like a new bill in content) agreed to limit the number of U.S. military people in Europe to 315,600 (a cut, *but* they also provided that the president could waive the limit if he found and stated that "overriding national security requirements" necessitated expansion or retention beyond the limit.

The second issue had to do with a tiny amount of money ($35 million) and the attempt to disband one specific brigade of one specific cavalry division stationed in West Germany. The provision in the bill agreed to by the conferees and signed by the president deleted the money, which represented the operating funds for the brigade (which had about 4,000 troops in it). But once again Congress was deferential. The bill gave the Defense

Department several months (until March 30, 1983) to decide whether to save the $35 million by disbanding the brigade *or* by making the cuts elsewhere if it judged the brigade to be "essential." And, of course, finding $35 million in a budget the size of the U.S. Army's was hardly an onerous task, if that was the final military judgment.

Turkish Aid

Two hostile ethnic communities (Greeks and Turks) occupy the island of Cyprus, and Turkey and Greece have long disputed which country has rightful claim to the island. In July 1974 Turkey invaded the island, using weapons supplied through the U.S. military assistance program. This violated provisions of U.S. statutes prohibiting the use of weapons for other than defensive purposes.

During the autumn of 1974 Congress engaged in a running battle with the administration over what response the United States should make to this action. The level of final decision was the full floor of the House and Senate rather than in a quiet bureau-subcommittee setting. As was true in the case of Soviet trade restrictions, Congress also got involved in part because of the presence of a group of American voters—those of Greek extraction—who were vocal in demanding anti-Turkish action. There was no competing set of American voters of Turkish extraction. Despite the fervent protests of the president, secretary of state, and other high-ranking executive branch officials, Congress made the strategic policy decision that a cutoff of military aid to Turkey (presumably coupled with U.S. mediation of the Greek-Turkish dispute over Cyprus) would be a better means of forcing a solution to the military situation on Cyprus than quiet diplomatic moves alone. But as in the Soviet trade and troop cut decisions, there was enough self-doubt in Congress about this strategic decision that it still allowed the administration some flexibility by giving it the option to postpone the cutoff date.

The parliamentary maneuvering over Turkish aid from mid-September through mid-December 1974 was elaborate and intricate. Each house took numerous roll call votes on the issue and always took an anti-Turk, antiadministration position. The entire story of the maneuvering throughout the autumn need not be told here, but the kinds of compromises that were reached are interesting and show the reluctance of Congress to be overly rigid on strategic issues when caught between the crosspressures of voters, moral principle, and forceful arguments from the president and secretary of state that the national interest and national security demand a minimum of overt restriction on a valued and important ally.

The first restriction voted by Congress and accepted unhappily by the administration was contained in a temporary law—an appropriations continuing resolution—signed in mid-October. The key congressional concession was to delay the aid cutoff until December 10, thus giving Ford and Kissinger time to put diplomatic pressure on the Turks so the cutoff would be moot. The final Ford agreement to the compromise came in a telephone call to the House minority leader. The language of the bill allowed the president to delay imposing the ban as long as Turkey observed the cease-fire on the island and did not add either troops or U.S. weapons to its forces on Cyprus.

The same kind of debate resumed when Congress reconvened after the 1974 elections for a "lame duck" session. Proponents of an aid cutoff sought to add mandatory language to the foreign aid and military assistance authorization bill, thus making the cutoff part of permanent law rather than just a continuing resolution. Both houses voted for the cutoff. The House insisted on making the cutoff take effect December 10. However, the Senate passed a provision allowing the president to suspend the cutoff until February 14, 1975, in the interest of giving the president and Kissinger more latitude to continue quiet work with the Turks and Greeks. The conferees chose February 5, and both houses approved. The new law provided that, if the cutoff took place on February 5, it could be lifted if the administration could certify that "substantial progress" was being made toward a solution to the Cyprus problem.

As February 5 approached, Kissinger met with four Democratic leaders of the pro-cutoff forces. He asked them to arrange another extension of the deadline in the interests of national security and to avoid jeopardizing American bases in Turkey and the Turkish-American alliance, but he indicated he could not certify substantial progress in the Cypress negotiations. The senator and three representatives present refused and indicated the cutoff would have to take effect on schedule. They also indicated, however, their support for a speedy resumption of aid once the certification of substantial progress could be made.

When the cutoff of military aid to Turkey went into effect on February 5, 1975, the administration continued to press for a lifting of the ban. In the next three months an impressive coalition was built in the Senate that included the majority leader, the minority leader, the minority whip, the chairmen and ranking minority members of the Foreign Relations Committee and the Armed Services Committee. These individuals cosponsored a bill allowing resumption of aid but retaining an active oversight role for Congress, which the Senate narrowly passed, 41 to 40. The House narrowly (223 to 206) upheld the ban in late July 1975, however, and the Turkish government retaliated by ordering American bases closed.

In October 1975 Congress agreed to a partial lifting of the arms embargo in order to give the president latitude in negotiations to prevent the Turks from making the base closings permanent. Reporting requirements preserved an important congressional role in monitoring U.S. relations with both Greece and Turkey. The permitted sales were to be related to North Atlantic Treaty Organization (NATO) defenses.

In his 1976 campaign, Jimmy Carter supported the partial arms embargo, but as president in 1978 he took the position that the partial embargo should be lifted because it was threatening Turkey's continued membership in NATO and because Turkey was talking of making the U.S. base closings permanent (Maxfield, 1978a, 1978b, 1978c, 1978d, 1978e). Turkey had not, however, changed its position on Cyprus and remained in control of about 40 percent of the island. In early June 1978 the president labeled his request for repeal his top foreign policy priority. The president personally lobbied members of the House and Senate and was aided by such other high-ranking officials as NATO commander General Alexander Haig, Secretary of State Cyrus Vance, and Secretary of Defense Harold Brown.

The denouement of the 1978 debate took place along lines familiar to strategic issues: decisions in congressional committees had no finality. Final decisions were made on the floors of the House and Senate after heated debates. Those decisions required compromises that left Congress with the illusion of being important in continued decision making on the subject, and the president got the essence of what he wanted.

In the Senate the Foreign Relations Committee voted against ending the embargo eight to four. When the issue came to the Senate floor it was clear that some compromise language to accompany the repeal would be needed. The majority leader and others offered such language, which provided that when the president requested any funds for Turkey, Greece, or Cyprus, he must simultaneously certify that U.S. goals for resolving the conflict over Cyprus were being achieved. The language also noted disapproval of continuing Turkish military presence on Cyprus. The president was required to report to Congress every sixty days on progress toward a solution to the Cyprus question.

The House had always presented a tougher pro-embargo stance than the Senate. The International Relations Committee voted narrowly (eighteen to seventeen) to end the embargo but only because two pro-embargo members did not vote.

On the House floor the pro-embargo forces would have won had not an even more "pro-Congress" compromise than the one the Senate had forged been found. Even it passed only 208 to 205. This compromise, drafted by the majority leader (working with the White House), did not formally repeal the embargo but allowed it to be put aside by the president if he certified to Congress that resumption of aid was in the "national interest of the United States and in the interest of NATO." He also had to certify to Congress that Turkey was "acting in good faith" in settling a number of the Cyprus-related issues on a permanent basis. Like the Senate, the House required the president to report every sixty days.

The conference committee took the harder House line in framing the final bill—calling it a "de facto repeal" rather than an outright repeal. This was done to avoid another bruising battle on the House floor.

By 1981 the issue had receded so far that the conferees on a foreign aid bill simply dropped a House amendment that required the president to take into account whether Greece, Turkey, and Cyprus were working toward a peaceful settlement in Cyprus before supplying aid to them. Even this mild reminder of the stresses of the past—now lumping both Greece and Turkey with Cyprus—proved to be more meddling in a strategic matter than Congress ultimately wanted to undertake. In 1982 the president requested a large military aid appropriation for Turkey—$465 million. He got "only" $400 million, but he also got no policy language at all.

In retrospect, the importance of the Greek-American community in generating congressional interest in a cutoff and in sustaining such a cutoff despite strong appeals from the president and Kissinger in 1974–76 should be stressed (*Washington Post,* October 25, 1974). This had never been a politically active community before, and yet on this issue an impressive organization was put together to lobby members of the House and Senate. There were also several members of the House and Senate willing to take the lead in pressing the issue, including several members of Greek extraction. Of course, the issue was more complex than simple ethnicity, but the strength of the Greek-American lobby was important in sustaining congressional interest in an aid cutoff. The strength of that lobby continued to be apparent in Congress into the mid-1980s as Congress insisted on maintaining a seven to ten ratio between Greece and Turkey in military aid to the two countries. The Turks were displeased with this. They remained the third-largest recipient of American military aid in the world, behind Israel and Egypt, but they believed they were getting well below what they needed and deserved.

Foreign Economic Policy

A careful study of the making of foreign economic policy from 1929 through 1976 (Pastor, 1980) reaches a number of important conclusions. It finds, for example, that interest groups have a limited role in this strategic area. This accords with our general expectations about the strategic-policy arena. It also finds that both the executive branch and the Congress have reasonably well-established corporate views of issues in areas such as trade policy, foreign aid policy, and investment policy. Sometimes these views clash, sometimes they are not far apart. In all cases final outcomes are forthcoming through bargaining and compromise. These findings are generally in accord with our earlier articulated expectations about political relationships in the strategic area.

Another finding is that the internal divisions in executive branch views of these various matters seem to be relatively few and of low intensity. Again, this is in rough consonance with our view that disaggregated bureaus have only a modest influence and the more centralized parts of the executive branch, including the president, have more influence. This study suggests, however, there is something like a "natural" tendency on the part of the various pieces of the executive to see the world the same way (Pastor, 1980: 345):

> The foreign economic policies analyzed in this study were the product of a continuous, interactive process involving both the legislative and executive branches. While coalitions were sometimes organized between bureaus and committees, the rule in many of the policies analyzed was that Congress and the Executive approached issues as coherent, unitary organizations with decided preferences and predispositions in each issue. Whether these preferences were molded into a single policy depended to a great extent on the degree of trust and responsiveness which flowed in both directions between the branches.

The study also identifies a number of specific instances in which interest groups and classic bureau-subcommittee alliances sprang up and hived off some aspect of foreign economic policy to treat as structural. Thus, those both in Congress and the executive branch pushing for broad policy sought to keep issues defined as strategic. Those trying to pursue narrower domestic interests continually tried to redefine pieces of the total turf into the domain of structural policy. Congress could withstand these parochial pressures better when the president and executive branch were providing considerable pressure for keeping the definition strategic rather than letting it slip—either by inattention or inadvertence (rarely, preference)— into the structural realm. The detailed instances offered in this study— much too lengthy and detailed to summarize here—support the general view of the differences between strategic and structural policy that we have offered.

On the substance of policy, it is fair to say both that the executive tends to prevail when there is conflict and that, through the compromises necessary to reduce or resolve conflict, congressional impact on the "big picture" of policy is also sizable, even if not controlling. Congress made a difference in the substance of many policies, although the executive branch thrust was strong and relatively consistent through time. When interest groups appeared in force, got access, and were taken seriously, usually a subissue got redefined as structural. The essence of the issue that remained defined (perceived) as strategic, however, continued to get defined in the process of negotiation between Congress and the executive branch, with the latter getting a fair proportion—but not all—of its preferences.

Aid to Nicaraguan Contras

In dealing with administration policy toward Nicaragua between 1981 and the end of 1985, Congress has been a major and strong-willed partner; questioning, restricting, and at times denying administration requests. Only in the last half of 1985 did Congress begin to relax some of the restraints placed on U.S. policy toward Nicaragua.

Throughout the Reagan presidency, congressional-presidential disagreement in this strategic area has arisen over recurring issues: the use of the Central Intelligence Agency (CIA) in dispensing aid; the role of the U.S. government in efforts to destabilize and overthrow another government; the reliance on military rather than diplomatic solutions to achieve policy aims; and the possibility of the United States becoming embroiled in another Vietnam-like war.

Reagan came to office in 1981 enunciating a hard-line, anti-Communist policy for Central America, and he consistently espoused that position during his tenure. Although initially seeking the limited aim of suppressing the flow of arms from Nicaragua to El Salvador's leftist guerrillas, Reagan's aims and rhetoric quickly expanded to a denunciation of Nicaragua as the source of political instability for the entire region. He authorized covert CIA actions to overthrow the Sandinista government of Daniel Ortega.

In 1982 the Boland amendment (named for Democratic Congressman Edward P. Boland of Massachusetts, a consistent critic of administration policy in Nicaragua) was added to the 1983 continuing appropriations bill. The amendment prohibited the CIA and the Defense Department from participating in activities designed to overthrow the Nicaraguan government. However, Congress did not reduce or eliminate aid for the contras.

In 1983 Congress gave only half the amount of aid sought by the president but did not include restrictions on the CIA. The House had initially refused to go along with any aid.

In 1984 the administration's policy suffered a major setback due to publicity about the role of the CIA in mining Nicaraguan harbors. The action had been undertaken without consultation with the congressional intelligence committees, and Congress passed a cutoff of all aid, although it expressly included a provision allowing the president to seek funding again in 1985.

In 1985 the battle continued as the president again asked for aid for the contras. Facing stiff opposition in both houses, the president compromised, asking for "humanitarian" aid rather than military aid. The House continued to resist, voting twice in April against the president, but in June the House voted for the aid. The House shift was a negative reaction to

Daniel Ortega's visit to Moscow in the spring to seek funds from the Soviets; it also reflected fears that Congress would be perceived as lacking the will to fight Communism in Central America. The Reagan administration also compromised on two important political issues to gain the victory—by restricting the funds to nonmilitary, "humanitarian," purposes and by agreeing to prohibit the CIA from dispensing the aid, an issue on which the House refused to compromise.

At nearly the same time as the vote on the supplemental appropriation, Congress passed a foreign aid authorization bill (P.L. 99–83), the first since 1981. That bill also prohibited CIA and DOD involvement in distributing aid to contras, but it authorized $27 million in funding for humanitarian aid for fiscal years 1986 and 1987.

A second breakthrough for the president occurred with passage of an intelligence authorization bill (P.L. 99–169) late in 1985. That bill permits the CIA to provide advice and information to contras and also broadens the definition of "humanitarian" material to include such quasi-military items as trucks and radios.

The pull and tug between Congress and the president continued in 1986 with Reagan asking for $100 million in military aid for the Nicaraguan contras. The House in March narrowly rejected the request, 222 to 210, but included a provision for a subsequent vote later in the spring. Few people in or out of Congress in the spring of 1986 regarded the issue of American aid as settled conclusively. Public perceptions about the depth of the Communist threat in Nicaragua will affect how Congress votes. The persistence of the president in the long run will both set the agenda and will produce at least part of what he wants in this strategic policy area.

CRISIS POLICY

The typical pattern in crisis decision situations is one congressional legitimation of presidential action after it has occurred. Occasionally, the congressional reaction is not positive. When President Johnson decided in 1965 to send U.S. marines to the Dominican Republic, allegedly to prevent a Communist takeover (Evans and Novak, 1966, chapter 23), he had not engaged in even symbolic consultation with any members of Congress, but instead simply told some of the leaders an hour after the landing was ordered that the decision had been made. No formal congressional legitimating action was either requested or received. The event marked the public defection of the chairman of the Senate Foreign Relations Committee, William Fulbright (also a Democrat), from the president's foreign policy in general—both in the Dominican Republic and then in Vietnam.

There is also the possibility that congressional leaders will be consulted before action is taken in a crisis situation. When consulted they may take a variety of positions—either with or without effect. Two incidents, briefly described here, illustrate different kinds of response when Congress is consulted before presidential action. In the first case, involving a decision about Vietnam in 1954, the congressional response to the administration proposal was critical and negative in the sense of wanting no action rather than the proposed action; the administration finally bowed to the congressional view (although other factors intervened too). In the second case, involving the U.S. response in Cuba in 1962, congressional response was also critical and negative, this time in the sense of wanting more action than that proposed by the administration. But in this instance the president remained firm and proceeded with his initial decision.

In an effort to prevent a repetition of U.S. involvement in a foreign war because of executive action without formal congressional consent, as in Vietnam, Congress in 1973 passed the War Powers Act, which required the president to consult with Congress when making decisions involving the commitment of U.S. forces abroad. The act was envisioned by its supporters as a tool for ensuring congressional participation in crisis decisions involving armed forces before they became policy commitments. The last two examples in this section both involve (or could have involved) the War Powers Act.

Vietnam, 1954

In 1954 the administration pondered becoming involved militarily in Southeast Asia in support of what proved to be the losing French effort to keep Indochina French and non-Communist (Roberts, 1973). In April of that year the secretary of state, John Foster Dulles, called a meeting attended by five senators and three representatives—leaders from both parties in both houses—and a few Defense Department officials, including the chairman of the joint chiefs of staff, Admiral Arthur Radford. Dulles proposed at this meeting that Congress pass a resolution giving the president the authority to use American sea and air power to support the French in Indochina. The members of Congress who had been summoned questioned Dulles and Radford searchingly. Two key points were established: first, that the other members of the joint chiefs of staff did not agree with Radford that military action was essential and, second, that the United States had not consulted any allies about their support for the move. As events spun out, the United States could not generate support—especially critical support from Great Britain—and Dien Bien Phu (the French stronghold in Southeast Asia) fell before further action was taken.

The lesson of this episode should not be overstated. This was, after all, primarily a crisis for the French, and it did not have to become a crisis for the United States unless we chose to define it so. Radford and Dulles tried unsuccessfully to establish such a definition, but the congressional leaders' resistance and hard questioning persuaded President Eisenhower to shrink from action until Dien Bien Phu had fallen, at which time action became moot. Nevertheless, it shows that, when top administration officials consult congressional leaders, the questions and/or advice they receive may have considerable impact.

Cuban Missiles

On October 16, 1962, President Kennedy received undeniable proof that the Soviet Union had established offensive missile bases in Cuba. He and his closest advisers viewed this as a grave threat to American security and pondered their response for six days before deciding on a naval quarantine and a demand that existing bases be closed and the missiles be dismantled and returned to the Soviet Union. If the Soviets did not bow to these demands, the president was prepared to take direct military action against the bases. And, in his own private calculations, he figured the chances of a general nuclear war with the Soviet Union at between one in three and one in two. But he thought what was at stake demanded such a gamble, and his advisors agreed.

Until he had decided to make a public announcement concerning the U.S. reaction to the discovery of the missiles, President Kennedy's consultations had been limited to a group of fewer than twenty individuals from the highest levels of the executive branch (Kennedy, 1971: 8). Although some congressional critics had been claiming knowledge of the existence of Soviet missiles in Cuba for more than a month before the president was convinced of their presence and had been demanding strong action, the president did not consult with anyone from Capitol Hill until he had made his decision and was ready to announce it to the American people. Shortly before making the announcement, the president met with leaders of Congress to inform them of the course of action he was to take. Robert Kennedy described that meeting (Kennedy, 1971: 31–32):

> Many congressional leaders were sharp in their criticism. They felt that the President should take more forceful action, a military attack or invasion, and that the blockade was far too weak a response. Senator Richard B. Russell of Georgia said he could not live with himself if he did not say in the strongest possible terms how important it was that we act with greater strength than the President was contemplating.
>
> Senator J. William Fulbright of Arkansas also strongly advised military action rather than such a weak step as the blockade. Others said they were skeptical but would remain publicly silent, only because it was such a dangerous hour for the country.

The President, after listening to the frequently emotional criticism, explained that he would take whatever steps were necessary to protect the security of the United States, but that he did not feel greater military action was warranted initially. Because it was possible that the matter could be resolved without a devastating war, he had decided on the course he had outlined. Perhaps in the end, he said, direct military action would be necessary, but that course should not be followed lightly. In the meantime, he assured them, he had taken measures to prepare our military forces and place them in a position to move.

The *Mayaguez* Incident

After disillusionment with Vietnam policy had set in, many individuals in Congress were discontented with the minimal role of Congress in crisis situations involving the use of armed force. Even if that use began on a limited basis, it always posed the threat of expanding. Thus, in November 1973 Congress passed, over a presidential veto, the War Powers Act. This law provides that the president must report overseas commitments of American troops to combat within forty-eight hours. He must order the end of such combat after sixty days unless Congress has given specific approval for continuation, although he is given the power of extending the period for thirty more days if he determines American troops are in danger. The act also provides that the president should "in every instance possible . . . consult with Congress" before ordering actions that might risk military hostilities.

An early test, fortunately a limited one, of the impact of the War Powers Act on congressional involvement in a crisis situation occurred in May 1975. Forces of the new Communist government of Cambodia seized an American merchant ship, the *Mayaguez*, in waters claimed by the Cambodians but interpreted by the United States to be international waters. The president, as is typical in crisis situations, consulted with officials from the White House, State Department, and Defense Department and then informed a few leading members of Congress of his decision. The president opted for a limited use of force, although somewhat more force than that counseled by the Defense Department. He used Marines to seize the ship and rescue the crew from an island where they were being held. He also ordered bombing of selected Cambodian mainland targets as a preemptive measure to prevent retaliation.

However, the decision was made without the consultation suggested by the War Powers Act. As Senator Mansfield said, "I was not consulted. I was notifed after the fact about what the administration had already decided to do. . . . I did not give my approval or disapproval because the decision had already been made" (*Congressional Quarterly Weekly Report*, May 17, 1975: 1008.) The Republican floor leader in the Senate, Hugh Scott, agreed that he had not been consulted either.

He said he had merely been advised of the administration's intentions after they had already been decided. It was not until after the administration members had themselves decided on a course of action that any members of Congress were informed by White House congressional liaison officials.

The president, although not consulting, complied with the reporting requirements of the act by sending a letter to the full Congress explaining the provocation and the course of action. By the time the letter was received, the incident was over, and the *Mayaguez* and its crew had been rescued, although close to twenty American servicemen died in the process. Congressional reaction to the letter was moot because the hostilities had already ceased.

The reaction from Congress to the president's handling of the crisis was generally congratulatory. Except for some not-too-seriously voiced skepticism about having been "informed" rather than consulted, and despite a few skeptics who questioned whether negotiation had been explored sufficiently before force was used, the praise for the president was general from both parties and from members of all ideologies. There was a superfluous resolution of support from the Senate Foreign Relations Committee.

There is no agreement within Congress itself on what the War Powers Act of 1973 is supposed to do. On the one hand, critics of the act argue that if consultation with Congress were taken literally, executive flexibility to maneuver in a crisis would be seriously reduced. Supporters of the act argue that at a minimum it guarantees Congress the right to review executive decisions involving armed forces and to decide whether or not to continue them. Potentially, the Wars Powers Act gives to Congress a greater role in crisis decision making, but the *Mayaguez* incident does not reflect any change from the usual very limited role for Congress. The euphoria of having escaped a serious international incident was so great that serious reflection on the efficacy of the War Powers Act seems to have escaped attention.

After he left the presidency, Gerald Ford reflected on the use of the War Powers Act in his administration (Ford, 1977). He made it clear that the provisions really had very little impact on how he conducted himself in six specific incidents, including the *Mayaguez* case. The most accurate comment on the War Powers Act, given Ford's testimony and what else we know of the six cases he mentions, is that it remains an unclear and probably ineffective congressional attempt to control war-making powers. It is a symbol of congressional frustration in facing a world in which a genuine large-scale crisis could destroy much of the world's population in a matter of minutes or a few hours at most.

The Aborted Rescue of the Iranian Hostages

The seizure of more than fifty American hostages in the U.S. embassy in Teheran, Iran, in late 1979 set off a continuing crisis. The longer it lasted, the greater the number of U.S. actors who became involved in trying to figure out a way to free the hostages. Only the first few days or weeks possessed the classic attributes contained in the definition of a crisis. But presidential dominance of continuing aspects of the problem was again demonstrated forcefully in April 1980 when President Carter and those few people he chose to involve decided to rescue the hostages in a commando raid using helicopters. The raid failed even to reach Teheran, and eight would-be rescuers died. It was successful, however, in being carried out without any public knowledge beforehand. And it was also successful in driving another nail into the coffin of the War Powers Act. To put the same point another way, the lack of usage of the War Powers Act demonstrated again that the act contained rhetoric about the president reporting to Congress before using troops but that, under real world conditions as they perceived them, presidents probably had no intention of doing so.

The brief postraid debate over whether the War Powers Act applied and, therefore, whether it had been illegally ignored produced no definitive results. Both constitutional and legal opinion on the meaning of the act and its applicability or nonapplicability in this case were divided and inconclusive (Kaiser, 1980). The strongest analytic message from the incident, however, is clear: the president dominates in crisis situations; the War Powers Act is not likely to be operational in the real world.

CONCLUSIONS

In general the expected patterns of congressional-executive interaction can be observed in the illustrations chosen for this chapter. Subgovernments are very important in structural decisions, although when those decisions also have major strategic implications (as in the case of most major weapons systems), the scope of conflict is widened. Congress as a whole typically gets involved in strategic decisions, although the tendency to defer to the executive branch or at least to preserve considerable flexibility for the executive branch is very strong. Where Congress wants more clout it pushes, in effect, to redefine matters as structural. In crisis situations congressional participation tends to be only symbolic if it is present. The War Powers Act potentially claims more for Congress, but the *Mayaguez* case and the Iranian hostage case raise the question of whether anything has changed. There is serious doubt whether significant congressional involvement in any crisis situation is likely except for involvement in the form of endorsing presidential action. On the other hand, a president who is genuinely willing to consult congressional leaders before action is decided on and who is willing to listen to what they say may be swayed toward a different course of action than he would pursue if he had not asked or listened. Often, however, the press of events does not seem to allow time for consultation or the president involved is simply not disposed to consult.

The largest deviation from our expectations is the degree to which Congress gets involved in strategic decisions. This can be explained largely on two grounds. First, there is often a blurring between structural and strategic issues. The defense budget presents a number of structural decisions to Congress each year, but some of the decisions, particularly those on new weapons systems, are also strategic in impact. At the nadir of congressional willingness to challenge the executive branch on strategic matters, a period from roughly 1955 to 1965 (Ripley, 1983: 417–20), the tendency was for Congress to back off from any involvement. Since then Congress has been much more willing to get involved, even though strategic matters are at stake.

Second, if domestic political considerations are involved, then Congress is usually willing to render judgments on strategic issues that may vary from those coming from the executive branch and the services. This tendency was illustrated when Jewish voters and interest groups influenced the tie made between expanded U.S.–Soviet Union trade and Soviet emigration policy for Jews and when Greek-American voters and interest groups influenced the Turkish aid ban. It is also apparent—although not in terms of an identifiable potential voting bloc—in the case of troop cuts where balance-of-payments deficits, tied to the domestic economy, is one of the principal motivating factors behind the congressional drive to reduce the number of U.S. troops stationed abroad. But in all of these cases there was also congressional concern for allowing the executive branch, and particularly the president, flexibility in decision making.

Presidents wishing to have an impact on structural decisions can enhance their chances of success by stressing the strategic aspects of those decisions. When Congress wishes to intervene in strategic matters, it is most likely to oppose the president, at least in part, when it focuses on structural aspects or when there are domestic lobbies and groups of voters pushing in such a direction.

8

Congress, the Bureaucracy, and the Nature of American Public Policy

In general, American public policy can be characterized as slow to change, as more responsive to special interests than to general interests, as more responsive to the privileged in society than to the underprivileged, and as tending to be defined and treated as distributive when possible. The reasons for this situation are rooted in the importance of subgovernments in much of American policy making, the great premium placed on cooperation between Congress and the bureaucracy, the lack of meaningful congressional oversight on a continuing basis for many policies, and the greater strength of forces pushing for no change or minimal change in policy as opposed to the forces pushing for greater change.

When the United States is compared to Western European countries, it also becomes apparent that the relative weakness of central departmental (ministerial, in Europe) management in the United States and the enormous relative strength of disaggregated units (*bureaus* is the generic term) that goes with the central weakness both help to foster the situation we have portrayed. In addition, when the United States is compared to Western European nations, the lack of a strong, coherent left-wing (*social democratic* would be the most descriptive term) political party in the United States, coupled with the presence of a very strong right-wing party, helps to keep the already privileged protected and also helps to explain the American stress on distributive issues. Likewise, our party situation, when compared to that in European countries, helps explain they we define redistribution as running only in one direction (toward the disadvantaged) and, simultaneously, why we tend to view it as suspect or perhaps illegitimate much of the time.

Yet, given that the world is gray rather than black or white and that features of man-made institutions, processes, and policies are manipulable rather than inevitable, our examination of the congressional-bureaucratic relationship has also found some exceptions to the above generalizations. The facts of the policy-making system in operation support these generalizations more often than not, but at times counter-pressures develop that produce different results.

It is our aim in this final chapter to summarize the principal analytic themes we have developed in the preceding chapters in order to explain both the predominance of slow-changing, largely distributive policy catering mainly to special interests and the more privileged members of society and the exceptional conditions that produce some policies that do not fit the predominant mold. We also wish to underscore some normative concerns in the course of the discussion, although we do not pretend to have pat answers to the problems we see.

In the sections that follow we will first address in summary fashion the relative influence of various participants in different policy areas. Second, we will discuss the rewards of cooperation compared to the rewards of conflict in policy making. Third, we will offer some final thoughts on congressional oversight of bureaucratic policy performance. Fourth, we will summarize the relative strength of the forces pushing for stable policy and the forces pushing for changed policy.

PARTICIPANTS, INFLUENCE, AND ISSUES

The argument has been made in Chapters 4 through 7 that different relationships have varying degrees of importance in determining final policy statements, depending on the kind of issue at stake. That argument is summarized graphically in comparative terms in Figures 8–1 through 8–6. These figures portray the relationships between five clusters of actors in six policy areas. The five clusters of actors are the president and centralized bureaucracy (the president personally, his top advisors and cabinet appointees); the bureaus (symbolizing the bureaucracy in its decentralized state); Congress (as a whole); subcommittees (symbolizing Congress in its decentralized state); and the private sector (with actors including individuals, corporations, interest groups, and peak associations).

Figures 8–1 through 8–6, when coupled with the material in Tables 1–3 and 4–1, present an overview of the relative influence of all participants in the six different policy areas and also specify the changing role of the bureau-subcommittee-private sector subgovernments from area to area. The expectations we summarized in Table 4–1 were, in general, supported by the cases we examined. Thus, it would be accurate to say that ordinarily subgovernments dominate distributive and structural policy making. They play lesser roles in the other four policy areas but do not disappear except in crisis situations involving foreign and defense policy. They play a moderately important role in protective regulatory policy and are at least sporadically important in handling redistributive issues and strategic questions. Given that there is both a natural tendency for all domestic issues to

FIGURE 8–1
Relative Importance of Relationships for Determining Distributive Policy

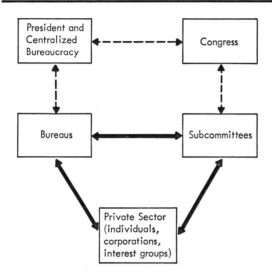

Key

= Very important relationship.

= Moderately important relationship.

= Relatively unimportant relationship.

Lack of an arrow indicates a relationship
that occurs only rarely.

be defined or redefined as distributive if possible and for strategic issues often to involve some structural aspects, this creates a very large role for subgovernments.

Some would argue that the dominance of subgovernments in much policy making is good and works in the public interest because genuine experts are placed in charge of issues. In addition, it is sometimes argued that the mechanisms for redressing excesses of subgovernment self-indulgence exist because access to various pressure points is open.

We would not entirely agree with this sanguine view, both because the incentives for using the mechanisms of redress are low most of the time and because the self-defense mechanisms possessed by most subgovernments are so strong. We would not argue that subgovernments can or

FIGURE 8-2
Relative Importance of Relationships for Determining Protective
Regulatory Policy

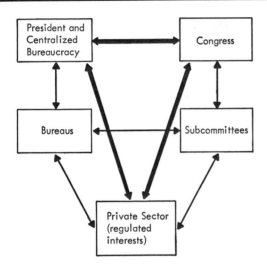

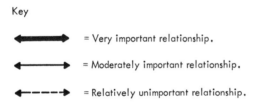

Key

◄██████►   = Very important relationship.

◄─────►   = Moderately important relationship.

◄───►   = Relatively unimportant relationship.

Lack of an arrow indicates a relationship
that occurs only rarely.

should be eliminated from the policy-making process in the United States. However, we think that better and more responsive public policy can result from broader oversight of subgovernment functioning and the involvement of "outsiders" in at least some subgovernment deliberations. At minimum, the policies of distributive subgovernments have implications for many sectors of the society and economy beyond the direct beneficiaries of the policies. Expanding the participants in subgovernment deliberations would help to spell out those impacts (such as sugar subsidies on the grocery store price of sugar, price supports on the cost of various foods, water resources subsidies on the environment). Such expansion

FIGURE 8-3
Relative Importance of Relationships for Determining Redistributive Policy

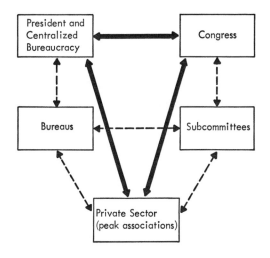

Key

= Very important relationship.

= Moderately important relationship.

= Relatively unimportant relationship.

Lack of an arrow indicates a relationship
that occurs only rarely.

might also help to relate the disaggregated policies of numerous dispersed subgovernments into a more coherent pattern. Bargaining, negotiation, and compromise are the hallmarks of the American decision-making system on public policy. Our preference is to open the bargaining and negotiation that occur within subgovernments more broadly than is often the case, particularly in the distributive and structural areas.

One general pattern we found that did not quite conform to our initial expectations in Table 4-1 was that Congress in general (not only at the subcommittee level) was a more important actor in all areas than the literature had led us to expect. In the protective regulatory area, for example, members of Congress get involved, not only in seeking weaker regulation for favored interests but also, in some cases, in seeking stiffer

FIGURE 8-4
Relative Importance of Relationships for Determining Structural Policy

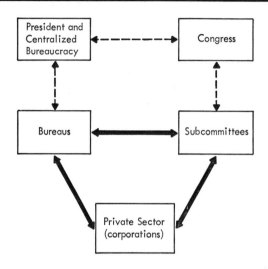

Key

= Very important relationship.

= Moderately important relationship.

= Relatively unimportant relationship.

Lack of an arrow indicates a relationship
that occurs only rarely.

regulation than that being favored by the relevant regulatory agencies or by the administration. In the redistributive area we found, as expected, that presidential initiation was often essential to action and that vigorous presidential support was virtually always essential to action. However, in several of the redistributive cases, we observed an important role for Congress in quiet negotiations. These quiet negotiations often took place directly within what might be called a redistributive subgovernment—individuals from relevant congressional committees and subcommittees, bureaus, and interest groups (often peak associations). This role for subgovernments is not nearly as frequent as in distributive policy, but it was often necessary at some critical juncture during a debate that might already have lasted for years.

FIGURE 8-5
Relative Importance of Relationships for Determining Strategic Policy

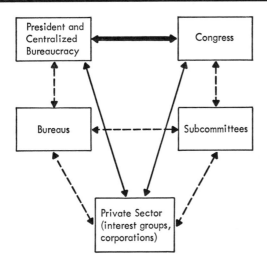

Key

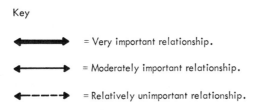

= Very important relationship.

= Moderately important relationship.

= Relatively unimportant relationship.

Lack of an arrow indicates a relationship
that occurs only rarely.

Congress played an unexpectedly large role in strategic decisions, both because there was a blurring of strategic and structural issues and because domestic political considerations often motivated congressional involvement. Even in crisis situations, it was suggested that individuals from Congress—senior leaders from the foreign policy and defense-oriented committees and the party leaders—might give relevant advice that could be important *if* the president chose to ask for the advice and chose to listen to it. Presidents often have neither the time nor the disposition to ask or listen, but the potential is there. The War Powers Act is at least a paper reminder from Congress that it would like to be consulted and a stronger reminder that it does not again wish to abdicate its power of declaring war as it did in Vietnam.

FIGURE 8-6
Relative Importance of Relationships for Determining Crisis Policy

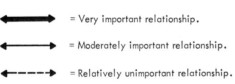

| President and Centralized Bureaucracy | ◄— — — — — —► | Congress |

| Bureaus | | Subcommittees |

| Private Sector |

Key

◄━━━━━━━► = Very important relationship.

◄━━━━━━━► = Moderately important relationship.

◄— — — —► = Relatively unimportant relationship.

Lack of an arrow indicates a relationship
that occurs only rarely.

Some analyses of the role of Congress in policy making proceed as if the source of the initiation of legislative ideas is all that matters and that somehow Congress and the executive branch are involved in a zero-sum game over initiation. The conclusion is usually drawn that because the executive initiates more than Congress, it has "won" the game, and the importance of Congress in policy making has declined. At least three things are wrong with this often-repeated formula. First, Congress can and does get involved in initiation on a broad range of issues (Chamberlain, 1946; Moe and Teel, 1970; and Orfield, 1975). For example, Congress was responsible for initiation in the following policy areas in recent years: medicare, social security disability insurance, pension reform, voting rights for eighteen-year-olds, political campaign reform, air pollution (including automobile pollution), reduction and cessation of the U.S. role in the Indochina war, chemical additives in foods, the creation of a consumer-protection agency, mandatory automobile safety standards, food programs for the poor, and increases in the minimum wage (Rich, 1975). Congress also initiated major investigations of the drug industry, multinational corporations, organized crime, and labor racketeering.

Second, and more important, Congress does much more than initiate. Even granting that the executive branch initiates a great deal on a piecemeal basis and that the president is probably the only possible source for a genuinely comprehensive and integrated legislative program, the power that Congress has and uses to legitimate, or amend, or reject executive and presidential initiatives is both extensive and extremely important.

Third, and perhaps most important, congressional-executive relations cannot reasonably be interpreted as a zero-sum game. Congress and the executive branch (both the president and the bureaucracy) can be creative together or can fall on their faces together. In most instances policy making involves at least some efforts from both of them. It is a cooperative venture.

A more systematic way of thinking of the interaction of the executive branch and Congress in making policy involves positing four basic "models" of the relationship (Ripley, 1983: 28–31, 410–26).

The first model is one of *executive dominance.* In this relationship the executive branch is the principal source of the initiation of legislative ideas and also shapes most of the details. Congressional participation in the shaping of details is low. Legislation results.

The second model is one of *joint program development.* In this relationship either the executive branch or Congress can be the principal source of initiation. Both branches are heavily involved in shaping the details of the final decision. Legislation results.

The third model is one of *congressional dominance.* In this relationship, Congress provides the chief source of initiation and also shapes most of the details of the final legislation, which is passed.

The fourth model is one of *stalemate.* In this relationship, principal initiative can come from either branch. Often it comes from both branches, but they disagree substantively. Both branches get involved in shaping details. Again they do not agree. The short-term result is that no legislation results because the disagreements are too great.

Table 8–1 summarizes the models of policy formulation and legitimation. Table 8–2 examines domestic cases from recent years that generally fit each model (see Anderson, Brady, Bullock, and Stewart, 1984, for more examples).

TABLE 8-1
Models of Policy Formulation and Legitimation

Model	Principal Source of Initiation	Degree of Congressional Participation in Shaping Details	Degree of Executive Participation in Shaping Details	Final Legislative Product
Exicutive dominance	Executive	Low	High	Yes
Joint program development	Executive or Congress or both	High	High	Yes
Congressional dominance	Congress	High	Low	Yes
Stalemate	Executive or Congress or both	High	High	No

Source: R. B. Ripley, *Congress: Process and Policy,* 3rd ed., (New York: W. W. Norton, 1983), 31.

COOPERATION AND CONFLICT BETWEEN CONGRESS AND THE BUREAUCRACY

In Chapter 1 we specified six conditions that promote either cooperation or conflict between Congress and the bureaucracy, depending on the state of the conditions at any given time. These were level of personal compatibility, level of ideological or programmatic agreement, level of genuine congressional participation in decision making, level of salience of an issue to constituents and organized groups, relative aggressiveness of agencies in requesting expansion, and nature of party control of the executive branch and Congress. The relative importance of these conditions varies by type of policy. Smooth subgovernment relations are dominant in the distributive and structural policy areas because personal compatibility is high, programmatic agreement is high (with ideology being almost totally irrelevant to all parties), the level of congressional participation is high, the issues are salient to constituents and organized groups that congressional and bureaucratic figures in key positions are eager to serve, there is a mutually agreed-on level of agency expansion, and differing party control of the two branches is often only a minor irritant.

In the protective regulatory, strategic, and redistributive arenas, there is more likely to be ideological or programmatic disagreement; the executive branch may try to exclude Congress or at least diminish its role; the salience of issues is likely to encompass larger groups and sets of individuals rather than small, tightly knit groups with common interests; desires

TABLE 8-2
Examples of Recent Domestic Policy Making Generally Fitting
Different Models

Executive dominance
　Economic Opportunity Act, 1964
　Model Cities, 1966
　Juvenile delinquency, 1963
　Tax act, 1981

Joint program development
　Area Redevelopment Act, 1961
　Humphrey-Hawkins bill, 1978
　Appalachia program, 1964
　Food stamps, 1963
　Aid to airports, 1950s and 1960s
　Mass transit, 1960s and 1970s
　Numerous education programs, 1940s–1960s
　Job Training Partnership Act, 1982
　Farm supports and Farm credit, 1985

Congressional dominance
　Air-pollution control, 1950s–1970s
　Water-pollution control, 1950s–1970s
　Strip mining regulation, 1977
　Health research, 1950s, 1960s
　Tax act, 1982

Stalemate
　Housing, early 1970s
　Aid to elementary and secondary education, 1940s–early 1960s
　Medicare, 1940s–early 1960s
　Creation of an Urban Affairs Department, 1961–1962
　Welfare reform, 1970s
　Enterprise-zone bill, 1980s
　Tax bill, 1985
　Deficit reduction, 1983–1985

for expansion will be articulated without prior agreement; and differing party control of the two branches makes increased conflict much more likely.

Cooperation is certainly needed, or else effective government cannot exist in the United States. We do not denigrate the values of cooperation. But we also do not denigrate the values of conflict. Conflict can produce incisive questions about public policy, more oversight and evaluation of program performance, and more awareness of what is at stake in public policy decisions. The desire of most participants, however, is for cooperation whenever possible and sometimes at all costs. The price paid for this desire is often an uncritical attitude about specific public policies on the part of public officials, both elected and nonelected. The incentives are heavily loaded in favor of cooperation. As suggested in Chapter 2, the background of our officials, both in Congress and in the executive branch, is such that a fairly homogeneous group of mostly middle-aged, middle-class white males makes most decisions. This may mean there is a built-in bias to see things from a single perspective. This is not to suggest a conspiracy but only that relative homogeneity in a set of officials helps produce relative homogeneity in an outlook on some crucial policy questions.

Even more important, as suggested in Chapter 3, a number of institutional incentives contribute to the desire to see policy in a nonconflictual light. Both members of Congress and members of the bureaucracy usually have more to gain from cooperation than from conflict (Ripley, 1983: chapter 10).

LEGISLATIVE OVERSIGHT

Why Oversight Is Less Than Systematic: Resources and Motivations

Oversight as a congressional activity can be thought of in two senses. In a random and nonsystematic sense, oversight can be described as a continuous activity, because there are many opportunities for individual members and for subcommittees and committees to inquire into specific activities of the bureaucracy, and these opportunities are exercised. However, in a more systematic and continuous sense—such as would occur in a "rational," constant evaluation of program performance and/or impact—oversight by Congress happens only occasionally. Some of the reasons for this have already been suggested. In general, members of the House and Senate have a variety of interests, and the motivation to engage in detailed, continuous oversight is often missing or weak at best. (For a good review of the literature on oversight and a proposal for how to study it systematically see Rockman, 1984: 414–439.)

Ogul (1973: 2–3) discusses specific legislative oversight activities in terms of these motivations (see also Ogul, 1976, 1981):

> When any action is perceived to contribute directly and substantially to political survival as well as to other legitimate functions, it is likely to move toward the top of any member's priority list. Extra incentives to oversee come from problems of direct concern to one's constituents or from issues that promise political visibility or organizational support. Conversely, problems not seen as closely related to political survival are more difficult to crowd onto the member's schedule. . . .
>
> Not all congressional activity is linked directly to political survival. A congressman seems to gain interest in pushing oversight efforts onto his active calendar under the following conditions: New executive requests are forthcoming

calling for massive new expenditures or substantial new authorizations in controversial policy areas; a crisis has occurred that has not been met effectively by executive departments; the opposition political party is in control of the executive branch; he has not been treated well either in the realm of personal attention or in the servicing of his requests; he has modest confidence in the administrative capacity of departmental or agency leaders.

Ogul also points out that when a member has high confidence in a set of leaders and/or agrees with the policies they are pursuing, the motivation for oversight lessens. If favored policies are being ignored or contradicted, however, the member has relatively high incentive to get involved with the bureaucracy to try to alter their policy behavior in a desired direction.

Davis (1970: 133–34) adds some reasons that oversight is weak and sporadic:

> For all the formal power of Congress, Congress does operate under important restraints in playing its role of administrative overseer. Congress is relatively small compared to the executive branch; it does not meet continuously, it is made up (at best) of intelligent laymen, and it has limited staff. These characteristics mean that Congress is unable to review the performance of executive branch organizations in any regular and systematic way. Because of its limited staff Congress cannot collect all the information it would need to review agency performance systematically and, if it could collect the needed information, it could not analyze and interpret it. Congress can at most spot-check what is going on in the executive branch. It can react to complaints, respond to fires. But it may be able to spot fires only when they have reached considerable proportions. . . .
>
> An additional limit on Congress's ability to oversee administration is the potential ability of a government executive to avoid the close examination of his organization and its budget by maintaining friendly personal relations with relevant committee chairmen. If a bureau chief can build an atmosphere of confidence and trust, then Congressmen may not ask him many questions and may accept on faith his answers to any questions asked.

Ralph K. Huitt (1966: 20), a careful student of Congress and a former assistant secretary of health, education, and welfare, reaches much the same conclusion as Davis about the extent of congressional oversight and also indicates the conditions under which it is most likely:

> Not much "oversight" of administration, in a systematic and continuous enough manner to make it mean very much, is practiced. The appropriations committees probably do more than the legislative committees. . . . Most legislative oversight occurs when hearings on new bills or authorizations occur. Closer scrutiny is likely to result from the personal interest of a chairman or ranking member, the sudden interest of the public in a program or a member's hunch that interest can be aroused, or the relationship (amounting virtually to institutional incest in a separation-of-powers system) which arises when a

chairman fills the agency's top jobs with his own former staff members. The individual member's interest in administration is likely to be spurred by a constituent's protest, which subsides when the matter is taken care of.

Surprisingly, only a few systematic studies of congressional oversight have been undertaken. One such study is of the relations between three congressional committees and seven independent regulatory commissions from 1938 to 1961 (Scher, 1963). Another is a study of the relations between the Senate Banking and Currency Committee and three agencies (the Small Business Administration, the Federal Reserve Board, and the Housing and Home Finance Agency) from 1954 through 1962 (Bibby, 1966). The Scher study supports the Davis and Huitt positions by observing that long periods of time would pass between serious reviews of the various agencies by the committees. The Bibby study examines specific conditions promoting greater oversight. These include the presence of a committee chairperson devoted to "serving" the other members of the committee rather than imposing personal views on the committee; a relatively high degree of subcommittee autonomy within the committee; a sufficient and aggressive staff for the committee; members highly interested in the work of the committee and experienced in Congress and in interacting with the executive branch; and a committee with a basic orientation toward oversight of the administration of existing statutes rather than the development of new basic legislation. Because few committees meet all of these conditions often or for long periods, the relative paucity of systematic oversight is easy to understand and explain.

A study by Ogul (1976) of three House committees (the Post Office and Civil Service Committee, a judiciary subcommittee, and a Special Subcommittee of the Government Operations Committee) in the mid- and late-1960s produced similar findings: only one of these three committees had much oversight impact and that was a short-term special subcommittee. He also summarizes the conditions most likely to foster oversight, although the presence of any one or all of these conditions in no way guarantees a strong oversight performance (Ogul, 1976: 21–22). His general conclusion is that nothing can guarantee effective oversight, and idiosyncratic features probably explain a great deal about its occurrence.

A thorough study of the intergovernmental grant system—one of the largest and most important sets of domestic programs—concluded that congressional oversight performance in this area, despite verbiage showing interest, had been "disappointing" (Advisory Commission on Intergovernmental Relations, 1978: 86). Specifically, a provision for periodic review of grants contained in the Intergovernmental Cooperation Act of 1968 has simply been ignored by Congress.

General and special revenue sharing programs and block grants also present new challenges to already weak oversight. Because these programs are not directly controlled or implemented by federal bureaucracies, but are instead controlled largely by seemingly innumerable state and local governments, Congress has great trouble in getting a "handle" on how to oversee them and also has little incentive to do so. When Reagan became president, he pushed for even more devolution of federal power to states and localities. Oversight of various forms of special revenue sharing and block grants has been minimal. One of the reasons for the minimal oversight was the federal agencies did not collect data that would allow systematic evaluation of programs, *even if* Congress asked the right questions. The block grant programs created under the Reagan presidency were even less likely to require data appropriate for systematic evaluation and oversight.

Even in the area of covert intelligence, in which extremely disturbing revelations about the practices of the Central Intelligence Agency, the Federal Bureau of Investigation, and other agencies have been made, protestations of changed congressional attitudes toward the intelligence function—which took considerable time to develop (Elliff, 1977; Ransom, 1975)—were followed up with little concrete, sustained oversight (Horrock, 1978; Marro, 1977). Both houses have shown interest by creating select committees on intelligence, but continuing productivity of these committees has not been forthcoming. Structural protections for covert agencies and shifting public attention, as well as shifting personal interest, views, experience, and stamina on the part of individual members of Congress, all work to minimize oversight in these areas (Johnson, 1980).

One very concrete problem Congress faces in trying to oversee many fields is that the delegations of power by Congress to the executive branch agencies are so broad they contain no standards against which performance can be measured, even at a very general level (Lowi, 1979; Woll, 1977). Broad delegations of power also blur the intended focus of oversight, and as a result oversight can ask widely varying questions, focusing on issues such as management efficiency, bureaucratic procedures, programmatic impact on clients and beneficiaries, degree of programmatic goal achievement, or justification for a program. Yet another obstacle to oversight is an attitude among legislators who agree that oversight is necessary and important but who do not want their pet programs to be the object of oversight activities. This can lead to a reverse form of back-scratching—"you don't investigate my program and I won't investigate yours"—that diminishes the incentives for and the frequency of oversight.

In the 1970s, after Watergate, there was an unquestioned increase in interest in oversight on the part of Congress. There was also a quick conclusion by some journalists (and even a few political scientists, who should have known better) that a new, permanently high level of congressional oversight had become part of the American political landscape. However the post-Watergate burst of interest proved to be largely a flash in the pan and did not really lead to a permanent increase in oversight or removal of any of the fundamental barriers to serious oversight (Dodd and Schott, 1979). Oversight does not come naturally or easily to Congress, and there is no reason to expect it ever will.

Altering Patterns of Resources and Motivations to Promote Oversight

The reasons for sporadic or absent congressional oversight relate both to the capacity and resources of Congress, on the one hand, and to the motivations of legislators on the other. Problems of capacity or resources are easier to affect than problems of motivation, but still not easy.

Resources.   At both the verbal level and the formal statutory level, Congress has shown considerable interest in oversight since World War II, and that interest intensified, at least verbally, in the 1970s (Aberbach, 1979; Freed, 1975; Havemann, 1976).

The first explicit congressional legislative attempt to create both an oversight mandate and capacity came in the Legislative Reorganization Act of 1946. In that act (which also reduced the number of standing committees, rationalized their jurisdiction in relation to the governmental agenda in 1946, and provided professional staffs for committees and members) all committees were charged with "continuous watchfulness" of executive branch performance in administering public laws and with studying agency reports submitted to Congress. The government operations committees in both houses were given a special mandate to make sure all government programs were meeting the twin traditional criteria of economy and efficiency.

In the Intergovernmental Cooperation Act of 1968, committees were specifically required to oversee the operations of federal grant-in-aid programs to states and localities, including those that had no firm expiration dates in the initial statutes. Congress has ignored this provision. The Legislative Reorganization Act of 1970 gave oversight capacity, at least in principle, to the General Accounting Office (GAO) and the Congressional Research Service. It also required virtually all committees to report every two years on their oversight activities.

In 1974 Congress passed two statutes that showed substantial concern with oversight. The Congressional Budget and Impoundment Control Act created staff capacity in the two budget committees and the Congressional Budget Office. In addition, the GAO was mandated to establish an Office of Program Review and Evaluation and to recommend to Congress methods to be used in such review and evaluation. The Treasury and the Office of Management and Budget in the executive branch were also required to provide special information to committees, the GAO, and the Congressional Budget Office.

Perhaps most important, the budget act got at least some members of the House and Senate themselves—the members of the budget committees—intimately involved in the details of the federal budgets. This involvement could lead to a greater concern with systematic oversight. And, given the procedures of the budget act requiring some critical budget resolutions each year passed by the entire House and Senate, there was at least some potential in the act for creating a similar concern in all members of the House and Senate.

One critical resource Congress has done well in providing itself in recent years is adequate and high-quality professional staff (Fox and Hammond, 1977; Ripley, 1983: 260–76). Staff limits are no longer a major constraint on oversight potential in most areas. Individual senators and representatives and all committees and subcommittees have sizable staffs.

In addition, Congress has created some new central support offices and strengthened some preexisting ones in an effort, in part, to create a more professional staff structure that could help sustain more effective and continuous oversight. The Congressional Budget Office has already been mentioned as one new office that has some potential for enhancing congressional oversight. Another new office with at least limited potential is the Office of Technology Assessment, although in its early years it was mired in charges of political empire building and had not built a constituency supporting it that would help guarantee some attention to its analytic products.

An old organization, the Congressional Research Service, was required by the 1970 Legislative Reorganization Act to provide committees of Congress (in effect, chairpersons) with lists of expiring legislation and also with "a list of subjects and policy areas which the committees might profitably analyze in depth." Another established organization, the General Accounting Office, was authorized by the same law "to review and analyze 'the results of government programs and activities, including the making of cost benefit studies,' on its initiative or when ordered by either house or a committee." The use of the GAO is not governed by a rational plan, however. A Wisconsin Republican member of the House, William Steiger, complained that the GAO "is not used properly because there is no comprehensive, rational approach to how it should be used. By and large, a congressman will tell GAO, 'Here's a problem, look at it and report back.' There's no understanding of the types of questions that should be asked or how programs should be evaluated." (All quotes in this paragraph are from Freed, 1975: 597–98.)

Both houses reorganized their committee systems in the 1970s—the House in 1974 and the Senate in 1977. The Senate reorganization had no particular relationship to oversight potential. In the House, one provision required standing committees with more than twenty members to set up special oversight subcommittees or to require their standing subcommittees to engage in oversight. It also gave special oversight responsibilities and powers to seven standing committees (Budget, Armed Services, Education and Labor, International Affairs, Interior and Insular Affairs, Science and Technology, and Small Business). These committees were specifically authorized to cross normal jurisdictional boundaries in pursuing their oversight duties. This formal requirement has not improved either the quality or quantity of oversight, however.

Motivations. A more subtle and difficult problem in improving oversight lies in altering the motivations of members to conduct it. The motivations of members are set in institutional contexts that are fairly rigid, although not impervious to change. One way to increase the amount of oversight that gets done would be to stress the linkages between oversight and other, higher-priority tasks of legislators. This would help improve members' motivations to perform oversight. The performance of oversight should have payoffs for members' other priorities or goals—such as getting reelected. For example, constituents' problems raise issues that spark legislative oversight. By seeking patterns among constituents' problems with agencies' programs (for example, social security eligibility and payments) more systematic oversight of client-oriented programs would result. Staff and others can argue that such patterns are present. But, ultimately, members have to see the patterns themselves to change their behavior.

Congressional perception of the public mood may help stimulate oversight, as the burst of post-Watergate activity demonstrates. But the normal lack of public interest in oversight also helps stimulate congressional apathy, because there is no apparent political reward for pursuing activities diligently if few people in the voting public value those activities. And there may be political incentives for pursuing what amounts to phony or toothless oversight conducted primarily to impress the home folks. Some congressional questions about and inquiries into the performance of some bureaucracies and programs is almost purely to build an image of effectiveness and hard-nosedness back in the district. Such "oversight" is, by definition, much too sporadic to have any genuine impact on the agencies or programs presumably involved.

Another way of creating motivation for legislative oversight would be to tie oversight to the desire of members to initiate and develop legislation. Because most members derive a feeling of accomplishment from authorizing legislation, that pride of parenthood might be tapped to motivate the members of a committee involved in creating legislation to follow through on oversight of the implementation and impact of that legislation. This would be facilitated if the legislation mandated stiff reporting and evaluation requirements for the administering agency.

In those areas in which Congress has been most important in initiating it has often been most aggressive in oversight. Air- and water-pollution legislation offer good examples. We disagree at least partially with Huitt (1966) and Bibby (1966) when they suggest there is a necessary trade-off between performing oversight and developing new legislation and a committee interested in the latter will not have much time for the former. This may be true if the committee is not subsequently forced, in effect, to consider performance because of the receipt of agency reports and evaluations. But with the automatic, scheduled receipt of such reports and evaluations, the opportunity for oversight would be created, and we would place our bets on the most aggressive initiating committees also performing most aggressively as overseers.

An additional provision of new statutes that might also enhance oversight would be an automatic termination date coupled with reporting and evaluation requirements that would force the committee to consider the statute periodically and at the same time provide data and agency views that would be considered in the deliberations about whether to terminate, extend, or amend a program (Lowi, 1973b). This notion of "sunset" legislation was relatively popular in Congress in the late 1970s, although the movement to pass it collapsed in the 1980s. Through a combination of attention to developing congressional resource capacity and increasing members' motivations for performing legislative oversight, the quality and continuity of oversight could improve. No magic formula will cure all problems, however, and congressional oversight is never likely to become everything critics want.

FORCES FOR AND AGAINST CHANGE

There are a number of powerful forces working against policy change of any sizable magnitude. And yet some sizable shifts do occur.

The status quo forces are most likely to be higher civil servants, especially those in older, larger, well-established agencies, and members of Congress and staff members working on the subcommittees related to the individual agencies and their programs. Their disposition to make only moderate or small changes in policies is seconded by the impact of the representatives of already advantaged interest groups working in the same substantive field. These individuals are all characterized by long service and usually by long-established patterns of personal interaction. They are highly specialized in the substantive business of their particular subgovernment. And their loyalties tend to be primarily institutional (to the subcommittee or agency itself) or, in the case of members of Congress, to a limited electoral constituency (the "most important" voters in a district or state).

The forces that are more likely to be mobilized in support of substantial policy change on at least some occasions consist of a few bureau officials, a few congressional staff members, a few members of Congress (usually outside of the subgovernment dominating policy in the area), and—selectively—the president and some of his appointees in relevant portions of the executive establishment. These individuals tend to have a shorter tenure (this is most evident in the case of presidents and their appointees) and probably do not have long-established patterns of personal relations with one another (the forces that coalesce to work in favor of major change are likely to do so on an *ad hoc* basis, whereas the subgovernments supporting the status quo with only minor changes tend to be more institutionalized and permanent). The degree of specialization is much lower than for the members of the typical subgovernment. And the principal loyalties of these individuals are more likely to be ideological or programmatic (to a vision of "good policy") than narrowly institutional. The president (and perhaps ambitious senators who want to be president) also presumably takes some major policy initiatives with a national electoral constituency in mind.

The sheer complexity of getting new policies adopted in the United States when compared to a number of other developed countries with open political systems also helps explain why "new departures" seem to be relatively rare in the United States. After studying policies on regional development and population distribution in the United States, Great Britain, France, Italy, the Netherlands, and Sweden, one careful student of policy making (Sundquist, 1978: 79) reached these conclusions:

> Because the institutional structure of policymaking in the United States is more complex and pluralized than those of the other industrial democracies of the Atlantic community, because the policymaking circle is broader and more amateur and less disciplined, public participation more intense, and the points of potential veto of policy innovation more numerous, and because political parties are weaker as integrating mechanisms, a higher degree of national consensus and a more intense commitment of political leadership are necessary before new departures can be developed and approved, and a narrower range of innovation can be successfully attempted at any one time.

What effect did the Reagan presidency have on the basic patterns of policy making we have analyzed in this book? How much change did Reagan bring to the underlying patterns of policy formulation and legitimation in the United States?

At one level the answer is that Reagan has been just another president, and the underlying patterns and activities have proceeded with only marginal adjustments. That answer is basically correct. However, it is also important to notice that Reagan clearly changed the mix of policies being addressed by the formulation and legitimation apparatus centered in

Congress and the bureaucracy. In that sense the very different policy agenda on which he insisted—different, at least, from the basic agenda of the preceding half century—did have an impact. By the same token, however, when he is replaced by a president with a different agenda—perhaps more in line with the pre-Reagan half century, perhaps in line with Reagan himself, and conceivably with some third thrust—the "Reagan revolution" will appear to be very transient.

However, the temporary changes wrought by Reagan because of the content of his administration's agenda are worth noting. Three major phenomena should be noted. First, his antipathy to social programs brought a halt to redistributive policy making aimed at greater social equality. Without presidential backing, such initiatives either are not taken or go only a very short distance. His efforts at redistributing in favor of the already well-off were substantial and are well documented. But, in American political parlance, these efforts are not generally viewed as redistributive.

Second, his lack of interest and, indeed, his strong opposition blocked consideration of new protective regulatory legislation. But he did not get statutory changes in laws he did not like. Various coalitions protected some of the laws already on the books, although the president and key appointees demonstrated that administrative action or nonaction during implementation could achieve changes without legislation.

Third, Reagan engaged in rhetoric against subgovernments. But, when examined, his antisubgovernment statements were directed primarily against coalitions supportive of redistributive policy, not against the classic subgovernments clustered around subsidy packages. The Reagan focus on the primacy of national defense strengthened the hand of most of the subgovernments working in structural defense areas.

There is a chance that the most important relatively long-run Reagan impact on government will have to do with personnel, structure, and morale in the bureaucracy. Analytically, little is known about the impact of elections—especially "realigning" elections that may reveal widespread changes in political beliefs—on bureaucracy in the United States (Meier and Kramer, 1980). Nor is anyone sure how quickly pieces of the domestic bureaucracy can reestablish pre-Reagan equilibrium upset by reductions in force, mass shifting of senior and middle-level personnel, budget cuts, and attitudes unsupportive of agency missions and purposes. For that matter, no one is sure agencies would want to reestablish such equilibrium. It is certainly too early to assert that the Reagan period has changed either the content or the machinery of American policy making for longer than the period itself lasts. But there are some signs that this president has unleashed some forces, developments, and values that will need to be monitored closely by those interested analytically in how the American system of government functions to produce different kinds of public policies.

A CLOSING WORD

We end this chapter and this book both on an analytical note and on a moderately hopeful note. The analytical note is that conservatism in the sense of support of the status quo is dominant in the national policies of the United States for reasons that we hope we have made clear: the pervasive need for compromise built into the system, the widespread desire to minimize conflict, and the desire to protect personal careers on the part of individuals throughout the executive and legislative branches. The hopeful note is twofold: not all the status quo is bad or undesirable policy, and, more important, the status quo policy is not completely rigid, nor are the status quo forces completely dominant. Bursts of creativity can and do occur and may come from either branch. Too much is often claimed for the "genius of American government." Likewise, indictments are often too sweeping. Conservative, distributive policies are likely to prevail unless deliberate action to the contrary is taken. Even though the system does not encourage such deliberate action, it at least permits it when men and women of energy with differing policy commitments become policy actors.

References

Aberbach, J. D. (1979) "Changes in Congressional Oversight." American Behavioral Scientist 22 (May/June): 493–515.

Aberbach, J. D., R. D. Putnam, and B. A. Rockman (1981) Bureaucrats and Politicians in Western Democracies. Cambridge, Mass.: Harvard University Press.

Aberbach, J. D., and B. A. Rockman (1976) "Clashing Beliefs within the Executive Branch: The Nixon Administration Bureaucracy." American Political Science Review 70 (June): 456–468.

_____ (1977) "The Overlapping Worlds of American Federal Executives and Congressmen." British Journal of Political Science 7 (January): 23–47.

_____ (1978) "Bureaucrats and Clientele Groups: A View from Capitol Hill." American Journal of Political Science 22 (November): 818–832.

Adams, G. (1982) The Politics of Defense Contracting: The Iron Triangle. New Brunswick, N.J.: Transaction Books.

Advisory Commission on Intergovernmental Relations (1978) Categorical Grants: Their Role and Design (publication A-52). Washington, D.C.: U.S. Government Printing Office.

Anderson, J. E. (ed.) (1970) Politics and Economic Policy-Making. Reading, Mass.: Addison-Wesley.

Anderson, J. E., D. W. Brady, C. S. Bullock III, and J. Stewart, Jr. (1984) Public Policy and Politics in America, 2nd ed. Monterey, Cal.: Brooks/Cole.

Armacost, M. H. (1969) The Politics of Weapons Innovation. New York: Columbia University Press.

Arnow, K. S. (1954) The Department of Commerce Field Service. Indianapolis: Bobbs-Merrill. ICP Case #21.

Baumer, D.C., and C. E. Van Horn (1984) The Politics of Unemployment. Washington, D.C.: Congressional Quarterly Press.

Beam, D. R. (1984) "New Federalism, Old Realities: The Reagan Administration and Intergovernmental Reform." In L. M. Salamon and M. S. Lund (eds.), The Reagan Presidency and the Governing of America. Washington, D.C.: The Urban Institute.

Bendiner, R. (1964) Obstacle Course on Capitol Hill. New York: McGraw-Hill.

Bernstein, M. H. (1958) The Job of the Federal Executive. Washington, D.C.: Brookings Institution.

Bibby, J. F. (1966) "Committee Characteristics and Legislative Oversight of Administration." Midwest Journal of Political Science 10 (February): 78–98.

Bird, K. (1978) "Food for Peace—Or Politics?" Washington Post (January 4).

Bonafede, D. (1979) "The Tough Job of Normalizing Relations with Capitol Hill." National Journal (January 13): 54–57.

Brady, D. W. (1981) "Personnel Management in the House." In J. Cooper and G. C. Mackenzie (eds.), The House at Work. Austin: University of Texas Press.

Carper, E. (1965) The Reorganization of the Public Health Service. Indianapolis: Bobbs-Merrill.

Carroll, H. N. (1966) The House of Representatives and Foreign Affairs, rev. ed. Boston: Little, Brown.

Cater, D. (1964) Power in Washington. New York: Random House.

Chamberlain, L. H. (1946) The President, Congress and Legislation. New York: Columbia University Press.

Chubb, J. E. (1985) "Federalism and the Bias for Centralization." In J. E. Chubb and P. E. Peterson (eds.), The New Direction in American Politics. Washington, D.C.: Brookings Institution.

Chubb, J. E., and P. E. Peterson (eds.) (1985) The New Direction in American Politics. Washington, D.C.: Brookings Institution.

Cohen, R. E. (1974) "Senate Seeks to Modernize Workings of the Patent Office." National Journal (March 30): 475–482.

Congressional Budget Office (1984) U.S. Shipping and Shipbuilding: Trends and Policy Choices. Washington, D.C.: U.S. Government Printing Office.

Congressional Quarterly (1965) Congress and the Nation, 1945–1964. Washington: Congressional Quarterly Service.

Cooper, A. (1978) "Congress Approves Civil Service Reform." Congressional Quarterly Weekly Report (October 14): 2945–2950.

Corrigan, R. (1977a) "The Senate Plays 'Let's Make a Deal' with Carter's Energy Plan." National Journal (September 24): 1486–1489.

——— (1977b) "Lobbyists Are Putting the Blitz on Carter's Energy Program." National Journal (November 26): 1836–1840.

——— (1978) "Chalk One Up for the President's Energy Lobbyists." National Journal (September 30): 1556–1559.

Corrigan, R., and D. Kirschten (1978) "The Energy Package—What Has Congress Wrought?" National Journal (November 4): 1760–1768.

Corson, J. J., and R. S. Paul (1966) Men Near the Top. Baltimore: Johns Hopkins.

Craig, B. H. (1983) The Legislative Veto: Congressional Control of Regulation. Boulder, Colo.: Westview Press.

Culhane, P. J. (1981) Public Lands Politics: Interest Group Influence on the Forest Service and the Bureau of Land Management. Baltimore: Johns Hopkins.

Davidson, R. H. (1967) "Congress and the Executive: The Race for Representation." In A. De Grazia (ed.), Congress: The First Branch of Government. Garden City, N.Y.: Doubleday.

——— (1969) The Role of the Congressman. New York: Pegasus.

_____ (1972) The Politics of Comprehensive Manpower Legislation. Baltimore: Johns Hopkins.

_____ (1975) "Policy Making in the Manpower Subgovernment." In M. P. Smith et al. (eds.), Politics in America. New York: Random House.

_____ (1977) "Breaking Up Those 'Cozy Triangles': An Impossible Dream?" In S. Welch and J. G. Peters (eds.), Legislative Reform and Public Policy. New York: Praeger Publishers.

Davidson, R. H., and W. J. Oleszek (1977) Congress against Itself. Bloomington: Indiana University Press.

Davis, J. W. (1970) The National Executive Branch. New York: Free Press.

Davis, J. W., and R. B. Ripley (1967) "The Bureau of the Budget and Executive Branch Agencies: Notes on Their Interaction." Journal of Politics 29 (November): 749–769.

Dodd, L. C., and B. I. Oppenheimer (eds.) (1977) Congress Reconsidered. New York: Praeger Publishers.

Dodd, L. C., and R. L. Schott (1979) Congress and the Administrative State. New York: John Wiley & Sons.

Donovan, J. C. (1973) The Politics of Poverty, 2nd ed. Indianapolis, Pegasus.

Drew, E. B. (1970) "Dam Outrage: The Story of the Army Engineers." Atlantic (April): 51–62.

_____ (1982) "Legal Services." New Yorker (March 1): 97–113.

Eidenberg, E., and R. D. Morey (1969) An Act of Congress. New York: W. W. Norton.

Elder, S. (1978) "The Cabinet's Ambassadors to Capitol Hill." Congressional Quarterly Weekly Report (July 29): 1196–1200.

Elliff, J. T. (1977) "Congress and the Intelligence Community." In L. C. Dodd and B. I. Oppenheimer (eds.), Congress Reconsidered. New York: Praeger Publishers.

Evans, R., and R. Novak (1966) Lyndon B. Johnson: The Exercise of Power. New York: New American Library.

Fenno, R. F., Jr. (1959) The President's Cabinet. New York: Vintage.

_____ (1966) Power of the Purse. Boston: Little, Brown.

_____ (1973) Congressmen in Committees. Boston: Little, Brown.

_____ (1978) Home Style: House Members in Their Districts. Boston: Little, Brown.

Fiorina, M. P. (1977) Congress: Keystone of the Washington Establishment. New Haven, Conn.: Yale University Press.

Fisher, L. (1974) "Reprogramming of Funds by the Defense Department." Journal of Politics 36 (February): 77–102.

_____ (1985a) Constitutional Conflicts between Congress and the President. Princeton, N.J.: Princeton University Press.

_____ (1985b) "Judicial Misjudgments about the Lawmaking Process: The Legislative Veto Case." Public Administration Review 45 (November): 705–711.

Ford, G. R. (1977) "The War Powers Resolution: Striking a Balance between the Executive and Legislative Branches." Reprint #69. Washington: American Enterprise Institute.

Foss, P. O. (1960) Politics and Grass. Seattle: University of Washington.

Fox, H. W., Jr., and S. W. Hammond (1977) Congressional Staffs: The Invisible Force in American Lawmaking. New York: Free Press.

Franck, T. M., and E. Weisband (1979) Foreign Policy by Congress. New York: Oxford University Press.

Franklin, G. A., and R. B. Ripley (1984) CETA: Politics and Policy, 1973–1982. Knoxville: University of Tennessee Press.

Freed, B. F. (1975) "Congress May Step Up Oversight of Programs." Congressional Quarterly Weekly Report (March 22): 595–600.

Freeman, J. L. (1965) The Political Process, rev. ed. New York: Random House.

Frey, A. (1975) A Responsible Congress: The Politics of National Security. New York: McGraw-Hill.

Friedman, K. M. (1975) Public Policy and the Smoking-Health Controversy. Lexington, Mass.: Lexington Books.

Fritschler, A. L. (1983) Smoking and Politics, 3rd ed. Englewood Cliffs, N.J.: Prentice-Hall.

Froman, L. A., Jr. (1968) "The Categorization of Policy Contents." In A. Ranney (ed.), Political Science and Public Policy. Chicago: Markham.

Getler, M. (1974) "The Great Warplane Charade." Washington Post (September 20).

Gist, J. R. (1978) "Appropriations Politics and Expenditure Control." Journal of Politics 40 (February): 163–178.

Goldenberg, E. N. (1984) "The Permanent Government in an Era of Retrenchment and Redirection." In L. M. Salamon and M. S. Lund (eds.), The Reagan Presidency and the Governing of America. Washington, D.C.: The Urban Institute.

Green, H. P., and A. Rosenthal (1963) Government of the Atom: The Integration of Powers. New York: Atherton.

Greenberg, D. S. (1967) The Politics of Pure Science. New York: New American Library.

Greider, W. (1978) "After Squeezing through Hill Pipeline, Gas Bill Now Skewed toward Industry." Washington Post (July 30).

Harris, J. P. (1964) Congressional Control of Administration. Washington, D.C.: Brookings Institution.

Havemann, J. (1976) "Congress Tries to Break Ground Zero in Evaluating Federal Programs." National Journal (May 22): 706–713.

_____ (1977) "Congress Opens Floodgates in the SBA's Disaster Loan Program." National Journal (December 31): 2001–2003.

_____ (1978) Congress and the Budget. Bloomington: Indiana University Press.

Hayes, M. T. (1981) Lobbyists and Legislators: A Theory of Political Markets. New Brunswick, N.J.: Rutgers University Press.

Heclo, H. (1977) A Government of Strangers: Executive Politics in Washington. Washington, D.C.: Brookings Institution.

Holtzman, A. (1970) Legislative Liaison: Executive Leadership in Congress. Skokie, Ill.: Rand McNally.

Horn, S. (1970) Unused Power: The Work of the Senate Committee on Appropriations. Washington, D.C.: Brookings Institution.

Horrock, N. M. (1978) "Intelligence Oversight: Congress Tries Again." New York Times (February 12).

Huitt, R. K. (1966) "Congress, the Durable Partner." In E. Frank (ed.), Lawmakers in a Changing World. Englewood Cliffs, N.J.: Prentice-Hall.

Huntington, S. P. (1961) The Common Defense. New York: Columbia University Press.

_____ (1973) "Congressional Responses to the Twentieth Century." In D. B. Truman (ed.), Congress and America's Future, 2nd ed. Englewood Cliffs, N.J.: Prentice-Hall.

Jantscher, G. R. (1975) Bread upon the Waters: Federal Aids to the Maritime Industries. Washington, D.C.: Brookings Institution.

Johannes, J. R. (1976) "Executive Reports to Congress." Journal of Communication 26 (Summer): 53–61.

Johnson, L. (1980) "The U.S. Congress and the CIA: Monitoring the Dark Side of Government." Legislative Studies Quarterly 5 (November): 477–499.

Jones, C. O. (1967) Every Second Year. Washington, D.C.: Brookings Institution.

_____ (1984) An Introduction to the Study of Public Policy, 3rd ed. Monterey, Cal.: Brooks/Cole.

Kaiser, R. G. (1980) "In Stunned Congress Wariness and Concern over War Powers Act." Washington Post (April 26).

Kanter, A. (1972) "Congress and the Defense Budget, 1960–1970." American Political Science Review 66 (March): 129–143.

Katzmann, R. A. (1980) Regulatory Bureaucracy: The Federal Trade Commission and Antitrust Policy. Cambridge, Mass.: Harvard University Press.

Kaufman, H. (1981) The Administrative Behavior of Federal Bureau Chiefs. Washington, D.C.: Brookings Institution.

Keefe, W. J., and M. S. Ogul (1985) The American Legislative Process, 6th ed. Englewood Cliffs, N.J.: Prentice-Hall.

Keisling, P. (1982) "Old Soldiers Never Die." Washington Monthly (March): 20–29.

Keller, B. (1980) "How a Unique Lobby Force Protects over $21 Billion in Vast Veterans' Programs." Congressional Quarterly Weekly Report (June 14): 1627–1634.

_____ (1981a) "Fast-Food Industry Expands Its Lobby Franchise to Cover Jobs and Commodities Issues." Congressional Quarterly Weekly Report (June 20): 1095–1098.

_____ (1981b) "Executive Agency Lobbyists Mastering the Difficult Art of 'Congressional Liaison.'" Congressional Quarterly Weekly Report (December 5): 2387–2392.

_____ (1981c) "Many Invincible Programs Again Spared the Budget Ax in Spite of Reagan Campaign." Congressional Quarterly Weekly Report (July 18): 1271–1282.

_____ (1982) "Some Sacred Cows of the Past Turn Out Not to Be Immortal as a Year of Budget Cuts Ends," Congressional Quarterly Weekly Report (January 2): 6–8.

Kennedy, R. F. (1971) Thirteen Days. New York: W. W. Norton.

Kilpatrick, F. P., M. C. Cummings, and M. K. Jennings (1963) The Image of the Federal Service. Washington, D.C.: Brookings Institution.

Kirst, M. W. (1969) Government without Passing Laws. Chapel Hill: University of North Carolina Press.

Kluger, R. (1976) Simple Justice. New York: Alfred A. Knopf.

Kofmehl, K. (1977) Professional Staffs of Congress, 3rd ed. West Lafayette, Ind.: Purdue University Studies.

Kolodziej, E. A. (1975) "Congress and Foreign Policy: The Nixon Years." In H. C. Mansfield, Sr. (ed.), Congress against the President. New York: Academy of Political Science.

Kristof, N. D. (1982) "Scorned Legal Services Corporation on the Rebound." Washington Post (July 21).

Landis, J. M. (1938) The Administrative Process. New Haven, Conn.: Yale University Press.

Lanoutte, W. J. (1978) "Who's Setting Foreign Policy—Carter or Congress?" National Journal (July 15): 1116–1123.

Lawrence, S. A. (1965) "The Battery Acid Controversy." In E. A. Bock (ed.), Government Regulation of Business. Englewood Cliffs, N.J.: Prentice-Hall.

—— (1966) United States Merchant Shipping Policies and Politics. Washington, D.C.: Brookings Institution.

LeLoup, L. T. (1980a) Budgetary Politics, 2nd ed. Brunswick, Ohio: King's Court.

—— (1980b) The Fiscal Congress: Legislative Control of the Budget. Westport, Conn.: Greenwood Press.

Levantrosser, W. F. (1967) Congress and the Citizen-Soldier. Columbus: Ohio State University Press.

Levitan, S. A. (1969) The Great Society's Poor Law. Baltimore: Johns Hopkins.

Lewis, E. (1977) American Politics in a Bureaucratic Age: Citizens, Constituents, Clients, and Victims. Cambridge, Mass.: Winthrop.

Light, L. (1979) "White House Lobby Gets Its Act Together." Congressional Quarterly Weekly Report (February 3): 195–200.

Loftus, J. A. (1970) "How the Poverty Bill Was Saved in the House." In J. E. Anderson (ed.), Politics and Economic Policy-Making. Reading, Mass.: Addison-Wesley.

Lowi, T. J. (1964) "American Business, Public Policy, Case-Studies, and Political Theory." World Politics 16 (July): 677–715.

—— (1967) "Making Democracy Safe for the World: National Politics and Foreign Policy." In J. N. Rosenau (ed.), Domestic Sources of Foreign Policy. New York: Free Press.

—— (1972) "Four Systems of Policy, Politics, and Choice." Public Administration Review 32 (July/August): 298–310.

—— (1973a) "How the Farmers Get What They Want." In T. J. Lowi and R. B. Ripley (eds.), Legislative Politics U.S.A., 3rd ed. Boston: Little, Brown.

—— (1973b) "Congressional Reform: A New Time, Place, and Manner." In T. J. Lowi and R. B. Ripley (eds.), Legislative Politics U.S.A., 3rd ed. Boston: Little, Brown.

—— (1979) The End of Liberalism, 2nd ed. New York: W. W. Norton.

Lynn, L. E. (1984) "The Reagan Administration and the Renitent Bureaucracy." In L. M. Salamon and M. S. Lund (eds.), The Reagan Presidency and the Governing of America. Washington, D.C.: The Urban Institute.

Lytle, C. M. (1966) "The History of the Civil Rights Bill of 1964." The Journal of Negro History 51 (October): 275–296.

Maass, A. A. (1950) "Congress and Water Resources." American Political Science Review 44 (September): 576–593.

Manley, J. F. (1970) The Politics of Finance. Boston: Little, Brown.

_____ (1971) "The Rise of Congress in Foreign Policy-Making." Annals of the American Academy of Political and Social Science, no. 337: 60–70.

Marmor, T. R. (1973) The Politics of Medicare, rev. ed. Chicago: Aldine Publishing.

Marro, A. (1977) "Watching over Intelligence Involves New Fears and Doubts." New York Times (March 22).

Maxfield, D. M. (1978a) "Carter Plan to End Turkey Arms Sale Embargo Faces Tough Opposition in House." Congressional Quarterly Weekly Report (April 15): 872–873.

_____ (1978b) "Carter Steps Up Lobbying for Turkey Arms Sales." Congressional Quarterly Weekly Report (June 10): 1464.

_____ (1978c) "Senate Backs End to Turkey Arms Embargo." Congressional Quarterly Weekly Report (July 29): 1919–1920.

_____ (1978d) "House Votes End to Turkey Arms Embargo." Congressional Quarterly Weekly Report (August 5): 2041.

_____ (1978e) "Military Aid Bill Cleared Authorizing $2.8 Billion; Turkey Arms Ban Lifted." Congressional Quarterly Weekly Report (September 23): 2561.

Mayhew, D. R. (1974) Congress: The Electoral Connection. New Haven, Conn.: Yale University Press.

Meier, K. J. (1979) Politics and the Bureaucracy. North Scituate, Mass.: Duxbury.

Meier, K. J., and K. W. Kramer (1980) "The Impact of Realigning Elections on Public Bureaucracies." In B. A. Campbell and R. J. Trilling (eds.), Realignment in American Politics: Toward a Theory. Austin: University of Texas Press.

Meier, K. J., and L. G. Nigro (1976) "Representative Bureaucracy and Policy Preferences: A Study in the Attitudes of Federal Executives." Public Administration Review 36 (July/August): 458–469.

Meisol, P. (1978) "Has the Disaster Loan Program Hit Its High-Water Mark?" National Journal (September 16): 1462–1463.

Moe, R. C., and S. C. Teel (1970) "Congress as Policy-Maker: A Necessary Reappraisal." Political Science Quarterly 85 (September): 443–470.

Moe, T. M. (1985) "The Politicized Presidency." In J. E. Chubb and P. E. Peterson (eds.), The New Direction in American Politics. Washington, D.C.: Brookings Institution.

Moreland, W. B. (1975) "A Non-Incremental Perspective on Budgetary Policy Actions." In R. B. Ripley and G. A. Franklin (eds.), Policy-Making in the Federal Executive Branch. New York: Free Press.

Morgan, R. J. (1965) Governing Soil Conservation. Baltimore: Johns Hopkins.

Morrow, W. L. (1969) Congressional Committees. New York: Charles Scribner's Sons.

Munger, F. J., and R. F. Fenno (1962) National Politics and Federal Aid to Education. Syracuse, N.Y.: Syracuse University Press.

Nadel, M. V. (1971) The Politics of Consumer Protection. Indianapolis, Bobbs-Merrill.

Nelson, G. (1975) "Change and Continuity in the Recruitment of U.S. House Leaders, 1789-1975." In N. J. Ornstein (ed.), Congress in Change. New York: Praeger Publishers.

Neustadt, R. E. (1954) "Presidency and Legislation: The Growth of Central Clearance." American Political Science Review 48 (September): 641-671.

―――― (1955) "Presidency and Legislation: Planning the President's Program." American Political Science Review 49 (December): 980-1021.

―――― (1973) "Politicians and Bureaucrats." In D. B. Truman (ed.), Congress and America's Future, 2nd ed. Englewood Cliffs, N.J.: Prentice-Hall.

Nivola, P. S. (1980) "Energy Policy and the Congress: The Politics of the Natural Gas Policy Act of 1978." Public Policy 28 (Fall): 491-543.

Ogul, M. S. (1973) "Legislative Oversight of the Bureaucracy." Paper prepared for the Select Committee on Committees, U.S. House of Representatives, 93rd Congress, 1st session. Washington, D.C.: U.S. Government Printing Office.

―――― (1976) Congress Oversees the Bureaucracy. Pittsburgh: University of Pittsburgh Press.

―――― (1981) "Congressional Oversight: Structures and Incentives." In L. C. Dodd and B. I. Oppenheimer (eds.), Congress Reconsidered, 2nd ed. Washington, D.C.: Congressional Quarterly Press.

Oleszek, W. J. (1978) Congressional Procedures and the Policy Process. Washington, D.C.: Congressional Quarterly Press.

Orfield, G. (1975) Congressional Power: Congress and Social Change. New York: Harcourt Brace Jovanovich.

Ornstein, N. J., T. E. Mann, M. J. Malbin, A. Schick, and J. F. Bibby (1984) Vital Statistics on Congress, 1984-1985 Edition. Washington, D.C.: American Enterprise Institute.

Page, B. I. (1983) Who Gets What from Government. Berkeley: University of California Press.

Palmer, J. L., and I. V. Sawhill (eds.) (1982) The Reagan Experiment. Washington, D.C.: Urban Institute.

―――― (eds.) (1984) The Reagan Record. Cambridge, Mass.: Ballinger.

Pastor, R. A. (1980) Congress and the Politics of U.S. Foreign Economic Policy. Berkeley: University of California Press.

Pechman, J. A. (ed.) (1983) Setting National Priorities: The 1984 Budget. Washington, D.C.: Brookings Institution.

Pelham, A. (1978a) "Gas Pricing Bill Passes Second to Last Test." Congressional Quarterly Weekly Report (September 30): 2615-2616.

―――― (1978b) "Energy Bill: The End of an Odyssey." Congressional Quarterly Weekly Report (October 21): 3039-3044.

Peterson, G. E. (1984) "Federalism and the States: An Experiment in Decentralization." In J. L. Palmer and I. V. Sawhill (eds.), The Reagan Record. Cambridge, Mass.: Ballinger.

Pincus, W. (1974) "Reforming Oversight Functions." Washington Post (December 23).

Pipe, G. R. (1966) "Congressional Liaison: The Executive Branch Consolidates Its Relations with Congress." Public Administration Review 26 (March): 14-24.

Polsby, N. W. (1968) "Institutionalization in the House of Representatives." American Political Science Review 62 (March): 144-168.

Price, H. D. (1971) "The Congressional Career—Then and Now." In N. W. Polsby (ed.), Congressional Behavior. New York: Random House.

Rankin, B. (1977) "House Gives Carter Major Energy Victory." Congressional Quarterly Weekly Report (August 6): 1623-1628; 1694-1695.

Ransom, H. H. (1975) "Congress and the Intelligence Agencies." In H. C. Mansfield, Sr. (ed.), Congress against the President. Proceedings of the Academy of Political Science 32: 153-166.

Rauch, J. (1985) "Farmers' Discord over Government Role Produces a Farm Bill That Pleases Few." National Journal (November 9): 2535-2539.

Rich, S. (1975) "Congress Has Lead in Major Programs." Washington Post (February 14).

_____ (1980) "America as a 'Depressed Area,'" Washington Post (May 4).

Rieselbach, L. N. (1977) Congressional Reform in the Seventies. Morristown, N.J.: General Learning Press.

Ripley, R. B. (1965) "Congressional Government and Committee Management." Public Policy 14: 28-48.

_____ (1969a) Power in the Senate. New York: St. Martin's Press.

_____ (1969b) "Congress and Clean Air: The Issue of Enforcement, 1963." In F. N. Cleaveland and Associates (eds.), Congress and Urban Problems. Washington, D.C.: Brookings Institution.

_____ (1972) The Politics of Economic and Human Resource Development. Indianapolis: Bobbs-Merrill.

_____ (1983) Congress: Process and Policy, 3rd ed. New York: W. W. Norton.

Ripley, R. B., and G. A. Franklin (1986) Policy Implementation and Bureaucracy, 2nd ed. Homewood, Ill.: Dorsey Press.

Roberts, C. M. (1973) "The Day We Didn't Go to War." In T. J. Lowi and R. B. Ripley (eds.), Legislative Politics, U.S.A., 3rd ed. Boston: Little, Brown.

Rockman, B. A. (1984) "Legislative-Executive Relations and Legislative Oversight." Legislative Studies Quarterly 9 (August): 387-440.

Rothman, S., and S. R. Lichter (1983) "How Liberal Are Bureaucrats?" Regulation (December): 16-22.

Rothschild, E. (1977) "Is It Time to End Food for Peace?" New York Times Magazine (March 13): 15, 43-48.

Rudder, C. E. (1977) "Committee Reform and the Revenue Process." In L. C. Dodd and B. I. Oppenheimer (eds.), Congress Reconsidered. New York: Praeger Publishers.

Ruttenberg, S. H., and J. Gutchess (1970) Manpower Challenge of the 1970's: Institutions and Social Change. Baltimore: Johns Hopkins.

Salamon, L. M., and M. S. Lund (eds.) (1984) The Reagan Presidency and the Governing of America. Washington, D.C.: Urban Institute.

Salisbury, R. H. (1968) "The Analysis of Public Policy: A Search for Theories and Roles." In A. Ranney (ed.), Political Science and Public Policy. Chicago: Markham.

Sanders, M. E. (1981) The Regulation of Natural Gas: Policy and Politics, 1938-1978. Philadelphia: Temple University Press.

Sawyer, K. (1982) "A 'Tough Cop' on Private Sector, but Few Arrests in Own Precinct." Washington Post (April 13).

Schattschneider, E. E. (1960) The Semi-Sovereign People. New York: Holt, Rinehart & Winston.

Scher, S. (1963) "Conditions for Legislative Control." Journal of Politics 25 (August): 526–551.

Schick, A. (1980) Congress and Money: Budgeting, Spending and Taxing, Washington, D.C.: Urban Institute.

———— (1981) Reconciliation and the Congressional Budget Process. Washington, D.C.: American Enterprise Institute.

———— (ed.) (1983) Making Economic Policy in Congress. Washington, D.C.: American Enterprise Institute.

Schlozman, K. L., and J. T. Tierney (1986) Organized Interests and American Democracy. New York: Harper & Row.

Scott, A. (1977) "Veterans' Clout Extracts Extraordinary Benefits." Washington Post (November 1).

Scott, S. (1981) "Consumer Advocates Wait Anxiously for the Pendulum to Swing Their Way." National Journal (January 10): 57–58.

Seidman, H. (1980) Politics, Position, and Power: The Dynamics of Federal Organization, 3rd ed. New York: Oxford University Press.

Sharkansky, I. (1965a) "Four Agencies and an Appropriations Subcommittee: A Comparative Study of Budget Strategies." Midwest Journal of Political Science 9 (August): 254–281.

———— (1965b) "An Appropriations Subcommittee and its Client Agencies: A Comparative Study of Supervision and Control." American Political Science Review 59 (September): 622–628.

Smith, R. A. (1973) "TFX: $7 Billion Contract That Changes the Rules." In M. H. Halperin and A. Kanter (eds.), Readings in American Foreign Policy. Boston: Little, Brown.

Special Analyses, Budget of the United States Government, Fiscal Year 1984 (1983). Washington, D.C.: U.S. Government Printing Office.

Stanley, D. T. (1964) The Higher Civil Service. Washington, D.C.: Brookings Institution.

Stanely, D. T., D. E. Mann, and J. W. Doig (1967) Men Who Govern. Washington, D.C.: Brookings Institution.

Strickland, S. P. (1972) Politics, Science, and Dread Disease. Cambridge, Mass.: Harvard University Press.

Stokes, B. (1985) "A Divided Farm Lobby." National Journal (March 23): 632–638.

Sundquist, J. L. (1968) Politics and Policy. Washington, D.C.: Brookings Institution.

———— (1978) "A Comparison of Policy-Making Capacity in the United States and Five European Countries: The Case of Population Distribution." In M. E. Kraft and M. Schneider (eds.), Population Policy Analysis. Lexington, Mass.: Lexington Books.

Talbot, R. B., and D. F. Hadwiger (1968) The Policy Process in American Agriculture. San Francisco: Chandler.

Tate, D. (1982) "Use of Omnibus Bills Burgeons Despite Members' Misgivings; Long-Term Impact Is Disputed." Congressional Quarterly Weekly Report (September 25): 2379–2383.

U.S. Civil Service Commission (1976) Executive Personnel in the Federal Service. Washington, D.C.: U.S. Government Printing Office.

Welch, S., and J. G. Peters (eds.) (1977) Legislative Reform and Public Policy. New York: Praeger Publishers.

Wildavsky, A. (1984) The Politics of the Budgetary Process, 4th ed. Boston: Little, Brown.

Wilensky, H. L. (1967) Organizational Intelligence. New York: Basic Books.

Wilson, G. C. (1981) "Opponents Find Vought Corporation's A7 Impossible to Shoot Down." Washington Post (March 13).

Wilson, J. Q. (1975) "The Rise of the Bureaucratic State." The Public Interest (Fall):77–103.

_____ (ed.) (1980) The Politics of Regulation. New York: Basic Books.

Witmer, T. R. (1964) "The Aging of the House." Political Science Quarterly 79 (December): 526–541.

Woll, P. (1977) American Bureaucracy, 2nd ed. New York: W. W. Norton.

Yates, D. (1982) Bureaucratic Democracy. Cambridge, Mass.: Harvard University Press.

Index

About the Authors

Randall B. Ripley is Professor and chairperson of the Department of Political Science and a Senior Faculty Associate at The Mershon Center, The Ohio State University. He has written extensively on many aspects of U.S. politics and policy. He received his Ph.D. in political science from Harvard University and spent five years at the Brookings Institution in Washington, D.C., before moving to Ohio State in 1967.

Grace A. Franklin is a Research Associate at and Assistant Director of The Mershon Center of The Ohio State University. She has been affiliated with The Mershon Center since receiving her M.A. in political science at Ohio State in 1970. She has published a number of books and articles on politics and policy in the United States, including (with Ripley) *Policy Implementation and Bureaucracy,* a companion volume to *Congress, the Bureaucracy, and Public Policy.*

A NOTE ON THE TYPE

The text of this book was set in 10/12 Palatino using a film version of the face designed by Hermann Zapf that was first released in 1950 by Germany's Stempel Foundry. The face is named after Giovanni Battista Palatino, a famous penman of the 16th century. In its calligraphic quality, Palatino is reminiscent of the Italian Renaissance type designs, yet with its wide, open letters and unique proportions it still retains a modern feel. Palatino is considered one of the most important faces from one of Europe's most influential type designers.

Composed by Carlisle Graphics, Dubuque, Iowa.

Printed and bound by Kingsport Press, Kingsport, Tennessee.